THOMAS PYNCHON AND COUNTERCULTU

Thomas Pynchon and American Counterculture employs the revolutionary sixties as a lens through which to view the anarchist politics of Pynchon's novels. Joanna Freer identifies and elucidates Pynchon's commentaries on such groups as the Beats, the New Left, and the Black Panther Party and on such movements as the psychedelic movement and the women's movement, drawing out points of critique to build a picture of a complex countercultural sensibility at work in Pynchon's fiction. In emphasising the subtleties of Pynchon's responses to counterculture, Freer clarifies his importance as an intellectually rigorous political philosopher. She further suggests that, like the graffiti in *Gravity's Rainbow*, Pynchon creates texts that are "revealed in order to be thought about, expanded on, translated into action by the people," his early attraction to core countercultural values growing into a conscious, politically motivated writing project that reaches its most mature expression in *Against the Day*.

Joanna Freer obtained her PhD in American literature from the University of Sussex in 2012. Freer has written for the *Journal of American Studies* and has published book reviews in *American Studies Today* and *Orbit: Writing around Pynchon*.

CAMBRIDE STUDIES IN AMERICAN
LITERATURE AND CULTURE

Editor
Ross Posnock, *Columbia University*

Founding Editor
Albert Gelpi, *Stanford University*

Advisory Board
Alfred Bendizen, *Texas A&M University*
Sacvan Bercovitch, *Harvard University*
Ronald Bush, St. John's College, *University of Oxford*
Wai Chee Dimock, *Yale University*
Albert Gelpi, *Stanford University*
Gordon Hutner, *University of Illinois, Urbana-Champaign*
Walter Benn Michaels, *University of Illinois, Chicago*
Kenneth Warren, *University of Chicago*

RECENT BOOKS IN THIS SERIES

168. GAVIN JONES
 Failure and the American Writer: A Literary History

167. LENA HILL
 Visualizing Blackness and the Creation of the African American Literary Tradition

166. MICHAEL ZISER
 Environmental Practice and Early American Literature

165. ANDREW HEBARD
 The Poetics of Sovereignty in American Literature, 1885–1910

164. CHRISTOPHER FREEBURG
 Melville and the Idea of Blackness: Race and Imperialism in Nineteenth-Century America

163. TIM ARMSTRONG
 The Logic of Slavery: Debt, Technology, and Pain in American Literature

162. JUSTINE MURISON
 The Politics of Anxiety in Nineteenth-Century American Literature

161. HSUAN L. HSU
 Geography and the Production of Space in Nineteenth-Century American Literature

160. DORRI BEAM
 Style, Gender, and Fantasy in Nineteenth-Century American Women's Writing

159. YOGITA GOYAL
 Romance, Diaspora, and Black Atlantic Literature

158. MICHAEL CLUNE
 American Literature and the Free Market, 1945–2000

THOMAS PYNCHON AND AMERICAN COUNTERCULTURE

JOANNA FREER
University of Sussex

CAMBRIDGE UNIVERSITY PRESS

CAMBRIDGE
UNIVERSITY PRESS

32 Avenue of the Americas, New York NY 10013-2473, USA

Cambridge University Press is part of the University of Cambridge.

It furthers the University's mission by disseminating knowledge in the pursuit of education, learning and research at the highest international levels of excellence.

www.cambridge.org
Information on this title: www.cambridge.org/9781107429710

© Joanna Freer 2014

This publication is in copyright. Subject to statutory exception and to the provisions of relevant collective licensing agreements, no reproduction of any part may take place without the written permission of Cambridge University Press.

First published 2014
First paperback edition 2016

A catalogue record for this publication is available from the British Library

Library of Congress Cataloguing in Publication data
Freer, Joanna, 1983–
Thomas Pynchon and American Counterculture / Joanna Freer.
pages   cm – (Cambridge studies in American literature and culture)
Includes bibliographical references and index.
ISBN 978-1-107-07605-1 (hardback)
1. Pynchon, Thomas – Criticism and interpretation.   2. Counterculture – United States.   I. Title.
PS3566.Y55Z653   2014
813'.54–dc23   2014014937

ISBN 978-1-107-07605-1 Hardback
ISBN 978-1-107-42971-0 Paperback

Cambridge University Press has no responsibility for the persistence or accuracy of URLs for external or third-party internet websites referred to in this publication, and does not guarantee that any content on such websites is, or will remain, accurate or appropriate.

Contents

Abbreviations		*page* ix
Introduction		1
1	On the Road to Anti-Structure: *V., The Crying of Lot 49*, and the Beats	14
2	Love, Violence, and Yippie Subversion in *Gravity's Rainbow*: Pynchon and the New Left	40
3	The Psychedelic Movement, Fantasy, and Anarchism in *The Crying of Lot 49* and *Against the Day*	65
4	The Black Panther Party, Revolutionary Suicide, and *Gravity's Rainbow*	102
5	Feminism Moderate and Radical in *The Crying of Lot 49* and *Vineland*: Pynchon and the Women's Movement	126
Conclusion: A "Little Parenthesis of Light": Pynchon's Counterculture		157
Notes		167
Bibliography		191
Index		203

Abbreviations

Frequently mentioned works by Thomas Pynchon, Jack Kerouac, Timothy Leary, and Huey P. Newton are cited parenthetically in the text using the following abbreviations.

ATD	*Against the Day* (2006)
L49	*The Crying of Lot 49* (1966)
GR	*Gravity's Rainbow* (1973)
IV	*Inherent Vice* (2009)
J	"A Journey into the Mind of Watts" (1966)
MD	*Mason & Dixon* (1997)
OTR	*On the Road* (1957)
PE	*The Politics of Ecstasy* (1968)
RS	*Revolutionary Suicide* (1973)
SL	*Slow Learner* (1984)
V.	*V.* (1963)
VL	*Vineland* (1990)

Introduction

The novels of Thomas Pynchon are recognised as among the greatest produced by a contemporary American writer. Each one is vast in scope, presenting the reader with a cornucopia of colourful characters, bizarre narrative twists, and delightfully comic moments, while displaying its author's formidable knowledge on topics as diverse as the German chemical industry during World War II, the use of the sector in eighteenth-century astronomy, and the location of legendary Buddhist holy lands. Pynchon is an originator of the postmodern style in literature: from his first novel *V.* (1963) to the recent *Bleeding Edge* (2013), his work exemplifies postmodernism in its irony and black humour, in recreating and adapting various generic modes, and in referencing high art and popular culture with equal enthusiasm. Integrating fiction with (often obscure) historical fact, Pynchon's encyclopaedic novels also largely fall into Linda Hutcheon's category of postmodern historiographic metafiction.[1] Yet postmodern texts are often seen as closed off from the world, as self-absorbed and apolitical, while quite the opposite is true of Pynchon's work. Indeed, Pynchon produces fiction laden with political critique and his novels are to be recognised as important works of political philosophy.

Pynchon is profoundly concerned with exploring and making vivid the mechanisms and motivators of oppression, and his narratives span continents and centuries in their attempts to trace historical developments in the tactics of repressive forces. Pitting themselves against such forces, the novels are carefully constructed so as to challenge preconceptions and prejudices, and encourage independent critical speculation or investigation. Formed of tangentially connected fragments and diegetic strands to be woven together and interpreted by a reader acting with relative autonomy, the work is innately anti-authoritarian. Concomitant with this post-structuralist promotion of the exercise of individual thought and imagination comes Pynchon's considerable interest in small-scale oppositional groups operating in the fields of literature, art, culture, or more traditional political arenas, and the alternatives they offer to current socio-economic systems. As his literary career has progressed, the author's antipathy to capitalism has become ever more visible, as has his relative sympathy for anarchist solutions, which is fully confirmed by *Against the Day* (2006). But Pynchon's politics are subtle and complex, and he must not be aligned too readily with any established ideology.

Although fully deserving of comprehensive critical attention, much of the political commentary Thomas Pynchon has offered still waits to be unravelled and appreciated. This is despite the fact that Pynchon's insights could represent a valuable contribution to political debate at a time when modern societies are growing more intertwined, the fortunes of each dependent on the courses taken by many others, and the imperative to learn historical lessons and avoid pathways leading to violence and the abuse of power is making itself ever more strongly felt. Whether literature can, in fact, play a significant role in fostering such understanding is a matter of long debate, and one to which Pynchon himself contributes in his 1984 introduction to the *Slow Learner* collection of his early short stories. Here, Pynchon claims that fiction writing lies on a "spectrum of impotence" with regard to political change, incapable of really doing anything about the "succession of the criminally insane" who hold power.[2] He is in good company in this contention, with fellow postmodern innovators as diverse as Kurt Vonnegut and Kathy Acker offering similar meditations on the problem.[3] Nevertheless, every one of Pynchon's novels is politically engaged, a fact which testifies to the author's ongoing struggle in the hope that literature can, in fact, exert an influence and promote social change. Whatever his assessment of their final political import, Pynchon stubbornly creates texts on the model of the graffiti which appear in the Weimar Germany of *Gravity's Rainbow*, texts which are "revealed in order to be thought about, expanded on, translated into action by the people."[4]

Acting from a position of (supposed) political neutrality, literary critics can of course facilitate the first stage of the process described in this quotation, clarifying the meanings embodied within novels and offering them up to the wider society for further reflection. *Thomas Pynchon and American Counterculture* thus offers an elucidation of certain elements of Pynchon's political philosophy, contributing to the critical dialogue on Pynchon's politics that has recently begun to gain ascendancy over thematic analyses of the author's work or considerations of its self-reflexively postmodern attributes. Sam Thomas's book-length study *Pynchon and the Political* (2007) is perhaps the most developed and notable expression of this new trend to date, offering a perspective on Pynchon's critique of society from the Enlightenment onwards, on his treatment of war as a literary subject, and on some of the potential alternatives to oppression he sets forth in his work. Other recent works of criticism approaching the political dimensions of Pynchon's fiction include Cyrus R. K. Patell's *Negative Liberties: Morrison, Pynchon, and the Problem of Liberal Ideology* (2001), Stefan Mattessich's *Lines of Flight: Discursive Time and Countercultural Desire in the Work of Thomas Pynchon* (2002), several of the essays collected in Niran Abbas's *Thomas Pynchon: Reading from the Margins* (2003), and Jeffrey Severs and Christopher Leise's *Pynchon's "Against the Day": A Corrupted Pilgrim's Guide* (2011), not to mention a number of articles that have been published on the subject.[5] In a 2005 review of Abbas's *Reading from the Margins*, Kathryn Hume called for more analysis in this field, claiming that the essays making up the collection's section on politics acted as "a prolegomenon to something that needs to be done, namely to map Pynchon's political views and social values and contextualize them in the sources of their time."[6] Significant contributions to this project have been made since the publication of Hume's comment, but much remains undone. In particular, as Hume emphasises, a greater sense of the *context* of the author's ideas is required. Several historical contexts are of course applicable to an analysis of Pynchon's politics, but the most relevant of these is, I suggest, the era of the sixties counterculture.

The 1960s enjoy a symbiotic relationship with postmodernism in general, whether seen as the form's generator or antithesis, and many critics and commentators have recognised the importance of the decade to Pynchon's fiction. For Sam Thomas "the experience of the sixties functions as the most significant juncture in Pynchon's political universe."[7] Thomas also quotes Cowart in his contention that "Pynchon's novels and other short stories revolve in planetary orbits around the sunlike moral intensity of the 1960s."[8] Similarly, Victor Strandberg "find[s] at the base of all Pynchon's work the temperament of a hippie rebel against tradition, convention, and all forms of social hierarchy."[9] When the sixties began, Pynchon was twenty-two years old and newly graduated from Cornell University. He was about to start his career as a professional writer; his first short story had been published in March 1959, and was followed by more stories and a novel in the early years of the following decade. In his article "Smoking Dope with Thomas Pynchon: A Sixties Memoir," Andrew Gordon underscores the importance of the sixties as a formative experience in the author's life, explaining that he "consider[s] Pynchon a quintessential American novelist of the nineteen sixties because he came of age as an artist during that entropic decade and shows its stamp in all his work."[10] We all attribute a routine significance to the era in which we reach maturity or choose our course in life, but this temporal convergence had unusually strong repercussions on the creative practice and political convictions of Thomas Pynchon.

The sixties was an era of extreme social and political turbulence that few within the United States could ignore. Attacking the moral and epistemological foundations of contemporary society, the colourful and impassioned protests of those heterogeneous oppositional groups and cultural innovators known collectively as the counterculture inspired and challenged many onlookers, Pynchon among them. Despite the wide-ranging eclecticism and broad scope of his work, the subversive fervour of the decade asserts its presence in all of Pynchon's novels. This is true as much of those written or published during the sixties – *V., The Crying of Lot 49*, and *Gravity's Rainbow* – as of the later production. Indeed, Pynchon's 2009 novel *Inherent Vice*, which is set in 1969–70, perhaps makes this point most clearly. (It should be noted here that, to some extent, a dialectic of inspiration operated between Pynchon and the counterculture, with whom his works enjoyed considerable popularity. Todd Gitlin describes how, given the surreality of the times, "the fiction that young freaks and radicals read in [1967–70] tended toward postmodern weirdness, the false calm of allegory, or the eerie simplicities of the saucer's-eye abstraction: Thomas Pynchon, Kurt Vonnegut, Jr., Hermann Hesse."[11] Even counterculture royalty like the leader of the psychedelic movement, Timothy Leary, admired Pynchon's work. In fact, Leary declared in a 1980s interview that Pynchon was, for him, "the finest writer living," and the person he would most like to meet.[12]) Yet although critics acknowledge the sixties character of much of Pynchon's fiction, surprisingly little relevant analysis has been published. Sam Thomas considers the sixties to inform Pynchon's politics in important ways, but his aforementioned study does not have a particular focus on that decade. Stefan Mattessich's *Lines of Flight* deals more directly with the subject, but is limited by its thematic focus on time. David Cowart dedicates a chapter of his book *Thomas Pynchon and the Dark Passages of History* to "Pynchon and the Sixties," complementing articles published in previous years by Jeffrey S. Baker and Frederick Ashe on Pynchon's affinities with the New Left and counterculture. However, these shorter pieces, limited in scope, are unable to go deep enough into the vast web of interconnections between Pynchon's novels and the era's various cultural and political innovations.[13] Because it offers a huge array of commentaries, tales, and histories relating to wildly divergent fields of human experience, Pynchon's work is of course by no means reducible to its connections to sixties politics, but there is a concrete lack of criticism addressing this important aspect of his fiction. The intention behind this book is to help in remedying this lack.

As noted earlier, historically Pynchon criticism has based itself primarily on analysis of the writing's postmodern qualities, the novels often considered as centrally concerned with formal and aesthetic innovation and having little to say on social or political issues. But while the majority might perceive Pynchon's narratives as curled in upon themselves in their complexity, fragmentation, and obscurity of allusion, as the list of commentators on Pynchon's politics given previously attests, not everyone agrees. Thomas Schaub took the opposing line relatively early on, stating in 1981 that: "Pynchon's books are not self-reflexive because they reveal and document the reality of history," and labelling Pynchon "the most compelling social writer we have."[14] A similar case is made by Sam Thomas, who points out that the novels contain numerous "innovative and unsettling discussions of freedom, war, labor, poverty, community, democracy, totalitarianism and so on [which] are often passed over in favor of constrictive scientific metaphors and theoretical play" by critics.[15] Because a substantial proportion of critical debate has been abstracted into the realm of the purely aesthetic, the author's ethics have received relatively scant attention. But I would agree with Alan Wilde in his contention that "[a]lthough some critics find an unbridgeable gap between Pynchon's postmodernism and his ethical concerns, he is, in fact, not only a moralist but an insistent, urgent, and sometimes (most notably in *V.*) a heavy-handed one."[16]

No writing can operate entirely independently of its social context, and the hermeticism of postmodern fiction has been overemphasised across the board, not only in the case of Pynchon. As Linda Hutcheon suggested in her 1989 study *The Politics of Postmodernism*, the dichotomy that critics of art and literature have tended to draw between the postmodern and the political is a false one:

> Postmodern art cannot but be political, at least in the sense that its representations – its images and stories – are anything but neutral, however "aestheticized" they may appear to be in their parodic self-reflexivity. While the postmodern has no effective theory of agency that enables a move into political *action*, it does work to turn its inevitable ideological grounding into a site of de-naturalizing critique.[17]

Pynchon's work certainly engages in such critique, seeking to destabilise all kinds of complacently held beliefs and naive assumptions, and demonstrates that postmodern literature can be playful, parodic, fragmentary, obscure, and self-referential, while at the same time having considerable political bite. However, the present study contends that Pynchon's novels do not fit entirely with Hutcheon's theory in that they *do* have agency, and courses of political action are proposed, however tentatively or provisionally.

In the chapters that follow I do not find it useful to read Pynchon as a "postmodern" author, partially because of this ongoing common false association of postmodernism with insularity, but also because the term "countercultural" seems more to the point. Many of the postmodern literary techniques employed in Pynchon's work and discussed in this study are, I suggest, motivated primarily by countercultural values. After all, as it was forming during the 1960s, before there was a well-recognised "postmodern" model to emulate, the new aesthetic in literature had to be the result of external factors, and I suggest that these were largely the same factors that spawned many counterculture movements. (Of course, to describe postmodernism as expressing nothing more than a reaction against literary modernism is untenable.) To offer some specific examples, Pynchon's emphasis on the participation and independence of the reader seems to be, as I mentioned earlier, an expression of anti-authoritarianism and a preference for the creative freedom of the individual. Likewise, his use of fantasy (or magical realism) is intended to promote the exercise of the imagination and the liberation of the mind from reified thought patterns, a major goal of the psychedelic movement in particular, as I discuss in Chapter 3. His metafictional incorporation of obscure histories of oppression and brutality often functions to critique capitalism, but also to endorse a process of continuous learning on the part of the reader, something at the core of countercultural ideology. This is also true of the numerous intertextual allusions made in Pynchon's novels. Even the more jocular elements of Pynchon's prose can have a deep political valence, and this is in line with the tactics of groups such as the Yippies, epitomising an emphasis recurrent within the counterculture on imbuing protest with pleasure.[18]

Another point on which my approach differs from much previous criticism is the degree of legibility I assign to Pynchon's politics within his works. Of course, a work of fiction is far from being a political manifesto and, as Seán Molloy points out, without any such clear and direct statement on Pynchon's part "any interpretation must perforce be partial and provisional."[19] But with every new work that appears the author is more forthcoming, expressing his political sympathies more directly. This progression is, I admit, decidedly relative; Pynchon has always preferred to veil his values somewhat. Yet it is an exaggeration to say, as Charles Hollander does, that from the short stories to *Gravity's Rainbow*, "Pynchon's politics are absent, or in deep code," and that "[n]ot until *Vineland* … did he explicitly articulate his political beliefs."[20] Contemporary readers of this earlier phase of Pynchon's production would not, I suggest, have had to "cryptanalyze" to discover these beliefs, although to some extent this is now necessary.[21] In his journalism and other non-fiction work both early and late, Pynchon is by no means evasive in this area – we need only think of his blunt criticism of the government agencies of the "humanitarian establishment" in his 1966 article "A Journey into the Mind of Watts" (discussed at greater length in Chapter 4). Likewise, in each of his novels, I suggest, Pynchon speaks his politics fairly clearly given the constraints of his anti-didactic approach.[22] If his values appear to us *deeply* encoded, it may be due either to our temporal (and perhaps also geographical) distance from the contemporary social scene of their production, or to an expectation that political ideas should be simple and one-sided, while Pynchon's are subtle and ambivalent.

Pynchon's ambivalence, his refusal to endorse any single viewpoint without qualifications, is an important reflection of his anarchic political philosophy, and indeed functions as a structural principle in his narratives. All of Pynchon's commentaries have an open-ended quality; there are very few, if any, final judgements in his work. Rather than asserting one or another particular perspective, Pynchon promotes habits of critical thought. For the Italian writer Italo Calvino, such an attitude is admirable: the literary object must "know itself and distrust itself," as must political discourse. If it achieves this, he argues, literature can be positively educative, offering "a type of education that can yield results only if it is difficult and indirect, if it implies the arduous attainment of literary stringency."[23] Confirming the importance of such stringency to Pynchon and his political goals, Schaub argues in his classic study *Pynchon: The Voice of Ambiguity* that "[t]he complexity of his understanding prevents opposition from declining into false division."[24] Pynchon's ambivalence bespeaks his intellectual rigour, his ability to think critically on all fronts, adopting the kind of questioning approach the best counterculture thinkers sought to foster. Throughout this book, I therefore make a concerted effort to underscore such doubts and ambiguities, so as to avoid misrepresenting or simplifying Pynchon's politics.

Turning to more practical matters, my method in the present study is essentially to unravel the significance of sections of Pynchon's novels containing apparent countercultural commentary via close textual analysis conducted with reference to particular texts, personalities, organisations, and ideologies of the era. The works of literature and social/political philosophy which function as intertexts in this book are each representative of a particular countercultural perspective that helped to shape and define the oppositional sixties. All were well known if not notorious in their time and are texts which Pynchon is either known to have read, or which my analysis demonstrates he must have been familiar with. Pynchon's commentaries sometimes refer more directly to countercultural figures, and I identify in what follows variously clear-cut references to Timothy Leary and Eldridge Cleaver, and to groups including the Black Panther Party (BPP), the Yippies, and radical feminist organisations. Occasionally, my analysis bases itself on certain ideological themes of the sixties; this is true particularly of Chapter 2's discussion of "love" in *Gravity's Rainbow*. Comments made by Pynchon in his journalism or other non-fiction are employed to reinforce my interpretations. In these ways *Thomas Pynchon and American Counterculture* attempts to demonstrate the extent to which Pynchon's novels (or parts thereof) align themselves with or, indeed, reject particular countercultural arguments, theories, and tactics. Within and between chapters, interconnections traced between seemingly disparate narratives and commentaries build a sense of the coherence and development of Pynchon's politics over the course of his career.

The overarching themes of this book, which tie together Pynchon's responses to the various manifestations of the counterculture discussed, are anarchism, escape and escapism, altruistic love, community, political violence, consciousness expansion, and the role of the rational intellect. Given that the dynamic of the sixties counterculture, the process by which its earnest hopefulness and positive activism turned to hedonism and violence, is so fundamental to the insights and lessons offered in Pynchon's political philosophy, the chapters which follow move chronologically through the late fifties and sixties in terms of their reference to particular movements and groupings. In terms of their reference to Pynchon's novels, however, the sequence is not chronological. Instead, chapters feature analysis of the work or works with most relevance to the subject matter at hand. As a result, *The Crying of Lot 49*, published in the middle of the sixties and revealing much about Pynchon's values at this juncture, features quite heavily, alongside *V.*, *Gravity's Rainbow*, *Vineland*, and *Against the Day*, whereas *Mason & Dixon* and *Inherent Vice* are less prominent. In the case of the latter, this is because, although set in the era and containing various direct comments on it, the action seems comparatively lacking in depth of signification with respect to the particular themes and movements at issue in this study. The former, *Mason & Dixon*, is an extremely well-respected member of the Pynchon canon, and its importance must not go unacknowledged. However, its manner of relating to the 1960s offers less in the way of the kind of specific commentaries and analogies on which my analysis of Pynchon's writing bases itself. Although its emphasis on love and community and its consistent critique of the oppressive behaviours of the powerful identifies its essential political concerns with those of many countercultural figures and groups, it treats the major issues, themes, and grand narratives of modernity more broadly than does Pynchon's other work, viewing these from an expanded historical perspective which is reflected in the novel's greater temporal distancing from the present moment. Pynchon's latest novel, *Bleeding Edge*, has been published too recently to allow inclusion in this study.

My analysis begins in the pre-countercultural 1950s, the first chapter of this book uncovering an originating source of Pynchon's left-wing values in his early enthusiasm for the Beat movement. A reading of Pynchon's introduction to his *Slow Learner* short story collection – in which he professes admiration for Beat writing and particularly Jack Kerouac's *On the Road* – suggests that what Pynchon found inspirational in the Beat project was its raw motive energy, which stood in stark contrast to the static purposelessness of the fifties mainstream. In *On the Road* the trajectory of Sal and Dean promises access to surprise, joy, freedom, and spiritual meaningfulness (later to become core countercultural values), as they disentangle themselves from the reified hierarchies of the familiar city. Pynchon's first two novels, *V.* and *The Crying of Lot 49*, depict characters who strain towards these same goals, seeking liminal, anti-structural spaces and marginal associations in order to achieve what the anthropologist Victor Turner described as *communitas*.[25] Yet there can be no easy escapes in Pynchon's prose, and he substantially problematises *On the Road*'s hedonistic model of liberation, latched on to by many within the counterculture. For Pynchon, I argue, neither flight along the highway nor pursuit of that ineffable high Dean calls "IT" bring one very far towards the attainment of real freedom. Rather than rejecting organisation entirely, it is a case of recognising those structures that are useful or indispensable – language, rational thought, and such like – while challenging the *excessive* capitalist superscription of both the physical and psychological landscapes of the times.

In Chapter 2 I explore Pynchon's treatment of subversion as conducted through more traditional political channels, gauging the extent of his novels' sympathy for the core values and methods of the New Left. Pynchon's early work is pervaded by a sense of apocalyptic urgency – imaged most forcefully in the final scene of *Gravity's Rainbow* – that was shared with major New Left groups such as Students for a Democratic Society (SDS), who considered themselves potentially "the last generation in the experiment with living" as a result of the development of the atomic bomb.[26] Analyses of the author's treatment of protest groups and direct action in *The Crying of Lot 49* and his article "A Journey into the Mind of Watts" suggest Pynchon's support for the egalitarian, non-paternalistic, cross-community approach New Left groups exercised particularly in the early to mid sixties, but also a preference for artistic commentary over the setting up of schemes. Pynchon's reaction to New Left groups' turn away from the commitment to love and non-violence expressed in key texts such as SDS's *Port Huron Statement* (1962) towards a more aggressive, idealistic, and communist-influenced stance in the late 1960s is clarified via a reading of the role of love in *Gravity's Rainbow* and the novel's treatment of the activism of Leni and her communist comrades in Weimar-era Germany. I argue that non-possessive, altruistic love (conceptualised in Chapter 1 as *communitas*) can effectively motivate political action for the Pynchon of 1973, but only if one remains staunchly aware of love's co-optive and manipulative potentialities. Regarding tactics, *Gravity's Rainbow*'s treatment of organised street protest points to the risks to self involved from an overzealous police force, while anarchic approaches like those of the Yippies are presented as more viable and effective.

The third chapter further develops arguments around the importance of community, heightened awareness, and anarchism to Pynchon's political philosophy. It begins with a discussion of commentaries on the early psychedelic movement and its leader Timothy Leary visible within *The Crying of Lot 49*, proposing that these demonstrate both the author's sympathy for a man demonised by the mass media, and his basic support for the careful, guided, and politically motivated use of LSD as a tool of consciousness expansion as promoted by Leary pre-1966 in interviews as well as in publications including *The Psychedelic Experience* (1964). Raising awareness is as important to Pynchon as it was to Leary, both men considering it a necessary precursor to political action and social reorganisation. However, psychedelic drugs are not the ideal means of achieving this for Pynchon, whose alternative approach is to invest his novels with consciousness-raising properties. This para-psychedelic method is epitomised in *Against the Day*, whose use of fantasy troubles our notions of the "real," offering a related thematic linking of light, illusion, and (capitalist) power that recalls the insights of Guy Debord's Situationist treatise *The Society of the Spectacle*. The chapter concludes with a discussion of the tendency of more conscious characters in *Against the Day* to move towards involvement with anarchism, a political theory prized by Pynchon for its resistance to centralised leadership and for its manner of balancing structure and anti-structure in a vision of the spontaneous synchronicity of ad hoc communities.

Returning to *Gravity's Rainbow*, Chapter 4 examines in more detail the potential problems of revolutionary leadership, discusses the role of violence in protest movements, and considers Pynchon's perspectives on Black Panther Party political theory as put forward through the speeches and writings of co-founder Huey P. Newton, with particular reference to his 1973 work *Revolutionary Suicide*. The first section centres on a dialogue in which "Marxist dialectics" and revolutionary suicide are discussed, two theories which were uniquely combined within the ideology of the Panthers. Pynchon's attack on a "racist" Marx is explained as resulting from his argument, put forward in an 1853 article, that colonial brutality must be borne as part of the dialectic that will inevitably move society towards communism.[27] *Gravity's Rainbow* demonstrates an aversion to Marxist dialectical materialism as a perverse (il)logical crutch used to garner authority in leadership, but the novel does not entirely dismiss the Panther project. An interest in race relations runs throughout Pynchon's work, and the egalitarianism and immediacy of Newton's concept of revolutionary suicide – the idea that, given no other options, one should risk death in a struggle against oppression rather than acquiesce in it – clearly appealed to him in 1973. Recounting the fictional history of a black revolutionary organisation in Second World War Germany, *Gravity's Rainbow*'s Schwarzkommando narrative anachronistically reveals the author's views on potential weaknesses within the BPP and other oppositional groups of the 1960s, particularly regarding their vulnerability to establishment forms of thought and power, as well as to more direct attacks via the media and FBI.

The final chapter of this study explores Pynchon's response to the emergence of second-wave feminism in the mid sixties and its subsequent development into a fully fledged women's movement. The chapter begins with an evaluation of the influence of the text most representative of early second-wave feminism, Betty Friedan's *The Feminine Mystique* (1963), on *The Crying of Lot 49*. Although the novel superficially supports calls for female liberation from the housewife role, I argue that it ultimately rejects the female-specific approach required by Friedan and the women's movement more broadly, implying, in fact, that working males tend to suffer greater oppression than housebound women in contemporary society. Moreover, the anti-capitalist fervour of Pynchon's writing implies a distaste for moderate, reformist approaches like that of Friedan. Like many within the male New Left at the time, I suggest, the Pynchon of *The Crying of Lot 49* prioritises the achievement of broad-scale social and economic reorganisation over the immediate attainment of female equality. Following on from this, reactions to more radical expressions of second-wave feminism are addressed via a discussion of passages from *Gravity's Rainbow* and *Vineland*, in which the author suggests that women can combine activism with mothering, defends male parenting rights – the family becoming a major potential site of *communitas* in Pynchon's later work – and destabilises notions of gender essentialism. Yet there is no outside to gender in Pynchon's novels, and his continuing predilection for pleasant-looking female characters and pornographic scenes demonstrates a lack of substantial maturation from the avowedly childish male sexism of his early stories, and troubles his countercultural credentials when it comes to the women's movement.

Defining the Counterculture

There is a considerable lack of consistency between commentators on the 1960s in their use of the term "counterculture," and given its centrality to the present study a working definition is called for. The term was originally coined by Theodore Roszak in his 1968 book *The Making of a Counterculture*, but he defines it rather vaguely as "a culture so radically disaffiliated from the mainstream assumptions of our society that it scarcely looks to many as a culture at all, but takes on the alarming appearance of a barbaric intrusion."[28] This does not tell us very much about where the practical limits of such a protean collection of movements should be drawn. One tendency is to consider the more traditional political activism of the era as somehow separate or distinct from its cultural manifestations. Thus the active protestors of the New Left early and late are placed in one bracket, while another is afforded to those, like the Beats, the psychedelic movement, and the hippies, who focussed on changing individual values and lifestyles. It is the latter group that is often termed the "counterculture," to the exclusion of the former. Others see the situation differently, preferring to describe the whole varied gamut of "radically disaffiliated" youth as one countercultural movement. The majority of authors take a middle road on the issue, maintaining the nominal distinction between political activism and counterculture while declaring that they are two sides of the same coin. Thus for Alexander Bloom, editor of *Long Time Gone: Sixties America Then and Now*, "[l]ost in the modern imagery of 'sixties' life is the interconnection of the political, the cultural, and the social. Individuals' lives, ideas, and actions wound together – the personal became political, and the cultural and political seemed to be two parts of a whole."[29] Roszak too describes the central unity of thought of the New Left and what he terms the "beat-hip bohemians," who share "the same insistence on revolutionary change that must at last embrace psyche and society."[30]

Political and cultural factions did diverge in terms of focus and approach, the former tackling the more tangible blights of entrenched poverty, racial discrimination, and the Vietnam War, while the latter looked more deeply, subverting what they considered to be the pillars supporting the alienated edifice of modern American life: conformity, aspirituality, and scientific rationalism. However, because the affinities between movements in terms of long-term aims and societal criticisms seem to me more significant than methodological differences, and given the era's important and thorough-going destabilisation of the categories of the "political" and "cultural" (something Pynchon certainly seems to invest in given the "truly holistic and global" nature of his politics[31]), I use "counterculture" in this book as a general term to designate the entire oppositional sixties, inclusive of the New Left, the psychedelic movement, the Black Panther Party, the Yippies, and even the women's movement. (The women's movement is often perceived as a development distinct from the counterculture, but I defend its inclusion on the basis that, like other protest movements, it had variously radical factions, including many seeking more widespread revolution, and its basic aim was an increase in individual and social freedom.) The Beats are the only group discussed in this study excluded from the category, their relevance being pre-countercultural and proto-countercultural. The core values which these movements tend collectively to endorse, albeit to greater and lesser degrees, are as follows. In society: personalism, egalitarianism, communitarianism, participation, and flexibility of structure. In the individual: openness, continuous attention to learning, creativity, wholeness, responsibility, the privileging of the moment over end goals, and a focus on the subjectivity of consciousness.[32]

CHAPTER 1

On the Road to Anti-Structure
V., The Crying of Lot 49, and the Beats

Every revolutionary era must have its pioneers, its precursors, its instigators. In the case of the youth movements of the 1960s, this role was filled in large part by the Beat poets, whose irreverent approach to accepted standards in both life and literature inspired a multitude to follow their example.[1] In 1956 Allen Ginsberg's "Howl" ruptured the comfortable complacency of the Eisenhower siesta, and was soon followed by similarly original and subversive works including Jack Kerouac's *On the Road* (1957) and William Burroughs's *Naked Lunch* (1959). Thus was spawned the Beat Generation, so named by Kerouac, who associated "beat" with both "beatitude" and poverty.[2] Studying English at Cornell during the late 1950s, the young Thomas Pynchon saw the Beats and other "emerging voices" as offering a stimulating alternative to the exclusivity and dogmatism of traditional modernist literary fiction (*SL* 7). For him, the new style proclaimed that writing "was not a case of either/or" and promised "an expansion of possibilities" in literature (*SL* 7). Reflecting in his 1984 introduction to the *Slow Learner* short story collection on the influences which helped to shape his early production, Pynchon lauds Kerouac's *On the Road* (along with recorded jazz and Norman Mailer's "The White Negro") as an exemplar of this counter-traditional impulse, describing it as "a book I still believe is one of the great American novels" (*SL* 7). These cultural innovations were "centrifugal lures" for the author, and the adjective is not incidental: Pynchon intimates that what attracted him to the art forms of the new generation was their affirmation of positive motion towards new geographical, musical, or literary horizons. He asserts that Helen Waddell's *The Wandering Scholars* had a "collateral effect" on him, being "an account of the young poets of the Middle Ages who left the monasteries in large numbers and took to the roads of Europe, celebrating in song the wider range of life to be found outside their academic walls" (*SL* 7–8).

"The Road Is Life": Motion, Transformation, and New Freedoms

Since the Beat Generation acted as a prologue to the countercultural sixties, its relevance to the novels of Thomas Pynchon is the natural focus of the first chapter of this book. My exposition of certain points of convergence and divergence between the philosophies and politics of Pynchon and the Beats takes as its starting point the author's retrospective emphasis on the inspirational quality of "the idea of motion, energy, and spontaneity" expressed by Beat writers, one of the major facets of their work.[3] Documenting in semi-autobiographical fashion the cross-continental journeys and frenetic lifestyles of its author and his social circle in 1947–50, Kerouac's *On the Road* is strongly representative of this impetus towards motion and transformation, the physical embodiment of which is the character of Dean Moriarty, who is invested with "the tremendous energy of a new kind of American saint."[4] His energy is forcefully depicted in the Kerouac character Sal Paradise's vision of the physical concentration of Dean running, with "bony face outthrust to life, his arms pumping, his brow sweating, his legs twinkling like Groucho Marx" (*OTR* 154). When he drives, as he loves to do, his vigour is expressed through his total concentration on the task and on maintaining his speed; he negotiates the road with his "rocky dogged face as ever bent over the dashlight with a bony purpose of its own" (*OTR* 234). (Dean's real-life counterpart Neal Cassady remained a mythic figure among the counterculture until his death in 1968, and his exploits as driver of "Further," the psychedelic school bus belonging to the LSD enthusiasts known as the Merry Pranksters, on an odyssey across America are documented by Tom Wolfe in another classic of the era, *The Electric Kool-Aid Acid Test* (1968).) Now comfortably ensconced within the American canon, Kerouac's novel is arguably the seminal text of the Beat Generation, positing movement as the "one and noble function of the time" (*OTR* 134), setting off a wave of copycat road trips, and defining many core tenets of the new literature. It is thus at the centre of my analysis in this chapter, a choice further justified by Pynchon's aforementioned professed admiration for the novel as an expression of the late fifties zeitgeist, as well as by the case already made for the influence of Kerouac's novel on Pynchon's work by Pierre-Yves Petillon in his essay "A Re-cognition of Her Errand into the Wilderness."[5] Here, Petillon claims that for *The Crying of Lot 49* "[e]verything, in a way, started with Kerouac."[6] In the present study, *On the Road*'s era-defining narrative is considered alongside Pynchon's first two novels, *V.* and *The Crying of Lot 49*, the latter of which is in turn "quintessentially a sixties document."[7]

Despite my emphasis on *On the Road*, dynamism and a motive logic characterised the Beat movement more broadly. Other Beat texts which captured the energy and spontaneity of their generation include John Clellon Holmes's *Go* (1952), the poetry of writers such as Gregory Corso and Lawrence Ferlinghetti, and William Burroughs's aforementioned *Naked Lunch*. In an interview given in 1974, Burroughs described his fiction as an embodiment of the *picaresque* tradition, a road genre whose heritage he considers to stretch back as far as the first century AD and the *Satyricon* of the Roman poet Petronius, while exemplified in more recent times by the work of Louis-Ferdinand Céline. (His reference is presumably to Céline's 1932 *Journey to the End of the Night*.)[8] *Naked Lunch* and the writer's other Beat novels, including *Junky* and *Queer*, express the ideal of motion largely through their form. According to Burroughs, "a picaresque novel has no plot," instead consisting of a loosely connected "series of incidents."[9] As Richard Pearce has pointed out, such shifts of focus in literature "stimulate us kinetically," producing a sense of rapid movement.[10] The "incidents" that populate Burroughs's fiction often range continents in their span, a journeying and questing motif being present as the protagonist searches for release from heroin dependence, or for the mythical hallucinogen known as "yage."

Ginsberg, the third member of the central Beat trio alongside Burroughs and Kerouac, generated a parallel sense of the frenzy which was so integral to the Beat lifestyle in his masterwork "Howl" through repetition and the intensely rhythmic pacing of the unrhymed and largely unpunctuated verses, a style with many affinities to Kerouac's own "spontaneous prose."[11] This technique was also turned to effect in other poems by Ginsberg. In the following lines from "Kaddish," for instance, first published in a collection of 1961, form closely mirrors content as the poet images speed in the flashing past of a landscape viewed from the road:

> Ride 3 hours thru tunnels past all American industry,
> Bayonne preparing for World War II, tanks, gas fields, soda factories, diners, locomotive roundhouse fortress – into piney woods New Jersey Indians – calm towns – long roads thru sandy tree fields -
>
> Bridges by deerless creeks, old wampum loading the streambed – down there a tomahawk or Pocohontas bone – and a million old ladies voting for Roosevelt in brown small houses, roads off the Madness highway –
>
> perhaps a hawk in a tree, or a hermit looking for an owl-filled branch –

> All the time arguing – afraid of strangers in the forward
> double seat, snoring regardless – what busride they snore on
> now?[12]

Ginsberg's use of dashes in this extract works to intensify the feeling of movement and rhythm implied by the subject matter. The dashes divide the events described into a Burroughsian "series of incidents," and the plotless nature of onrushing perceptions is also evocative of a similar quality in Kerouac's depictions of changing roadside landscapes in *On the Road*.

One might wonder why the Beat emphasis on centrifugal energy seemed so fresh, so original, for Pynchon and many of his contemporaries. After all, America's vision of both its present and its historical formation involves myriad images of movement and change. From the predominantly migratory Native American tribes through early pioneers and frontiersmen to modern car culture, spatial mobility – a nomadism of sorts – has long been an integral part of life on the North American continent. So too has the social mobility the country's democratic capitalist system supposedly ensured.[13] Furthermore, in the field of literature, the road novel functions as a kind of American Ur-narrative. Incorporating aspects of various road genres including the *picaresque*, the quest romance, the pilgrimage, and the *bildungsroman*, writers as innately canonical as Walt Whitman and Mark Twain have used the genre to reassert or renegotiate root concepts and ideals around what it means to be a citizen of the United States.[14] Yet the 1950s were something of an exception to this dynamic trend: the decade has entered the historical record as a time of post-war quietude and stability. Depending on one's perspective, stability can equate to stagnation; that Pynchon saw the era in which he spent his teenage years as problematically static and listless is signalled, as he himself points out, by the short story "Entropy" (1960), which looks pessimistically forward to a time when all change will cease and the universe will effectively die: "something like Limbo: form and motion abolished, heat-energy identical at every point in it" (*SL* 85). Pynchon explains in his introduction to *Slow Learner* that "[u]ntil John Kennedy ... began to get some attention, there was a lot of aimlessness going around. While Eisenhower was in, there seemed no reason why it should all not just go on as it was" (*SL* 14). Of course, Pynchon was by no means the only one to express such a viewpoint. In "The White Negro," first published in 1957, Norman Mailer described the recent past as "the years of conformity and depression," marred by "a collective failure of nerve," and, like the Beats, he proposed a solution in motion:

> Movement is always to be preferred to inaction. In motion a man has
> a chance, his body is warm, his instincts are quick, and when the crisis

comes, whether of love or violence, he can make it, he can win, he can release a little more energy for himself since he hates himself a little less, he can make a little better nervous system, make it a little more possible to go again, to go faster next time and so make more and thus find more people with whom he can swing.[15]

It is in this context that the Beats' investment in forms of spatial, social, and literary mobility, simultaneously hearkening back to bygone golden ages and reinvigorating old forms in a thoroughly modern manner, proved revolutionary. As Burroughs has said, "[t]he alienation, the restlessness, the dissatisfaction were already there waiting when Kerouac pointed out the road."[16]

V. and *The Crying of Lot 49*, fantastical accounts of their protagonists' quests for a shape-shifting muse and a mysterious underground courier service respectively, count amongst the many countercultural texts which latched onto and reimagined the Beats' inspirationally subversive cooption of the road narrative tradition, perpetuating the form's status and relevance throughout the 1960s and beyond. Others include Tom Wolfe's *The Electric Kool-Aid Acid Test*, Hunter S. Thompson's *Fear and Loathing in Las Vegas* (1971), James A. Michener's *The Drifters* (1971), and Gurney Norman's *Divine Right's Trip* (1972). In film, high-grossing movies like *Bonnie and Clyde* (1967) and *Easy Rider* (1969) drew on the rebellious and romantic associations of the road. The quest motif in Pynchon's work has been extremely well documented critically, being an important structural facet of each of his novels from the earliest to the most recent. In search of explanations and solutions both secular and transcendent pertaining to their personal histories and troubled presents, Pynchon's characters often rove across continents, undertaking convoluted voyages of discovery which lead them to a variety of unfamiliar locales. In some cases, characters are thrust out of the comfortable stasis of their lives by events beyond their control, in others, they are already habitual wanderers when we meet them; whatever the motive, Pynchon's protagonists rarely remain in any one place for long. Moreover, they often travel beyond the limits of the given world into the realms of the fictional, magical, or transcendent. As we have seen, Pynchon at Cornell was attracted by the cultural foment going on outside of the university, by what he describes as "alternative lowlife data that kept filtering insidiously through the ivy" revealing "that other world humming along out there" (*SL* 8); in his fiction such other worlds are equally promising and mysterious, and as I argue in Chapter 3, such concessions to the fantastical have an important political role in Pynchon's work.

In Pynchon's novels questing or wandering is necessitated by the emptiness of modern, Western society. Meaning seems to require movement, while stasis is aligned with the void. The image painted in *V.* is of a mid 1950s America ruled by superficial pleasures, populated on the one hand by those who ignorantly or cynically submit to this limited hedonism, and on the other by seekers after something more significant. Persisting into Pynchon's 1960s, the problem is summed up in *The Crying of Lot 49* by the protagonist Oedipa Maas's expression of the dire need for "a real alternative to the exitlessness, to the absence of surprise to life, that harrows the head of everybody American you know," her formulation explicitly linking the ability to leave or escape with access to variety and hence enjoyment of life.[17] If possible, *The Crying of Lot 49*'s San Narciso is even more vacuous than *V.*'s Norfolk, Virginia. Shaped entirely by the demands of financial profit, the area is characterised by an eerie stasis imaged in the "circuit card"-like "ordered swirl" (*L49* 14) of the city itself and the motionless swimming pool and blank windows of the Echo Courts motel. Amid this controlled, lifeless environment the protagonist Oedipa feels a "sense of buffeting, insulation" (*L49* 12). The absence of surprise is accompanied by "the absence of an intensity, as if watching a movie" (*L49* 12), the awareness of which leads Oedipa to imagine herself trapped Rapunzel-like within a perceptual tower created from without by some "anonymous and malignant" magic (*L49* 13).

As Burroughs suggested, Kerouac's road offered a clear alternative to such static, controlled confinement. Indulging in "[t]he purity of the road," promises his protagonist Sal, one can travel through America as "golden land," as a space in which "all kinds of unforeseen events wait lurking to surprise you and make you glad you're alive to see" (*OTR* 135). *On the Road* is largely untroubled by the sense of "exitlessness" that is so pervasive in Pynchon's work: when Sal is tired of the "confusion and nonsense" of the city, he and his comrades leave it behind by simply "performing [their] one and noble function of the time, *move*" (*OTR* 134). Situated beyond the familiar and apparently arbitrary coordinates of everyday life, Kerouac's unravelling road is a conductor of energy, a space of radical freedom acting as a healing salve for the modern condition. Concurrently taking to task rigid moralities and the imposition of arbitrary limits on behaviour, the book is a rallying cry for personal liberty, a value that was to be of central importance to the sixties counterculture. The car itself becomes a stage for scenes which subvert the rules of "proper" behaviour, such as when Dean has an epiphany regarding the pointlessness of clothes which results in the three of them, Dean, Sal, and

Dean's wife, Marylou, riding along naked, causing trucks to swerve in surprise as they pass (*OTR* 161). Yet of the "classic" Beat texts, *On the Road* is one of the least controversial. Edited pre-publication to remove some of the more risqué scenes, it was not subjected to the charges of obscenity levied against both "Howl" and *Naked Lunch*. Pynchon was well aware of these trials, and felt the influence of such "excesses of law enforcement" on his own early writing practice, which he considers marked by a resultant "tendency to self-censorship" (*SL* 6). Despite this, a Beat-like propensity to endorse "alternative" lifestyles and to question established norms is a major characteristic of his work. While his first novels may not quite approach the "obscene," even Pynchon's early fiction frequently puts contemporary morality to the test. Sympathetic characters might commit adultery, drink to excess, take drugs, associate with drifters and outcasts, or engage in unusual sexual practices with impunity in Pynchon's narrative worlds – all this in a time when it was considered a statement of subversive intent simply to have long hair or to grow a beard.

On the Road called for freedom to move, to travel, to transcend social norms and moral precepts, and it also called for the transformation of literature. As noted earlier, Beat literature, with its populism, its feverish passions, and its conspicuous rejection of the conventions of meter and punctuation, stood, for Pynchon as for many others, against the power of the established modernist literary tradition. It expressed a conception of both literary and social freedom predicated on the breaking down or rejection of reified structures, and the influence of this appears in the structural logic of Pynchon's narratives, which are built on the basis of rhizomatic forms, "open and connectable in all of [their] dimensions," much like the anarchist communities he depicts.[18] Yet although the literary revolution the Beats instigated was clearly a significant inspiration for Pynchon, he did not simply accept and mimic its formal tenets, as his ongoing commitment to reworking modernist forms suggests.[19] Nor did he consider the Beat message, albeit acknowledgedly "a sane and decent affirmation of what we all want to believe about American values" (*SL* 9), entirely unproblematic. In *Slow Learner* Pynchon describes himself as inhabiting (even in the late fifties) a "strange post-Beat passage of cultural time" in which he and his contemporaries could be little more than "onlookers" or "consumers," fed mediated and thus compromised versions of Beat culture (*SL* 9). He apparently regretted such temporal distancing, his inability to take a fuller part in the Beat "parade," but through his novels he does not hesitate to introduce a critical distance between certain elements of the Beat philosophy and his own. He seems to be strongly aware of Kerouac's tendency to myth making and exaggeration both in *On the Road* and in his public comments on the manner of its production. (As Howard Cunnell explains in his introduction to a new edition of *On the Road*, the legend that Kerouac wrote the novel in twenty days during various Benzedrine-fuelled high-speed typing sessions and all on one long scroll of paper obscures the previous three years of work done on the book since its conception, including the drafting of "three major proto-versions" and the revisions which followed its completion.[20])

That Pynchon's painstaking, research-heavy approach to writing is the virtual polar opposite of Kerouac's "spontaneous prose" production myth reflects the two writers' very different attitudes to freedom and escape. In both form and content, Pynchon's work problematises the idea that escape from oppressive social and economic structures can be as simple as *On the Road* seemed to suggest to many of those who read it, taking a cue, perhaps, from overlooked and underemphasised moments of sadness and defeat which recur throughout Kerouac's novel. A perspective on the difficulty of escape is expressed in *V.*'s narration of Herbert Stencil's addiction to the mystery of V., his use of this motivating principle as a means to "[a]pproach" yet also "avoid" facing up to larger realities.[21] Even more biting is the novel's commentary surrounding the character of Benny Profane, a "born pedestrian" (*V.* 356) whose name further positions him as a kind of anti-Sal Paradise, while also, potentially, referencing Kerouac's and other Beat poets' use of Benzedrine. Profane has a habit of "yo-yoing" on the subway and up and down the East Coast – a form of travel which, while subversive in its rejection of capitalist values relating to the use of time and the purpose of movement, yet fails to bring Benny into contact with any more meaningful way of life. His manner of riding the subway reflects a dulled anguish and a pessimistic refusal to struggle, contrasting markedly to that of Ginsberg's "best minds" in "Howl,"

> who chained themselves to subways for the endless
> ride from Battery to holy Bronx on benzedrine
> until the noise of wheels and children brought
> them down shuddering mouth-wracked and
> battered bleak of brain all drained of brilliance
> in the drear light of Zoo[22]

The monotonous movement of the yo-yo directly subverts Kerouacian motion; it represents not travel as adventure and exploration, but travel reduced to routine, an access of passivity. As Joseph Slade puts it, the yo-yo in *V.* represents "motion without meaning, or decadence."[23] The force which acts on a yo-yo is one of centripetal coercion rather than centrifugal liberation. Tugged at by a desire for Rachel Owlglass, Profane envisions himself as a yo-yo in "[h]ands it doesn't want to escape. Know[ing] that the simple clockwork of itself has no more need for symptoms of inutility, lonesomeness, directionlessness, because now it has a path marked out for it over which it has no control" (*V.* 217). Moreover, in *V.* twentieth-century civilisation is ruled not by the road but by "the Street," a negative, structured space, and its concomitant activity: tourism.

Pynchon's early pessimism over the possibility of liberating motion is matched, in *V.*, by a related scepticism regarding the potential for discovering any higher meaning in human existence. What questers discover in this novel most often concurs with Ludwig Wittgenstein's assertion that "The world is all that the case is" (*V.* 278), as Pynchon rejects what his character Fausto considers "the 'role' of the poet, this 20th Century" – to promote complacency by "cloaking [the] innate mindlessness with comfortable and pious metaphor" (*V.* 326).[24] Published three years later, *The Crying of Lot 49* is slightly more optimistic regarding the prospects of travel leading to meaningfulness, but it still substantially problematises the notion of spatial escape. Its protagonist Oedipa, who we first encounter inhabiting a bland suburbia, embarks on a journey which serves to liberate her from the reified patterns of her former life, but not necessarily to assimilate her into any supra-structural space of freedom. Unlike Profane, Oedipa is not pedestrian by nature, but finding a route out in the novel, even when one is behind the wheel of a Chevrolet Impala, is still a far more complex endeavour than it appears to be in *On the Road*. Initiated by the receipt of a letter requiring her to help execute the last will and testament of her ex-lover the real-estate mogul Pierce Inverarity, Oedipa's departure is not self-determined like that of Sal. Moreover, as she progresses on her journey, which soon turns from a legal investigation into a quest to make meaning out of the traces she uncovers of a shady organisation known as the "Trystero," the degree of free choice in her movements is brought into question as it is suggested that the late Pierce is somehow manipulating proceedings to his own dark ends. *Lot 49*'s enigmatic subject matter and tangled plot line are matched by the complexity of the forms of motion Oedipa undertakes. In place of a movement that is clearly directed towards freedom, we have in this novel a movement which is ambiguous in the etymological sense that it drives in both directions,[25] a journey which could lead to a revelation that would free Oedipa from the structures and doubts that bind her, or to some more or less straightforward form of destruction.[26]

Her inability to escape along the Kerouacian road works to frustrate Oedipa's chances of obtaining a clearer perspective on her situation and the reality of her entrapment. Rarely leaving the environs of a sprawling Los Angeles, she never makes it to anything which even remotely resembles the wildernesses described in *On the Road*. Every road journey she makes seems to lead her into spaces which are increasingly overburdened with structures, be they conceptual or physical. Experiencing the road as a space of radical freedom is, Pynchon suggests, no longer possible, if it was indeed ever anything more than a function of myth making in Kerouac's representation. *On the Road* recounted journeys made in 1947–50, but as John A. Kouwenhoven observes, by the early 1960s, "the 'interminable and stately prairies,' as Walt Whitman called them, [had been] ruled off by roads and fences into a mathematical grid," leaving us with "a technological landscape: subdivided by wire fences, smoothed by tractors, tied to the urban-industrial world by wires, roads, and rails, and by the invisible pulses felt in the lofty antennas."[27] San Narciso, the hub of Inverarity's property empire, consists of neighbourhoods that are built around the connective highways, which themselves become "little more than the road's skinny right-of-way, lined by auto lots, escrow services, drive-ins, small office buildings and factories whose address numbers [are] in the 70 and then 80,000s" (*L49* 15). Cities are now built to facilitate car travel, but Dean's dream of speed is subverted as businesses work to slow cars down in an attempt to pull in custom and streets stretch out into the suburban sprawl. The "illusion of speed, freedom, wind in your hair, unreeling landscape" is no more as "the road," reduced to a servant of the capitalist profit motive, is recognised as a "hypodermic needle, inserted somewhere ahead into the vein of a freeway, a vein nourishing the mainliner LA, keeping it happy, coherent, protected from pain" (*L49* 16).[28] The circuitousness of Pynchon's prose style, the digressions and lacunae in his complex plot lines and the tangled syntax of his multiple-clause sentences, reflects this lack of speed, freedom, and immediacy in American life.

Undermining Kerouac's idealism, Pynchon's representation of the road in this and other novels concurs more with that expressed in the work of another Beat poet, Lawrence Ferlinghetti. In a poem from his collection *A Coney Island of the Mind* Ferlinghetti declares:

> We are the same people
> >only further from home
> on freeways fifty lanes wide
> >on a concrete continent
> >>spaced with bland billboards
> >>>illustrating imbecile illusions of happiness.[29]

San Narciso, as its name suggests, reflects any attempt at escape back inwards, functioning like a hall of mirrors, and Oedipa is drawn into the "ordered swirl" of the city to the point where she completely loses her ability to orient herself. Towards the end of the novel, we find her standing between the anonymous symbols of the "public booth" and the "rented car," "pivoting on one stacked heel," unable to find the mountains or the sea (*L49* 122). Oedipa's disorientation culminates in the intimation that "there could be no barriers between herself and the rest of the land" (*L49* 122), a formulation which recalls Sal Paradise's similarly climactic experience of a state of oneness with the Mexican atmosphere achieved while sleeping on the roof of a car amid the intense humidity of the Tropic of Cancer: "For the first time in my life the weather was not something that touched me, that caressed me, froze or sweated me, but became me. The atmosphere and I became the same" (*OTR* 294). But while Sal's experience is "extremely pleasant and soothing" (*OTR* 294), a Romantic rapprochement with the natural world, Oedipa's leaves her stalled, still trapped between possibilities, structure paranoiacally layered on structure into the depths.

Yet despite such difficulties and frustrations, there can be little doubt that Oedipa, from Pynchon's perspective at least, is in a better position at the end of the novel than at the beginning. As the novel closes Oedipa is freer than before, her day is more open to unexpected intrusions. Although she has been unable to completely extricate herself from the structures of oppression, by disassociating herself from the familiar environment of Kinneret-Among-The-Pines she has at least solved the problem of the "absence of surprise to life": her experience is now characterised by a dramatic "expansion of possibilities." The same is of course true of all of Pynchon's questing characters across the entirety of his surreal and imaginative *oeuvre*. The liberatory potential of the road may be significantly compromised by the technologisation of the landscape, but characters are still positively motivated by the hope of attaining something valuable via motion. Paradoxically, although the road is now a structured and controlled space, and despite the early novels' intimations of the probable lack of any real meaning in life, as characters pursue their goals they are encouraged by proliferating *suggestions* of just such a transcendent significance encountered en route. In this sense, Pynchon's work quite strongly affirms the Beat faith in motion. Moreover, in countering his own assertions of the void, Pynchon expresses a fundamental optimism which reveals any nihilistic pronouncements as part of an assumed pose or protective stance.

Such optimism gradually gains ground in Pynchon's work, becoming more visible as the novels increasingly affirm potentialities beyond the given. *Mason & Dixon* is riddled with unexpected intrusions into the astronomers' reality – whether in the form of aggressive French frigates, pygmies claiming their right to inhabit the eleven days "lost" from the British year of 1752, or a fugitive mechanical duck that travels "between the Words ... shimmering into Visibility, for a few moments, then out again," while *Against the Day* imagines numerous other realities.[30] The epigraph chosen for Pynchon's recent novel *Inherent Vice* – "Under the paving-stones, the beach!" (a translation of the Situationist graffito from May 1968, Paris: "*Sous les pavés, la plage!*") – further confirms this emphasis on the wondrous unknown, and hints at its political significance. Other realities in Pynchon's fiction sometimes have a basis in the mathematical or physical sciences, but they are also given an important spiritual valence. This interest in the spiritual, this concern over meaningfulness, is, as we have seen, already present in *V.*, which deals, after all, with a quest whose object is finally a Bad Priest. In *The Crying of Lot 49* it is yet stronger: as Oedipa travels she experiences moments of near "hierophany" (*L49* 20), intimations of the sacred. (It is only a slight exaggeration to suggest, as Edward Mendelson does, that "[t]he manifestations of the Trystero ... and all that accompanies it, are always associated in the book with the language of the sacred and with patterns of religious experience").[31] In the following section, I suggest that Pynchon's investment in a spirituality which is intrinsically linked to discovery via motion in space serves to align his fundamental sensibility yet more closely with that of the Beats.

Transcendence, Liminality, and *Communitas*

Religious and spiritual experience was vital to many of the Beats, who can profitably be viewed as "spiritual protestors" lamenting modern society's lack of real engagement with the beyond.[32] Jack Kerouac, Gary Snyder, and Allen Ginsberg, among others, embraced and extolled the virtues of Eastern religion through their writings. Gary Snyder was the most thorough of the Beats in his engagement with the East, spending several years living as a Buddhist disciple in Japan and becoming "a living example of the counterculture's Zen ideal" and "San Francisco's off-shore representative."[33] Ginsberg became a great friend of Snyder, and Buddhist thought is one of the poles around which his poetry turns. Kerouac's own approach to religion was especially eclectic and experimental. Much of the Catholicism instilled in him during his French-Canadian upbringing was retained, and later came to be combined with elements of other religions, most notably Mahayana Buddhism.[34] This spirituality came through in his work clearly in novels like *The Dharma Bums* (1958) (a semi-autobiographical account of Kerouac's attempt to endure several weeks of complete solitude as a fire lookout atop a mountain named Desolation Peak), as well as in the collection of poetry entitled *The Scripture of the Golden Eternity* (1960), and non-fiction like *Some of the Dharma* (1997), but it was also present in *On the Road*, in which a large part of the motive energy discussed in the first section of this chapter was, in fact, directed towards a spiritual goal. As Beat poet and novelist John Clellon Holmes has attested, speaking of *On the Road*'s Sal and Dean, "the specific object of their quest was spiritual … their real journey was inward."[35] Although contemporary public reception largely bypassed this aspect of the work, which is primarily associated with Sal Paradise (Salvatore meaning "saviour"), focussing instead on the inspirational energy and largely secular passions of Dean Moriarty, the Beat interest in the spiritual came across more strongly in other works and fed through into the later counterculture; Pynchon recounts in *Slow Learner* how "the hippie resurgence" in Beat attitudes expressed renewed enthusiasm for "the wisdom of the East" (*SL* 9).[36] Thus the countercultural popularity of works such as Mircea Eliade's study of religious belief *The Sacred and the Profane*, and Herman Hesse's Buddhist novel *Siddharta*.

The spiritual bankruptcy of the West is as important a theme in Pynchon's early (and late) novels as it was in much Beat literature. In *V.*, for instance, the author expresses his disdain for both a degraded Catholicism and a widespread, empty hedonism. The poet Fausto Maijstral describes the post-war world in which the later parts of the novel are set as "physically and spiritually broken" (*V.* 307), and the process of its breaking is forcefully embodied in the trajectory of V., who metamorphosises from a "green" (*V.* 72) young girl at the turn of the century, eager to become a nun, into a corrupted "Bad Priest" who preaches that the men of Malta should be "like a crystal: beautiful and soulless" (*V.* 340), while advising the women to be celibate or to abort babies already conceived. (Such sermons eventually evince a cruel karmic payback on the Bad Priest, who, trapped beneath the rubble following a bombing, is picked apart by curious children and left to die as Fausto watches on, imbued with "passiveness," with the "characteristic stillness, perhaps, of the rock" (*V.* 445).) The predatory nature and, indeed, the insanity of the Catholic Church implied in the actions of the Bad Priest is further underscored by the tale of Father Fairing's "parish" in the sewers of Norfolk; in administering to his rat parishioners and providing them with "spiritual nourishment" we are told that he "considered it small enough sacrifice on their part to provide three of their own per day for physical sustenance" (*V.* 118).

Pynchon may criticise such perversions of faith, but atheism fares no better in *V.*. In the opening pages of the novel, set in "The Sailor's Grave" public house on Christmas Eve, the "militant atheist" Pig Bodine ruins a rare moment of communion in the singing of a hymn by calling for the commencement of the regular "Suck Hour" (in which sailors suck beer from taps concealed within large foam breasts), unleashing the temporarily subdued debauchery and bloodlust of those assembled (*V.* 15–16). Yet unlike the Beats, in his early work at least Pynchon does not offer up "the wisdom of the East" as a solution to the corrupt Catholicism or profane vulgarity he depicts.[37] In fact, *V.*'s only relevant allusion seems to be to a narrowly conceived Buddhism treated with considerable scepticism. As Ester Harvitz lies on an operating table undergoing rhinoplasty, she describes feeling herself "drifting down, this delicious loss of Esterhood, becoming more and more a blob, with no worries, traumas, nothing: only Being" and likens this to the attainment of "the highest condition" in "one of the Eastern" religions, that of becoming "an object – a rock" (*V.* 106). This scene implies a satiric rejection of the kind of "do-nothing" Buddhism the Kerouac character Ray Smith practised in *The Dharma Bums*, and a preference for the more restless spirituality that generally obtains in Kerouac's work. In promoting absolute passivity, Eastern logic so represented is undifferentiated from that of the Catholic "Bad Priest," and is therefore judged negatively.

The kinds of religious belief manifested in the world of *V.* are part of the problem, contributing to the lethargy of society, rather than motivating action or positive change. But the internal logic of the text and its critique of atheism suggest that we are in dire need of a more genuine spirituality. The novel's emphasis is on the idea that the world is running ever more "afoul of the inanimate" (*V.* 290): variations on the term "animate" appear again and again. Given the etymological associations of "animate," its links to the Latin *anima* (meaning "air, breath, life, soul") and *animus* (meaning "spirit"), this implies the desirability of spirit, of soul, and also of a related positive motion and activity, as opposed to a movement like Profane's yo-yoing, which causes him to "doubt his own animateness" (*V.* 217).[38] In *On the Road* motion is invested with a potentially positive spiritual value; it is broadly true that "[t]he essence of Beat divinity was motion as opposed to stasis."[39] So too in Pynchon's *V.*.

Pynchon's characters' desire for (spiritual) meaning makes their quests pilgrimages of sorts, something which, as manifested in *Against the*

Day, has received recent critical attention.[40] Meanwhile, evidence of a pilgrimage narrative lurking behind the scenes in *On the Road* (and in Beat texts more broadly) has been picked up on critically in articles including those by Stephen Prothero and Steve Wilson.[41] But Kerouac, like Pynchon, has a non-traditional, inventive approach to spirituality. Prothero points out that "[w]hat distinguished the beats from other pilgrims … was their lack of a 'center out there.' The beats shared, in short, not an identifiable geographical goal but an undefined commitment to a spiritual search. They aimed not to arrive but to travel."[42] Cities, coasts, and borders are merely secular substitutes for what I consider the real pilgrimage centre of Kerouac's novel, which Dean describes in a moment of linguistic inventiveness as "IT." An ecstasy of sorts, "IT" is an experience of freedom beyond structure, and also of the marvellous and of unity between people. IT is "a vital force in the experience of living that takes one by surprise, suspending for the moment belief in the 'real' concrete grey everyday facts of self and selfhood."[43] It can be achieved either via literal motion or via increased animation in speech, attention, or behaviour. Gunning down to Mexico with Sal, Dean proclaims his ultimate faith in the trip: "Man this will finally take us to IT!" (*OTR* 265). IT is a quality not only of a Mexico conceived in primitivistic splendour, but also of the reckless fluidity of Dean's driving, which, as described earlier, requires of him absolute concentration. In animated conversation, Dean claims that he has "IT," and when he encounters the "wild, ecstatic" Rollo Greb, he explains to Sal that Greb has "IT" too: "He's never hung-up, he goes every direction, he lets it all out, he knows time, he has nothing to do but rock back and forth. Man he's the end!" (*OTR* 126–7). Furthermore, in a lively jazz club, Dean explains that when the jazz soloist gets "IT" "[t]ime stops," and he "has to blow across bridges and come back and do it with such infinite feeling soul-exploratory for the tune of the moment that everybody knows it's not the tune that counts but IT – " (*OTR* 207–8).

Although not the concrete, sacred location we conventionally expect as the end goal of religious pilgrimages, this internal experience as described by Dean bears the core characteristics of the anthropologist Victor Turner's concept of a pilgrimage centre. For Turner, pilgrimage centres represent "a 'threshold,' a place and moment 'in and out of time,'" in which a pilgrim hopes for "direct experience of the sacred, invisible, or supernatural order, either in the material aspect of miraculous healing or in the immaterial aspect of inward transformation of spirit or personality."[44] The disruption of everyday conceptions of time is key in both this description and those offered by Dean. Dean repeatedly expresses the importance of "knowing time," understanding time on some higher plane, in *On the Road*. Turner's emphasis on reaching across to other orders of experience is matched by Kerouac's depiction of those who have "IT" transcending their situation in some way – whether this means pushing beyond the limitations of a melody, as in the case of the jazzman, being able to rise above everyday irritations, to go "in every direction" as Rollo Greb does, or crossing the physical border into foreign lands, like Sal and Dean. That Dean is unable to find a better name for the phenomenon further attests to its existence beyond all structural paradigms, including the linguistic. Escape into "IT" is the ultimate expression of liberation in the novel, and thus has an unquestionably healing and transformative value.

The connections embedded in *On the Road* and many other Beat and countercultural texts – and also taken up, it appears, by Pynchon – between motion, spiritual meaningfulness, freedom, and community feeling, can be elucidated further via Turner's anthropological analyses of the pilgrimage and the rite of passage put forward in his study *The Ritual Process*.[45] For Turner, both of these social phenomena are examples of "anti-structural" experience: in other words, experience that transcends the everyday social and routine structures of life. He identifies two principal characteristics of "anti-structure": *liminality* and *communitas*. The term "liminality" derives from Arnold van Gennep's notion of the *rite de passage* ("rites which accompany every change of place, state, social position and age") as a three-stage phenomenon moving from separation to margin (or *limen* meaning "threshold") to aggregation.[46] Liminality describes a state between states, a condition of ambiguity and indeterminacy in which ritual subjects lose the attributes of their former position but are yet to gain those of their new one. As such the liminal is associated with the womb state, with death, darkness, the wilderness, bisexuality, and invisibility.[47] Since they involve motion and hence a change of place, liminality is also a feature of pilgrimages.

Communitas, the second characteristic of anti-structure, was, Turner argued, a common result of accession to a liminal state. A feeling of oneness with humanity as a whole, "the spontaneous, immediate, concrete nature of communitas" comes most fully into focus, he suggested, when contrasted to "the norm-governed, institutionalized, abstract nature of social structure."[48] In other words, communitas is strongest when the fixed bonds of the social structure are felt to be at their weakest. In the liminal state, the ritual subject in a rite of passage characteristically has "no status, property, insignia, secular clothing indicating rank or role, position in a kinship system – in short, nothing that may distinguish them from their fellow neophytes or initiands."[49] Furthermore, they are made to endure humiliations and must "accept arbitrary punishment without complaint."[50] Subjects are thus "ground down to a uniform condition to be fashioned anew" ready for their new position, and this ground-down state, also achieved on pilgrimages, produces communitas – an "intense comradeship and egalitarianism."[51]

The cultural movement we have been considering, with its thrust towards a liminal state outside of the controlling frameworks of city or town life, seems then to be instinctively seeking after such feelings of intense comradeship. As Turner himself notes, writing in 1969, "the values of communitas are strikingly present in the literature and behavior of what came to be known as the 'beat generation,' who were succeeded by the 'hippies.'"[52] He identifies distinguishing features of these groups corresponding to a liminal and communitas-based lifestyle including their adoption of hobo-like dress, their itinerancy, love of folk music and sexual liberation, their use of religious terms stressing unity such as the Zen Buddhist formulation "all is one, one is none, none is all," their emphasis on spontaneity and immediacy, and their habits of casual, low-paid employment.[53] "Anti-structure" notionally shares a great number of qualities with "counterculture," and the works of Beat and counterculture writers express a sense of imbalance, a lack of opportunities for freedom, the necessity of anti-structure.[54] In *On the Road*, Kerouac's "IT" can thus be read as an experience of anti-structure and of communitas.

In attempting to redress the social balance, the Beat and counterculture movements were responding not only to the stagnation or spiritual poverty of society discussed earlier, but also to the lack of community, the pervasive isolation, and alienation of modernity. Thus William Burroughs's *Naked Lunch* represents human relationships operating in vicious indifference, and his fiction is populated with "fractured and dislocated figures."[55] A general tenor of suffering and incomprehension also underlies Ginsberg's poetry even as he celebrates the strength of his personal relationships in poems such as "Howl," "Sunflower Sutra," and "Many Loves." In "A Supermarket in California," Ginsberg more pointedly laments the "lost America of love" and the present "solitary streets."[56] In *On The Road*, while Dean, embodiment of communitas, exudes optimism and dynamism in his frantic energy, and in his long letters the hope that true communication and community are still possible, Sal's musings on "poor beat life itself in the god-awful streets of man" (*OTR* 199) suggest that loneliness and sorrow are ultimately indelible characteristics of modern American life.[57]

Pynchon's early production has a similar melancholy tone to it; *V.*'s emplotment of humanity's increasing *attraction* towards inanimateness (as literalised in Rachel Owlglass's lust for her MG) implies that human relationships are coming to function more and more on the basis of power dynamics, following a sadomasochistic model in which the "other" becomes an object of abuse, and lovers are distanced from each other as V. and Melanie are by "the mirror's soulless gleam" (*V.* 411). In *V.*, people may exist in close proximity, but their interactions are lacking in humanity. On the Norfolk subway, the routinisation of life has spawned "nine million yo-yos" who crowd the subways: "[v]ertical corpses, eyes with no life, crowded loins, buttocks and hip-points together" (*V.* 303). The Whole Sick Crew, a reincarnation of their predecessors the Crew of Foppl's siege party, are likewise sunk into a fruitless hedonism, an endless series of wild drunken parties which do not, one feels, substitute for a real community or make up for their participants' "deracinated" (*V.* 382) status. The novel laments this modern loss of roots, of a sense of home – a sentimentality which increases over the course of Pynchon's career, and which perhaps owes something to the work of Kerouac. In *V.*, Paola's choice of words to express her homesickness for Malta – "Benito, things are falling apart. The sooner I get home – " (*V.* 417) – strongly recalls Sal's repeated worry, at the end of the various cycles of disassociation and reaggregation which structure *On the Road*, to the effect that "[e]verything was falling apart" (*OTR* 77) or "[e]verything was collapsing" (*OTR* 99, 221). If Kerouac's characters are pilgrims seeking the "intense comradeship" of anti-structural communitas, so too are Pynchon's: in questing after V. (who may indeed be his mother) the reticent Stencil admits: "It may be that Stencil has been lonely and needs something for company" (*V.* 54).

Isolation is also central to Oedipa's experience in *The Crying of Lot 49*; as noted, her sense of a lack of "intensity" is accompanied by feelings of "buffeting" and "insulation." In seeking the Trystero, Oedipa hopes to uncover more than an underground postal service, rather "a network by which X number of Americans are truly communicating whilst reserving their lies, recitations of routine, arid betrayals of spiritual poverty, for the official government delivery system" (*L49* 117–18). Her quest is directed towards the attainment of communitas, and thus towards a society which might foster a new spirituality and new freedoms of action beyond the routine. In seeking this, Oedipa enters the liminal realms of America, and in doing so she comes into contact with communities of outsiders living permanently on the threshold of society, both "in and out of" official structures of account and control.[58] Progressing on her journey she becomes ever more aware of the vitality which often characterises such denizens of the margins. Treading the railroad sleepers towards the end of the novel, she realises the existence of an America not coded in Inverarity's will, not recognised by and hence not subject to the capitalist system. This leads her to think of

> other, immobilized freight cars, where the kids sat on the floor planking and sang back, happy as fat, whatever came over the mother's pocket radio; of other squatters who stretched canvas for lean-tos behind smiling billboards along all the highways, or slept in junkyards in the stripped shells of wrecked Plymouths, or even, daring, spent the night up some pole in a linesman's tent like caterpillars, swung among a web of telephone wires, living in the very copper rigging and secular miracle of communication, untroubled by the dumb voltages flickering their miles, the night long, in the thousands of unheard messages. She remembered drifters she had listened to, Americans speaking their language carefully, scholarly, as if they were in exile from somewhere else invisible yet congruent with the cheered land she lived in; and walkers along the roads at night, zooming in and out of your headlights without looking up, too far from any town to have a real destination. (*L49* 124–5)

This inventory of those Americans who remain living in relative anti-structure, and thus with communitas, inhabiting the interstices of the vast web of communications and transport networks which they have subverted from their original purposes in order to make homes of them, is all that is "left to inherit" (*L49* 124) once Inverarity's vast real estate empire has been apportioned out. Linked by the W.A.S.T.E. communications system, such liminal groupings offer Oedipa hope of escaping being "assumed full circle into some paranoia" (*L49* 126), hope of overcoming her isolation through access to a genuine community in which all communitas feelings have not been channelled into Ferlinghetti-esque "smiling billboards."

Oedipa's interest in such exiles parallels that of Sal and Dean in similar liminal communities in *On the Road*, an extremely well-documented aspect of both this novel and Beat culture more generally. As Stephen Prothero has suggested,

> the beats looked for spiritual insight not to religious elites but to the racially marginal and the socially inferior, "fellah" groups that shared with them an aversion to social structures and established religion. Hipsters and hoboes, criminals and junkies, jazzmen and African-Americans initiated the beats into their alternative worlds, and the beats reciprocated by transforming them into the heroes of their novels and poems.[59]

The travelling hoboes of the American railroads are objects of particular admiration, and, indeed, imitation, in Kerouac's novel, and Dean's attempt to find his father amongst them symbolises the quest to cast off the decrepit frameworks of a society headed towards self-annihilation, and re-establish a connection with the generative source of the basic human community. Another liminal community mentioned by Prothero which is celebrated in *On the Road* is the "fellahin," a group Kerouac treats as the guardians of a powerful regenerative energy. In Sal's words, hope for the post-apocalyptic future lies in the fellahin, "the essential strain of the basic primitive, wailing humanity that stretches in a belt around the equatorial belly of the world ... the source of mankind and the fathers of it," who "will still stare with the same eyes from the caves of Mexico" when "the Apocalypse of the Fellahin returns once more as so many times before" (*OTR* 280). The existence of a certain genealogy between Pynchon's interconnected W.A.S.T.E./Trystero organisations and Kerouac's fellahin has been pointed out by Petillon, and in *V.* Pynchon also pays direct tribute to the persistence of the "fellahin" amid deprivation and suffering (*V.* 79).[60]

Yet, in championing, even worshipping, such marginal groups, the Beats tended to stereotype them – an aspect of their work which has received considerable criticism.[61] Moreover, rather than promoting substantial integration, Kerouac's approach was more often to simply pillage these alternative cultures, taking from them certain insights and behavioural styles, while retaining the economic advantages of his own white, middle-class status. (This attitude comes across most forcefully in *On the Road* in Sal's planned abandonment of his Mexican girlfriend, Terry, a relationship closely modelled on Kerouac's real-life dalliance with Bea Franco.) Just as Pynchon's depiction of the road's subservience to capitalist imperatives problematises Kerouac's easy escapism, so does his treatment of marginal cultures work against this second weakness in Kerouac's prose, bringing clearly into view the role of powerful social forces (again, often resulting from a capitalist logic) in maintaining their distanced, alienated state.

As mentioned, one of those to get "IT" in *On the Road* is an African American jazz musician. In performing his solo, the jazzman expresses an individual creative freedom which is at the same time an affirmation of his sense of connection with both his fellow band mates and the audience.[62] Communicating his individual interpretation, the performer seems, in Dean's description, to unite and to liberate all those present. Constructed on the basis of flexibility, transformation, and animation, jazz is music on the anti-structural model, "egalitarian and open to all, a joint project where everyone is welcome to participate."[63] As was made clear in his introduction to *Slow Learner*, Pynchon too associated jazz with new freedoms, with "centrifugal" force. From his depiction of the African American jazz soloist

McClintic Sphere in *V.*, to the analogy made between jazz and the perfect anarchic organisation in *Against the Day* (anarchy being practically synonymous with anti-structure), wherever jazz appears in Pynchon's novels it is in connection with countercultural figures or philosophies, and it symbolises "right thinking." But Pynchon's representation of Sphere's experience of the V. Note jazz club (delivered, importantly, from Sphere's own perspective) differs markedly from Kerouac's portrait of the ecstatic jazzman in deep communion with his audience. While for Kerouac's alto "it was all great moments of laughter and understanding for him and everyone else who heard" (*OTR* 202), when Sphere solos on *his* alto saxophone, those in the bar are divided into various factions that either do not dig (the collegians), try to dig (the workers), or appear to dig (the people at the bar), "but this was probably only because people who prefer to stand at the bar have, universally, an inscrutable look" (*V.* 59). Later in the novel, when Sphere's "tired" horn man takes over the solo, Sphere himself is only "half listening," while musing on the patronising "Northern liberal routine" college students like to go through, and resenting what he considers their faked professions of admiration for black musicians. Moreover, we are told that those who "did or wanted to understand" were crowded out of the bar by rich kids and other musicians who did not (*V.* 280–1). In this way, *V.* critiques the Kerouacian and Beat idolisation and selective (mis)representation of African American culture, underscoring the ongoing social rift between many black Americans and their white contemporaries.

Pynchon's early novels express a Beat or "post-Beat" sensibility in proposing that freedom and spiritual meaningfulness may be gained by transcending the routine, by travel, by association with communities of exiles, or even by listening to jazz (in the right circumstances). But while Dean's promotion of "IT" in *On the Road* posits an extreme and prolonged transcendence of all structures of thought and action as a goal to aim for, Pynchon's approach is more tentative and more realistic, his idealism tempered by an awareness that even normative, functional communities are extremely hard to come by, that the kind of epiphanic *existential communitas* sought by Dean can only ever be fleeting, and that certain structures serve an inescapably practical purpose in human life.[64] Thus in *The Crying of Lot 49* the usefulness and even the safety of pursuing the promise of some highly obscure form of immediate, unstructured enlightenment is called into question. This is achieved primarily through the narrative regarding the alcoholic sailor that Oedipa encounters in a rundown lodging house, an old man whose delirium tremens allows him, Oedipa thinks, to experience "spectra beyond the known sun" (*L49* 89). Unlike Rollo Greb in *On the Road*, whose voiceless "spastic ecstasy" (*L49* 127) is an expression of his intense excitement and joy in life, the sailor's visions are "made purely of Antarctic loneliness and fright" (*L49* 89) and have left him a physical and mental wreck, unable to find a means of reconciling with the wife he left behind years before. While Rollo is somehow able to perpetuate his experience of "IT," a skill for which he is hero worshipped by Dean, the sailor's transcendent insights cannot be preserved, and he is a social outcast, isolated and suffering. If one attains an entirely anti-structural level of understanding, Pynchon suggests, one cannot use the conceptual paradigms we rely on – logical thought, time, language – to recall and pass on the insight. Thus, earlier in the novel, Oedipa muses on the similar plight of the epileptic, who recalls only what triggered his attack and never its revelations, and wonders whether at the end of her quest "she too might not be left with only compiled memories of clues, announcements, intimations, but never the central truth itself, which must somehow each time be too bright for her memory to hold; which must always blaze out, destroying its own message irreversibly" (*L49* 66). This image prefigures Oedipa's vision of the sailor burning amongst his soiled bedclothes, and suggests, furthermore, that frustrated insights can even have a destructive influence on those who experience them. In the case of the sailor, such dark visions perpetuate, perhaps, the vicious cycle of alcoholism that has alienated him from his wife.

In fact, there is a similar awareness of the final inaccessibility of meaning in *On The Road*, but again, as in the case of spirituality in the novel, this is largely expressed by the more pensive Sal, who tends to function as a foil for the brilliance and enthusiasm of Dean. One instance of this occurs when Sal witnesses the attempts of Dean and Carlo Marx (Allen Ginsberg) to communicate totally their every last thought and intention to each other, and realises that, reliant as they are on both a limited language and the inevitably selective human memory, they can never succeed: "That last thing is what you can't get, Carlo. Nobody can get to that last thing. We keep on living in hopes of catching it once for all" (*OTR* 48). Later in the novel, high on marijuana and swaying through the Mexican countryside, that site of maximum *communitas*, Sal himself seems to approach a revelation which yet eludes him. The liminal "passenger" in the rite of passage Dean is taking him on, Sal gets the feeling that the meaning of what he is experiencing is beyond the power of the human mind to grasp:

> [t]he mere thought of looking out the window at Mexico – which was now something else in my mind – was like recoiling from some gloriously

riddled glittering treasure-box that you're afraid to look at because of your eyes, they bend inward, the riches and the treasures are too much to take all at once. (*OTR* 284)

But while Sal treats the limitations of human expression and understanding as harmless frustrations, perhaps even heightening the wonder of the approach towards meaning, Pynchon's early work recognises that we must focus our action within the functional parameters given to us, making use of available conceptual and communicative frameworks however limited they may be. To continually seek after an elusive ultimacy is, Pynchon suggests, a potentially harmful distraction from the more practical possibilities available.

In line with such an approach, in *The Crying of Lot 49* Pynchon undermines to some extent the notion that the modern subject is able to enter into anti-structural liminality without psychological repercussions. As Turner explained, escape from structure and access to egalitarian community entails a "grinding down" of the self, the loss of common markers of identity. Oedipa's quest parallels Sal's in that as she travels she moves away from familiar structures and descends (or ascends) into the anonymity of liminality, but unlike Sal she is unnerved by the loss of her stable identity. When Sal wakes up near the beginning of his life on the road in a hostel by the railway tracks in Des Moines, "halfway across America, at the dividing line between the East of my youth and the West of my future" (*OTR* 15), he loses his identity completely for a moment. But he is not overcome by fear, instead he becomes "just somebody else, some stranger," his life "the life of a ghost" (*OTR* 15). Sal is like Turner's neophyte who has been stripped of all the attributes of his former life in order to be prepared for that to come, and the life to come, for Sal at this moment, is unquestionably positive. Oedipa's future prospects are not so clear to her, and she makes every attempt to preserve her identity as protection against the latent threat she feels lurking beneath the blank shimmering surface of San Narciso. The layers of clothes she puts on before engaging in a game of "Strip Botticelli" are an expression of this hesitance to forsake the buffering shield of her ego. As the clothes are slowly removed, paralleling the stripping of such secular proofs of rank and status in a rite of passage, Oedipa feels time slow down, her perceptions becoming "less and less clear." Going into the bathroom, she "tried to find her image in the mirror and couldn't," which results in "a moment of nearly pure terror" (*L49* 27). In characteristic Pynchon style, the joke is on Oedipa, as she realises with relief that she cannot see herself because the mirror had been broken in an earlier incident involving a flying aerosol can. Again, what is experienced positively in *On the Road* is fraught with difficulties in *The Crying of Lot 49*.

Into the Sixties

Pynchon was clearly inspired by the Beat movement, by its pure energy, its vigorous valorisation of communal experience, individual freedom, and the pursuit of spiritual meaning, its thrust towards liberation from the stifling structures of the military-industrial complex. However, as I hope to have made clear in my analysis, Pynchon perceived certain elements of the Beat attitude and approach as expressed within Kerouac's *On the Road* as naive, impractical, or misrepresentative of American reality. For Pynchon, as noted earlier, the Beat movement "was a sane and decent affirmation of what we all want to believe about American values" (*SL* 9). But rather than overlooking the problems and affirming what we *want* to believe, Pynchon's fiction attempts to throw into stark relief the obstacles that confront us on the road to freedom. Thus his emphasis on our entrapment within modern environments and modern mindsets, and his suggestion that there may be no ultimate meaning in life, or that the human mind may be incapable of apprehending, recalling, or communicating such meaning. Pynchon's relative seriousness in the early and mid sixties reflects his stronger sense of the imperative of change, a sense of urgency that potentially aligns him more with the politically activist student movements of the early sixties than with the more culturally radical Beats.

On this point Pynchon diverges strongly from Kerouac, who was among the least political of the Beats. While the Beat movement was not activist in any traditional sense, much Beat poetry contained social and political criticism – Allen Ginsberg's characterisation of capitalist America as a "Moloch whose blood is running money" in "Howl" being a prime example.[65] But Kerouac's work tended not to address such issues. Indeed, writing to Lawrence Ferlinghetti in May 1961, the author defends the United States as the site of "no Belsens ... no mortal purges, no decimations of population by starvation," suggests that "the 'Peace Marchers' [protesting Cold War atomic acceleration] are essentially marching *against america* [*sic*]," and exclaims that "[w]hile we're still young we should all join hands but not in politics, in God's name, in POETRY."[66] Indeed, he expressed anger at fellow Beats Corso and Ginsberg over their perversion of "beat" to political ends, labelling them in 1964 "frustrated hysterical provocateurs and attention-seekers with nothing on their mind but rancor towards 'America' and the life of ordinary people."[67] Although the sorrowful undertone to his novels evinces a degree of awareness of the distance that lies between the democratic dream that America was supposed to embody and the essentially alienated plutocratic reality of what it had become, when he wrote *On the Road*, Kerouac's view of the country which had long provided a comfortable home for his immigrant mother and himself was not nearly as negative as that of many of his contemporaries, or of Pynchon.[68] *On the Road* may have been radical in its reinvention of literary form, it may have helped create a cultural revolution in its vision of an alternative way of life, but deliberate political critique was not its intention. (This is true despite Kerouac's claim in a 1958 interview published in the *San Francisco Examiner* that "[t]he political apathy of the Beat Generation is in itself a 'political' movement; i.e., will influence political decisions in the future and possibly transfer politics to their rightful aims, i.e., sense."[69])

During the early sixties the student organisations of the New Left were offering an alternative to the individualism and predominantly cultural focus of the Beats, putting more emphasis on actively and immediately helping oppressed others and aiming for a society-wide revolution. An important indicator of the new political urgency that was beginning to imbue American youth, *The Port Huron Statement*, manifesto of the student activist group Students for a Democratic Society, was particularly concerned with the potential repercussions of the deployment of the atomic bomb and the escalation of the Cold War. Disaster was predicted, and SDS claimed that: "[o]ur work is guided by the sense that we may be the last generation in the experiment with living," that "we ourselves, and our friends, and millions of abstract 'others' we knew more directly because of our common peril, might die at any time."[70] Despair on this front was combined with frustration over the realities of institutionalised racism, then being brought to the attention of white America via the struggles and triumphs of the civil rights movement. Later in the 1960s, the Vietnam War was to become the major focus of the student Left. While Kerouac's *On the Road* had promoted the pursuit of the transcendent or ecstatic via escape into anti-structure, for Tom Hayden and his comrades in the burgeoning New Left the structures of the current social system, and particularly the regular patterns of thought and judgement, required immediate transformation if life itself was to be preserved. Although the establishment asserted that "there [was] no viable alternative to the present," that change was impossible, it was an urgent necessity for society's new rebels: the "invisible framework" which "seem[ed] to hold back chaos" for the average American had to be smashed, and to this end a non-violent activist agenda of sit-ins, marches, demonstrations, and the like was proposed.[71] *On the Road* inspired its readership with suggestions of the "kicks" that could be obtained via road travel and alternative lifestyles, but by the early sixties it seemed that much more was at stake, requiring a more direct methodology.

Pynchon was clearly influenced by the new instabilities and uncertainties of the times. His greater emphasis on practicality over idealism and his problematisation of various Kerouacian assumptions, reflects, no doubt, the deeper politicisation of his work. Despite having been admittedly "unpolitical" at college (*SL* 6), in *V.*'s critique of historical imperialist brutality abroad, and *The Crying of Lot 49*'s wider recognition of ongoing oppression within the American homeland, Pynchon's growing political engagement makes itself clearly felt. His narration of the troubled meanderings of the self-questioning postmodern subject, always unsure of the degree of free choice available, differs significantly from a figure like Kerouac's vital Dean, and is reflective of the marked sense in the 1960s that government control was encroaching into the everyday freedoms of its citizens. *The Crying of Lot 49* in particular dramatises what *The Port Huron Statement* describes as "the dominant conceptions of man in the twentieth century: that he is a thing to be manipulated, and that he is inherently incapable of directing his own affairs."[72] Moreover, an interest in non-violent direct action expresses itself explicitly in *The Crying of Lot 49* via Oedipa's encounter with campus politics on her visit to the University of Berkeley, and is also more subtly present in the underground W.A.S.T.E. postal system, uniting a network of social pariahs in an act of quiet rebellion against governmental monopolisation and control of lines of communication. That such liminal, anti-structural groups might pose a real threat to the powerful is suggested by Pynchon's imagining of their more violent potentialities (something which was to show itself in the New Left later in the 1960s) in his linking of the W.A.S.T.E. organisation with the brutally violent historical Trystero courier service (W.A.S.T.E. being an acronym for "We Await Silent Trystero's Empire"). It might thus be surmised that, like many within the student Left, Pynchon perceived in the early to mid sixties the need for a more deliberate and comprehensive approach to attaining a greater degree of freedom for all, in which activism towards political change must take precedence over apolitical aesthetic innovation. Pynchon's alignment with New Left ideals and methods is therefore the focus of the next chapter.

CHAPTER 2

Love, Violence, and Yippie Subversion in Gravity's Rainbow
Pynchon and the New Left

The legacy of the Beat movement was an ongoing trend of cultural subversion in America which gradually gathered pace and fed into the mass phenomenon of the hippie counterculture in the late sixties. During the earlier years of the decade, however, political activism became the primary manifestation of youthful unrest in America, taking its cue from the civil rights movement. The universities were at the centre of political protest in this era, spawning a number of student activist organisations. One of those with the highest profile was the Student Non-Violent Coordinating Committee (SNCC), whose members pitched in with the struggle for civil rights, developed the concept of Black Power, opposed the Vietnam War, and encouraged people to "use their energy in building democratic forms" within the United States.[1] Another was Students for a Democratic Society (SDS), who also stressed the need for the universal democratisation of society and called for the reassertion of the American values enshrined in the U.S. Declaration of Independence and Abraham Lincoln's Gettysburg Address: "[f]reedom and equality for each individual, government of, by, and for the people."[2] Collectively, student organisations came to form what was known as the New Left, of which SDS was the recognised figurehead. As explained in the introduction to this study, the New Left shared many core values and goals with contemporary cultural movements, envisioning an ideal society based on the tenets of personalism, egalitarianism, flexibility, "participatory democracy," and community.[3] Within this kind of society an open-minded individual could achieve wholeness through varied experience, creativity being combined with and stimulated through continuous learning. Pure hedonism was not of interest to the early sixties youth movements, whether culturally or politically focussed – that came later as the counterculture became a mass phenomenon. Rather, emphasis was laid on the responsibility of each individual to contribute and become an integral part of the social system. Fluidity between self and society was the aim, a unity that was to some extent achieved within youth groups at the time.

Despite this basic confluence in values, in terms of priorities and methods the New Left distinguished itself fairly sharply from the Beat generation that had gone before, and from the psychedelic, hippie, and commune movements that developed alongside it. Specifically, the New Left had narrower, more pragmatic goals, as well as being more other-directed. New Left organisations tended to locate sources of oppression within particular institutions, systems, and elites, finding meaning in attacking these directly through variously (un)traditional forms of political activism. Especially in its earlier manifestations, the New Left endorsed hard work and sacrifice towards effecting concrete reforms to elements of the American social, political, or economic structure, although the organisation was later to take on a more revolutionary bent. In contrast, cultural factions mounted a much broader critique of civilisation and its imposed limitations per se, questioning basic assumptions such as the reliability of sense perceptions and the nature of the rational. For them, reflecting the influence of the Beats, change was to spring from the self, and particularly from what might be considered a more "spiritual" relationship between man and nature (something hallucinogenic drugs helped many to envision). The emphasis was on spontaneity and the potential joy to be had in the moment rather than on future social improvements. Interest in the Third World was strong across the counterculture, but for the New Left this interest inhered in particular revolutionary movements, their tactics and leadership, rather than in the very different cultural and religious models offered by such countries.[4]

Early Reactions to the New Left

The idea that Pynchon would be in sympathy with certain aspects of New Left thought is confirmed fairly straightforwardly by his endorsement of Kirkpatrick Sale's 1973 study *SDS: Ten Years Toward a Revolution*, which Pynchon considers "the first great history of the American prerevolution," "a source of clarity, energy and sanity for anyone trying to survive the Nixonian reaction," and "one book that was there when we needed it the most."[5] Various critics approaching Pynchon's work from a historico-political perspective have asserted his ideological proximity to groups like SDS, an aspect of Pynchon's political philosophy which this chapter seeks to more fully describe the dimensions of.[6] My present analysis begins with *The Crying of Lot 49*, by the time of whose publication student-led subversion was flourishing across the United States. Pynchon's contemporary reaction to this can be glimpsed in the narrator's depiction of the Berkeley campus of the University of California, visited by Oedipa on her quest for information regarding the Trystero:

> It was summer, a weekday, and midafternoon; no time for any campus Oedipa knew of to be jumping, yet this one was. She came downslope from Wheeler Hall, through Sather Gate into a plaza teeming with corduroy, denim, bare legs, blonde hair, hornrims, bicycle spokes in the sun, bookbags, swaying card tables, long paper petitions dangling to earth, posters for undecipherable FSMs, YAFs, VDCs, suds in the fountain, students in nose-to-nose dialogue. (*L49* 71)

This proliferative catalogue of the imagery of student protest contains an energy, a forward momentum, which implies that the passage should be read as an enthusiastic judgement on the vibrancy of the movement. For Oedipa it is all a million miles away from her own experience of college life, albeit relatively recent: 1957 was "[a]nother world" (*L49* 71) by comparison. The "nerves, blandness and retreat" that had characterised Oedipa's education are explicitly contrasted here to the new order, under which "the most beloved of folklores may be brought into doubt, cataclysmic of dissents voiced, suicidal of commitments chosen – the sort that bring governments down" (*L49* 71). Writing this, Pynchon is expressing his own direct experience of a change in campus dynamic. In his 1983 introduction to college friend Richard Fariña's *Been Down So Long It Looks Like Up To Me* (1966), Pynchon discusses his years at Cornell studying English, describing the university in 1958 and 1959 as "another planet," one where sexual repression was enforced by the campus authorities, and protest was a novel and incongruous phenomenon, a "preview of the '60s."[7] (Cornell is also where Oedipa has apparently studied for her degree in English.) But although this passage appears to be predominantly supportive of student movements, of their emphasis on dialogue and their will to move forward in active pursuit of change, it contains qualifying elements which suggest that Pynchon's political philosophy may not be fully aligned with that of the New Left. For Pynchon's narrator organisational acronyms are "undecipherable" and commitments may be "suicidal." Within the orbit of the novel, the university campus is an isolated idyll amid a wider world which is reigned over still by the somnolence of the 1950s and held tightly in the exploitative grip of capitalist ideology. There is no hint that the student protestors at the University of California are in contact, via W.A.S.T.E. or other means, with other alternative and underground communities of the Bay area we learn about during the course of the novel.

Pynchon bluntly states the need for such cross-community involvement in his 1984 introduction to *Slow Learner*, in which he provides a retrospective judgement on the later developments of the student movement, asserting that "[t]he success of the 'new left' later in the '60's was to be limited by the failure of college kids and blue-collar workers to get together politically" (*SL* 7). Earlier in his career and at the peak of the New Left's success, Pynchon already expresses an awareness of the necessity of such interaction in his article "A Journey into the Mind of Watts," published in *The New York Times Magazine* shortly after *The Crying of Lot 49* first saw print. This piece of journalism offers a relatively unequivocal insight into Pynchon's view of certain forms of political action. In his discussion of the riots that had ravaged the Watts district of southern Los Angeles during the summer of 1965, Pynchon is most pointedly critical of the city's white population, which he considers wilfully ignorant of Watts and its problems, preferring to remain immersed in the unreality and transience of the so-called L.A. Scene.[8] The investigative strategy that Pynchon has followed in researching his article, involving travelling to Watts, observing the neighbourhood, and speaking directly to the locals, is offered up as a model for others to follow. Yet "A Journey" puts forward no easy solutions to such deeply ingrained social problems. Interpersonal understanding or identification are objectives endorsed here, but social projects which bring in outsiders seeking to ameliorate the situation in Watts via vocational training or educational measures are construed as meddlesome, patronising, and "strangely ineffective" (J 80). Although the area has been "seething with social workers, data collectors, VISTA volunteers and other assorted members of the humanitarian establishment" since the previous summer, according to Pynchon, "nothing much has changed" (J 35). In particular, the Economic and Youth Opportunities Agency of Greater Los Angeles (EYOA) is an object of indifference or mistrust for those tired of "The Man's" continual broken promises. For Pynchon, these proponents of Lyndon B. Johnson's "War on Poverty" are taking the wrong tack with their "inspirational mottoes" (J 81), corporate-style catchphrases, and statistical analyses because "they seem to be smiling themselves out of any meaningful communication with their poor" (J 82). Elaborating on his point, Pynchon contends that "[b]esides a 19th-century faith that tried and true approaches – sound counseling, good intentions, perhaps even compassion – will set Watts straight, [the EYOA volunteers] are also burdened with the personal attitudes they bring to work with them. Their reflexes – especially about conformity, about failure, about violence – are predictable" (J 82).

At the time Pynchon was writing, New Left groups were operating in the interests of poor black communities in the United States in ways distinct from those described earlier, using novel and creative methods predicated upon less conformist, more open-minded notions of what helping might entail. While government agencies maintained a professional distance, members of SNCC participating in voter registration drives in the South risked their lives (and some lost their lives) in their attempts to call attention to practices limiting black suffrage. On trips south from their Northern campuses, student activists lived within the communities they were seeking to help, either in rented "Freedom Houses" or in the homes of local families who took them in.[9] Inventive new forms of protest like the "sit-in" (with its associated "teach-ins," "be-ins," and so forth) and the "freedom ride" that had originated in the civil rights movement were enthusiastically adopted by student protestors in the early 1960s. In 1963 SDS began in earnest its efforts in community organising, developing the Economic Research and Action Project (ERAP) with the aim of reaching out to the wider community of oppressed peoples and creating "an interracial movement of the poor."[10] Again, this involved student staffers moving into rundown neighbourhoods. Responsibility, commitment, and respect were the foundations upon which ERAP based its presence in the slums; paternalism was to be avoided at all costs – even if that meant compromising the effectiveness of organising.[11]

Pynchon's approach to community involvement as embodied by "A Journey into the Mind of Watts," is clearly much more in line with New Left strategies at this point in the mid sixties than with the "tried and true approaches" of the government agencies. But his reportage is still methodologically distant from New Left organising and activist practices, and his exact perspective on these remains unclear. In *The Crying of Lot 49* Pynchon's particular choice of wording in his depiction of student protest suggested a hesitance to endorse New Left tactics too naively; his dismissal of "establishment" volunteers' projects in "A Journey" may imply some lack of enthusiasm for student-run versions of the same. It is notable that where the article affirms attempts to change things in Watts the emphasis is laid on more abstract and artistic political tactics: Simon Rodia's construction of "Watts Towers," a fantastical and utopian creation made out of collected and recycled debris from around Watts: "perhaps his own dream of how things should have been" (J 78); the "Renaissance of the Arts" festival held in memory of Rodia, among whose exhibits is an artwork entitled the "The Late, Late, Late show," offering an acerbic critique of L.A.'s deathly reliance on media illusion; and, reflexively, Pynchon's own journalistic attempt to provide insight into the psychology of Watts and to communicate this to a mass audience of *The New York Times* readers.

So much can be gleaned from Pynchon's mid sixties writings, but *Gravity's Rainbow*'s retrospective commentary on the New Left forms the major focus of this chapter. As noted earlier, during the later years of the decade the counterculture reached the peak of its influence, but in becoming a mass movement many of its early values were compromised and hedonism and violence took over. Change rocked the New Left as the Vietnam War became the firm focus of student protest, and as the Black Power movement gathered force. Student organisations generally became more radically left wing and amenable to communist theory, with a real fervour for revolution developing in the ranks alongside (justified) paranoia as FBI attention was drawn more fully onto student activists. With this came an increase in militancy; the guerrilla warfare of the Weathermen and armed self-defence of the Black Panther Party were two particularly divisive strategies New Left factions adopted in the late sixties, both of which resulted in a number of deaths within the movement. Even those groups which had earlier pledged to operate on peaceful principles largely followed the trend: having embraced Black Power, in 1969 SNCC changed its name from the Student Nonviolent Coordinating Committee to the Student National Coordinating Committee; SDS too renounced its earlier non-violence to engage in street riots that swept America in the final years of the decade. The most notorious of these were at the 1968 Democratic Convention in Chicago, resulting in the infamous "Chicago Eight" conspiracy trials in which charges were brought against members of SDS, the Yippies, the Black Panther Party, and others. Internal tensions between SDS old guard and new factions within the party (the Weathermen in particular) led to the organisation's fragmentation following its 1969 convention.[12] By the early 1970s the New Left had been toppled by FBI actions, by infighting, and by the conservative backlash, and the hippie movement had also burnt itself out. Published in 1973, *Gravity's Rainbow* is in substantial measure a response to the recent failure of the youth movements of the sixties, revealing to us the development of Pynchon's attitudes to the era, offering further insight into his assessment of the political values and methods of the New Left (as well as of the wider counterculture), and demonstrating a far greater attachment to the earlier manifestations of such movements.

Love as a Political Ideal

An analysis of *Gravity's Rainbow*'s thematic foregrounding of "love" (in the broadest sense of the word) helps to expose the novel's standpoint on these movements and the changes that occurred within them. In his review of Gabriel García Márquez's *Love in the Time of Cholera*, Pynchon laments "the postromantic ebb of the 70's and 80's," and recalls that love was "once the magical buzzword of a generation."[13] Love was at the core of the early counterculture, whose value systems as well as methods of seeking change can accurately be considered as based on a conception of love as altruism, as self-acceptance or self-exploration, as a relinquishing of control and authority over others. Non-violence in civil protest expressed a form of love which transcended the bounds of familial or romantic relationships; Martin Luther King and his followers in the SCLC championed the Christian ideal of loving one's enemy. In its founding statements SDS proclaimed that the "[l]oneliness, estrangement, [and] isolation" of modern life could be reversed "only when a love of man overcomes the idolatrous worship of things by man," and that the society they sought to found "would replace power and personal uniqueness rooted in possession, privilege, or circumstance by power and uniqueness rooted in love, reflectiveness, reason, and creativity," and SNCC professed to seeking "a social order of justice permeated by love," via a "corporate effort [that] must reflect a genuine spirit of love and good-will."[14] Popular music of the era gave its habitual focus on love a revolutionary twist: the Beatles evinced countercultural values when they sang "All You Need Is Love," as did Jefferson Airplane in another classic of the psychedelic era, "Somebody to Love." The word was of course also incorporated into the mottoes of the hippie movement: "Free Love," "Peace and Love," the "Summer of Love," the "Love-in." Later in the sixties and running on into the seventies, hippie commune culture established a link between love and working for one's community. Stephen Gaskin, founder of the Tennessee commune known as "the Farm," claimed, for example, that "love is not an abstract idea or something for a bumper sticker" but rather that, in the Farm, "work is the material expression of love."[15] Love was also the subject of two works of sociological and psychoanalytical criticism which proved highly influential on the counterculture, Herbert Marcuse's *Eros and Civilisation: A Philosophical Enquiry into Freud* (1955) and Norman O. Brown's *Love's Body* (1966). Both of these texts explored the limitations on love, especially erotic love, within modern society, considering whether such limitations (notionally imposed from above via cultural and educational processes) were strictly necessary – whether a non-repressive society was feasible. Brown went as far as to conceptualise a form of sexuality which would reject the traditional genital organisation in favour of "polymorphous perversity." Of course, when the movement turned violent in the late 1960s, this emphasis on love faded into the background.

Love as idea and practice is a constant presence in *Gravity's Rainbow*, which contains by my count 284 instances of the word "love" or closely related words ("lover," "beloved," etc.). Yet love has received relatively scant attention in scholarly criticism of this novel and indeed of Pynchon's entire *oeuvre*; for comparative purposes, "paranoia" and its related terms appears a mere forty-six times. *Gravity's Rainbow* narrates the love of couples and comrades, of music and the Word, of nature, and more obscurely, love of explosions or even of "be[ing] taken under mountains" (*GR* 299). Despite the enticingly enigmatic quality of the latter forms of love, it seems sensible to begin my present analysis with the conventional. There are various paired lovers in the novel, most of whose affairs are fleeting and unstable, Roger Mexico and Jessica Swanlake being the most strongly foregrounded couple, and the most commented on in the context of love in Pynchon. Extant criticism offers conflicting interpretations in terms of the political implications of their relationship, which is portrayed with a deliberate sentimentality on the part of the narrator. For Leo Bersani, Roger and Jessica's romance is one of the "appealing alternatives that *Gravity's Rainbow* offers to its own paranoiacally conceived apocalypses," and he recognises the "tender seriousness" with which Pynchon's narrator treats the couple.[16] However, he suggests that love's status in the novel is finally that of a "myth" which cannot be relied on to effect real political change.[17] Although the narrator seems to forcefully defend the couple's prioritising of their relationship by stating "They are in love. Fuck the war," their involvement is also described as a "gentle withdrawal" from "war's state" (*GR* 41–2), which for Bersani means that love is "discredited" in the novel (although simultaneously "venerated"), becoming in the end nothing more than a useless "fiction" which must be rejected.[18]

Nadine Attewell reads Pynchon's treatment of the lovers differently, suggesting that Roger and Jessica's withdrawal is more or less unambiguously positive because "If 'war's state' is Their domain, the instrument of a corporate elect whose reach extends to 'each of our brains' and whose 'mission [...] is Bad Shit,' secession would seem highly desirable."[19] In Attewell's interpretation,

> Roger and Jessica's idyll in an abandoned house becomes invested with a political potency that has everything to do with the sentimental discourse

it both encourages and depends upon. No longer entirely suspect, the escapist component of this literature acquires a new urgency, a new seriousness, and becomes not only the site for articulations of belief in the possibility of liberation but also, in some sense, the unlikely instrument of that liberation.[20]

Such divergent analyses reflect the complexity of love as a concept in *Gravity's Rainbow*. Asserted as a political solution and an ideal to aim for, it is yet tainted by the author's awareness of how easily this ideal crumbled amid the violence of the late 1960s, as well as his sense of how often the word "love" is used as a mask for those with avaricious, egotistical, or perverse motivations. *Inherent Vice*, set in 1969–70, contains a direct expression of the latter perspective in the thoughts of Pynchon's protagonist Doc, for whom "the word ['love'] these days was being way too overused. Anybody with any claim to hipness 'loved' everybody, not to mention other useful applications, like hustling people into sex activities they might not, given the choice, much care to engage in."[21] But exploitation under the guise of "free love" was not the worst manipulative use of love seen during the sixties. Charles Manson played on the hippie love ethos in creating a commune whose members carried out the shockingly brutal murders of eight people in 1969, just a few years before *Gravity's Rainbow* was published, the media frenzy surrounding this being an important context in *Inherent Vice*. In Simon Wells's study *Charles Manson*, one of the Manson Family murderers, Charles Watson, recounts his first meeting with Manson, during which he said "something about love, finding love, letting yourself love."[22] Watson's reaction was positive:

> I suddenly realised that this was what I was looking for: love. Not that my parents and brother and sister hadn't loved me, but somehow, now, that didn't count. I wanted the kind of love they talked about in the songs – the kind of love that didn't ask you to be anything, didn't judge what you were, didn't set up any rules or regulations – the kind of love that just accepted you, let you be yourself, do your thing whatever it was.[23]

He felt that "all the love in the room was coming from [Manson], from his music."[24] As Mason asks in *Mason & Dixon*, "How can Love conquer all, / When Love can be so blind?" (*MD* 144).

At the other end of the spectrum, committed and genuine lovers who seek escapist absorption in each other's love in a world where survival and struggle are the greater realities are also subjected to criticism in Pynchon's work. Thus Bersani's assessment of Roger and Jessica's relationship as a "harmless" fiction slightly misses the mark because the novel actually suggests the potential for pairs of lovers resorting to a "snuggled"

(*GR* 41) withdrawal from world affairs to compound the effects of oppressive forces.[25] This is signalled by the way the elongated SS/double integral form of the tunnels at the Nazi Mittelwerke arms plant mimics "the shape of lovers curled asleep" (*GR* 302), a description which appears in a scene in which Slothrop wishes he could abandon his own quest to discover the origin of the oppressions which have been targeted at him since he was a child, in order to return to his lover Katje. Yet at the same time, Nadine Attewell's point that love can have a liberating function is borne out, albeit with the additional proviso that it not be combined with escapism, by the fact that Slothrop does not return or withdraw, but continues onward with love as his sustaining ideal: "He wants to preserve what he can of [Katje] from Their several entropies, from Their softsoaping and Their money: maybe he thinks that if he can do it for her he can also do it for himself" (*GR* 302).

Love, for Pynchon, is as much of an ideal as it was for early proponents of the counterculture, but in the contemporary political climate (that of the conservative backlash and ongoing Vietnam War) it cannot be an end in itself. The notion of love as motivating principle expressed in the scene quoted earlier is not undermined by Pynchon's narrator's immediately following cynical quip that the American Lieutenant's reasoning in continuing his quest is "awful close to nobility for Slothrop and The Penis He Thought Was His Own" (*GR* 302). Rather, this assessment serves as a link to an earlier section in the novel, in which a fuller perspective on the role of love in a left-wing revolutionary context is elaborated. Towards the end of part one of *Gravity's Rainbow* we are taken back in time to 1929–30 and the years of the Weimar Republic, before the rise of Hitler to dictatorial power, where the reader is introduced to a small group of young German communist revolutionaries – Leni, Rudi, Vanya, and Rebecca – crouching in a cold, cheerless, derelict dormitory, nibbling on a crust of bread and discussing "street tactics" (*GR* 158), capitalism, and love.[26] Leni provides the consciousness through which the episode is filtered, its centrepiece being a series of daydreams or fantasies which Leni apparently drifts into as a form of escapism from the difficulties of her current situation; having just left her husband, she must now struggle to provide herself and her child, Ilse, with food and shelter. The narrator's insinuation of an external mechanism of control at work in Slothrop's romantic yearnings for Katje ("The Penis He Thought Was His Own") is an example of an attitude to love in the novel most fully elaborated by Vanya during the meeting described earlier. In a piece of persuasive rhetoric which recalls Leni's own musing a few lines earlier on her husband's "tranquil"

(*GR* 154) acquiescence to a lifestyle in which he is nothing but a deluded tool of the authorities, Vanya describes various forms of capitalist expression as "pornographies":

> "Pornographies: pornographies of love, erotic love, Christian love, boy-and-his-dog, pornographies of sunsets, pornographies of killing, and pornographies of deduction – *ahh*, that sigh when we guess the murderer – all these novels, these films and songs they lull us with, they're approaches, more comfortable and less so, to that Absolute Comfort." A pause to allow Rudi a quick and sour grin. "The self-induced orgasm." (*GR* 155)

As Wes Chapman asserts, pornography "is for Pynchon a means by which the state wields power over its citizens at the micropolitical level."[27] In other words, the term denotes material disseminated by the guardians of the capitalist system aimed at manipulating and directing the thoughts and behaviour of citizens into "useful" channels, channels which will help society run in such a way as to maximise profit for those in control.[28] Chapman's analysis foregrounds what Vanya describes as "pornographies of killing," the notion that "[p]ornography is one of the War's diversionary tactics, a means of drawing sexuality into its own service."[29] But in Vanya's speech the susceptibility of *love* to outside influence is emphasised most strongly. While Chapman interprets the passage as suggesting that "[t]he masturbator, physical or emotional, is the ideal citizen" for those in power because "he or she is unlikely to form the bonds with other people which threaten the effectiveness of the 'structures favoring death' by affirming the value of life,"[30] it actually implies that involvement may be as problematic as isolation because even if our relationships are apparently wholesome, we may be unwittingly engaging in a state-sponsored form of love, a romantic or erotic experience subtly directed by the will of the state. For love to be a positive force an awareness needs to be fostered as to the distinction between real love for others (or what might be called "revolutionary love") and capitalist "pornographies of love."

If there is any doubt as to the alignment between the novel's overall ideological stance on this front and that of Vanya, it is dispelled by Pynchon's inclusion of a critique of the kinds of novel which Vanya describes as "pornographies of deduction." Such works of literature allow their readers a closure ("*ahh*, that sigh when we guess the murderer") whose effect is likened to that of a "self-induced orgasm." It is this effect which Pynchon had been working specifically to frustrate in his first novels *V.* and *The Crying of Lot 49*, which feature detective-like characters seeking answers they cannot find, the moment of revelation being absent or denied to us.[31] In

Gravity's Rainbow this paradigm is pursued again but in a slightly different form: Slothrop does discover the truths he was looking for about his personal history, but he then fades from the novel, ending up "[s]cattered all over the Zone" (*GR* 712). His revelations do not lead to a neat denouement in which the reader can be satisfied that justice has been restored. Rather, the masturbatory satisfaction and orgasmic blankness with which Slothrop celebrates his discoveries atop a mountain, attended by pornographic visions of the natural landscape, parodies such ideals of closure, suggesting that they are ultimately destructive. Meanwhile, the narrative as a whole becomes less and less coherent as the novel approaches its end. Like all of Pynchon's writing, *Gravity's Rainbow* refuses to contribute to the capitalist establishment's effort to "lull" the masses into an apolitical somnambulist consumerism. Instead, the book is intended to have a parallel effect to that of the graffitied mottos appearing all over the communist districts of Berlin mentioned by the narrator immediately prior to, and apparently triggering, Vanya's anti-capitalist diatribe:

> AN ARMY OF LOVERS CAN BE BEATEN. These things appear on the walls of the Red districts in the course of the night. Nobody can track down author or painter for any of them, leading you to suspect they're one and the same. Enough to make you believe in a folk-consciousness. They are not slogans so much as texts, revealed in order to be thought about, expanded on, translated into action by the people. (*GR* 155)

"AN ARMY OF LOVERS CAN BE BEATEN": love is again a key term here, and there is also a countercultural reference. The original motto, "an army of lovers *cannot* be beaten," was used extensively in this or variant form within the gay rights movement in the years immediately prior to the publication of *Gravity's Rainbow*.[32] That Pynchon has reversed the logic of the slogan seems superficially to be further evidence of a desire to emphasise the potential weakness of love as a basis for revolutionary action, in line with Vanya's commentary. Bernard Duyfhuizen's similar interpretation is that the graffito "comments on the naiveté of the Vietnam War era slogan, 'Make love not war.'"[33] But the motto is ambiguous, and it may contain other meanings. As Stephen Mattessich has noted, its interpretation "depends on how one conserves its oblique and middle-voiced stress in the reading it provokes."[34] A possible interpretation which fits with my present analysis is that Pynchon is also criticising the idea of supposed "lovers" banding together to form an "army." An army, of course, connotes an aggressive attitude, and a limitation of love to those on one side of the dispute, all of which goes against the inclusive, egalitarian spirit of the early counterculture. The sentiment of the original form of the graffito is thus in one sense the opposite of "Make love not war," and Pynchon's alteration perhaps suggests his dissatisfaction with the militarisation of the movement during the late sixties as violent confrontation became methodologically commonplace.

Violence, Idealism, and Communism

This anti-militaristic interpretation of the graffito is at least partially borne out by an analysis of Pynchon's treatment of the street actions in which Leni and her comrades are involved. In one such action, whose depiction would certainly recall to contemporary readers' minds the violent protests of New Left elements at the 1968 Democratic Convention, Leni's lover, Peter Sachsa, is killed. The incident is depicted with particular vividness:

> here comes Schutzmann Jöche, truncheon already in backswing, the section of Communist head moving into view for him stupidly, so unaware of him and his power ... the Schutzmann's first clear shot all day ... oh, his timing is perfect, he feels it in arm and out the club no longer flabby at his side but tensed back now around in a muscular curve, at the top of his swing, peak of potential energy ... far below that gray vein in the man's temple, frail as parchment, standing out so clear, twitching already with its next to last pulsebeat ... and, SHIT! Oh – *how* –
> *How beautiful!* (*GR* 220)

In representing Peter's death as a murder effected by a zealously anti-communist member of the police force, Pynchon both highlights police brutality in the years prior to the publication of *Gravity's Rainbow* – an abuse of authority epitomised by the National Guard's killing of four students protesting at Kent State University in May 1970, followed within the same month by the deaths of two more at Jackson State College at the hands of the police – and expresses disdain for the anti-communist hysteria which was, of course, prevalent throughout the United States in the 1950s and '60s. The scene suggests sympathy with those drawn into such protests, while implying a criticism of the use of street violence as a political tactic. This is attested to by the very fact of Peter Sachsa's demise, which leaves Leni and her child vulnerable, resulting in their eventual internment in a Nazi labour camp within whose bounds Leni, it seems, loses her life.

The idea that radical commitments might be potentially "suicidal," proposed tentatively in *The Crying of Lot 49*'s depiction of campus politics, thus comes to narrative fruition in *Gravity's Rainbow*. And once more, interwoven with Pynchon's description of street protest we find a commentary on love which connects through to the ideology of the early sixties. Immediately prior to the scene quoted earlier, Pynchon's narrator meditates on the ambivalent dynamics of love in the street:

> there are two sorts of movement out here – as often as the chance displacements of strangers, across a clear skirmish-line from the Force, will bring together people who'll remain that way for a time, in love that can even make the oppression seem a failure, so too love, here in the street, can be taken centrifugally apart again: faces seen for the last time here, words spoken idly, over your shoulder, taking for granted she's there, already last words. (*GR* 219)

Here, the redemptive, recuperative power of love is foregrounded. However, as the narrator's commentary continues problematic connections between love and control are brought to light, dynamics of influence which can operate even without any deliberate manipulative intention. On this basis it is suggested that Peter's love for Leni was at least partially to blame for his death. Speaking from beyond the grave, Peter concedes that Leni did not quite "goad" him into violent protest, but claims that she did "set up male reverberations" (*GR* 220), piquing his sense of masculine pride by enjoying a moment when her daughter became confused over Peter's gender. He concludes that, "[i]n love, words can be taken too many ways, that's all" (*GR* 220). Taken as a whole, the passage thus reasserts the view that to be politically effective love must always be coupled with self-awareness and independence.

Delving further into the novel's treatment of the kinds of direct action undertaken by elements within the New Left during the late 1960s, the sections of *Gravity's Rainbow* concerning Leni and her communist comrades deserves further attention. Leni is perhaps the character in *Gravity's Rainbow* who is most enthusiastic about street protest (including violent action) as a means of attacking the forces of oppression and bringing about revolutionary change. In a much quoted passage, she rhapsodises about "the moment, and its possibilities":

> the level you reach, with both feet in, when you lose your fear, you lose it all, you've penetrated the moment, slipping perfectly into its grooves, metal-gray but soft as latex, and now the figures are dancing, each pre-choreographed exactly where it is, the flash of knees under pearl-colored frock as the girl in the babushka stoops to pick up a cobble, the man in the black suitcoat and brown sleeveless sweater grabbed by policemen one on either arm, trying to keep his head up, showing his teeth, the older liberal in the dirty beige overcoat, stepping back to avoid a careening

demonstrator, looking back across his lapel how-dare-you or look-out-not-me, his eyeglasses filled with the glare of the winter sky. (*GR* 158–9)

For Leni, during a street action, each moment is invested with a greater than normal potential, and determinism is no longer necessarily the rule as time seems to open up to a wide range of possible futures. In general, critical interpretations of this passage have tended to focus on the philosophies of temporal and spatial organisation it contains, suggesting a degree of sympathy between Leni's ideas here and Pynchon's own.[35] After all, Leni's related rejection of the cause-and-effect logic of her rather pathetic husband, Franz, who aids the Nazi war effort, parallels the narrator's clear distaste for Ned Pointsman, a scientist similarly reliant on that limited logical crutch. But Pynchon's attitude is not quite so clear cut when it comes to Leni's celebration of street protest. In fact, although Leni's understanding of how events might happen in space-time is clearly more sophisticated than her husband's, there are hints that her untamed idealism – reflected in the dream-like fluidity of Pynchon's prose in the passage quoted – is as problematic as Franz's steadfast practicality.

Leni is often portrayed as having wings, which embody both her strength and her attraction to the ideal. According to the narrator (describing the thoughts of a character called Carol Eventyr), the passive and masochistic Franz used to fantasise being "crouched on her back, very small, being *taken*" (*GR* 219), a fantasy metaphorically lived out in the end by Peter Sachsa as Leni guides him towards violent activism. Leni's utopian imaginings, her "dreams that will not grow up" (*GR* 218), the narrator suggests, swept Peter along, carrying him towards his death, as she hastened towards her own. Such symbolism is further related to Leni's viewing of Fritz Lang's *Die Frau im Mond* (a real film whose title has been translated into English as *By Rocket to the Moon* and *Woman in the Moon*), in which she sees "a dream of flight" (*GR* 159). Flight, in this novel, is more often negative than positive, with links to the V-2 rocket and to an unproductive yearning for transcendence. In these various ways the novel thus implies that Leni's idealism overreaches the politically useful, becoming, in fact, destructive. This is further attested to by Leni's lapses into escapist fantasy in the section immediately following Vanya's discussion of capitalist "pornographies." Rather than engaging in the ongoing dialogue with her fellow revolutionaries, Leni becomes absorbed in a series of daydreams, two of which – an erotic fantasy involving Leni's comrade Rebecca, and a romantic fantasy about a childhood sweetheart – could easily be described as pornographic delusions following Vanya's definition. In this sense Leni Pökler is much like Frenesi Gates of Pynchon's subsequent novel *Vineland* – a left-wing activist in the 1960s, Frenesi shuns reality in favour of sexual escapism.

All this would seem to discredit any notion that Pynchon would see street protest as Leni does, as a moment of rare opportunity for change. However, troubling this analysis are both similarly enthusiastic pronouncements on the subject appearing in other of Pynchon's novels – in *Mason & Dixon*, for example, Mason gets carried away telling Dixon about a weavers' rebellion he witnessed, with "thousands of angry men in Streets that ordinarily see no more than, oh, a dozen a day" and lauds "the great, crisp, serene Roar, – of a Mobility focus'd upon a just purpose" (*MD* 502) – and, within *Gravity's Rainbow* itself, Leni's allusions in her depiction of the riot to a spontaneous synchronicity that recurs in celebrations of the anarchic appearing throughout Pynchon's work. The idea that interactions between protestors can become fluid, seemingly "pre-choreographed," recalls the narrator's depiction of the deaf-mute ball in *The Crying of Lot 49* as an "anarchist miracle" in which dancers somehow avoid collisions, apparently expressing an "unthinkable order of music, many rhythms, all keys at once, a choreography in which each couple meshed easy, predestined" (*L49* 90–1). As the following chapter will argue, this anarchism, based on the possibility of a world "[w]here revolutions break out spontaneous and leaderless, and the soul's talent for consensus allows the masses to work together without effort, automatic as the body itself" (*L49* 83), is a pervasive ideal in Pynchon's novels, albeit appearing most forcefully in *Against the Day*. As mentioned in the previous chapter, in this later novel jazz is used as a metaphor for the "perfect Anarchist organization," the Irish anarchist Wolfe Tone O'Rooney describing "Dope" Breedlove's jazz band as embodying "the most amazing social coherence, as if you all shared the same brain."[36] And as Frederick Ashe notes, the very same idea is vaunted in "A Journey into the Mind of Watts."[37] Here Pynchon claimed that the dynamics of the rioting that had spread across the Watts district of Los Angeles the previous summer was being likened to art or music by those who had been involved:

> Some talk now of a balletic quality to it, a coordinated and graceful drawing of cops away from the center of the action, a scattering of The Man's power, either with real incidents or false alarms.
>
> Others remember it in terms of music; through much of the rioting seemed to run, they say, a remarkable empathy, or whatever it is that jazz musicians feel on certain nights: everybody knowing what to do and when to do it without needing a word or a signal: "You could go up to anybody,

the cats could be in the middle of burning down a store or something, but they'd tell you, explain very calm, just what they were doing, what they were going to do next. And that's what they'd do; man, nobody had to give orders." (J 84)

While such rioting thus seems to fit with Pynchon's anarchist ethos in 1966, it was treated differently in *V.*, where Victoria Wren impassively views a scene of street protest in which blood runs in the streets and soldiers bayonet a participant to death (*V.* 209). What emerges from this is a picture of Pynchon's changing perspective on activist violence across his first three novels. Initially sceptical, in the mid sixties the author apparently follows the countercultural trend and becomes more amenable to potentially violent action. Then, with a retrospective view of the failures of the New Left and of the counterculture more broadly, in *Gravity's Rainbow* he comes to occupy an awkward middle ground, associating street violence with failure and futility yet still lauding its aesthetic qualities and its ability to generate a feeling of unity akin to the spontaneous *communitas* discussed in Chapter 1.

That *Gravity's Rainbow* does, in fact, deliberately reference the New Left through its Weimar episode is more fully confirmed by the third of the fantasies in which Leni indulges while her companions discuss street tactics. Its depiction overlaps somewhat with the sequence that precedes it, in which Leni envisions herself and her lover Richard Hirsch living a bohemian lifestyle involving "exotic food and wine, new drugs, much ease and honesty in sexual matters" (*GR* 157), a lifestyle with very strong hippie connotations, especially for an early 1970s readership. It is in this context that the following fantasy appears:

> the President, in the middle of asking the Bundestag, with his familiar clogged and nasal voice, for a giant war appropriation, breaks down suddenly: "Oh, fuck it . . ." *Fickt es*, the soon-to-be-immortal phrase, rings in the sky, rings over the land, *Ja, fickt es!* "I'm sending all the soldiers home. We'll close down the weapon factories, we'll dump all the weapons in the sea. I'm sick of war. I'm sick of waking up every morning afraid I'm going to die." It is suddenly impossible to hate him any more: he's as human, as mortal now, as any of the people. There will be new elections. The Left will run a woman whose name is never given, but everyone understands it is Rosa Luxemburg. The other candidates will be chosen so inept or colorless that no one will vote for them. There will be a chance for the Revolution. The President has promised.
>
> Incredible joy at the baths, among the friends. True joy: events in a dialectical process cannot bring this explosion of the heart. Everyone is in love. (*GR* 158)

Clearly, the German president here is a parodic analogue to Richard Nixon, whose 1969 election pledge to end the Vietnam War had not been honoured by the time of *Gravity's Rainbow*'s publication.[38] The passage therefore reflects on such idealist imaginings within the anti-war movement, in which the New Left was prominent, painting them as intensely unrealistic. To underscore this point, Leni is abruptly brought out of her reverie by someone's mentioning, again, of the pessimistic graffito "AN ARMY OF LOVERS CAN BE BEATEN" (*GR* 158), as Rudi and Vanya continue their discussion of street tactics. However, despite its excessive utopianism (and its intimation of openness to semi-dictatorial election rigging on the part of the radical Left), the overall earnestness of the passage rules out parody of the basic ideals and values embodied within it. And love creeps into the picture once more. Leni's fantasy contains a very countercultural ideal of inclusive, collective, non-possessive love, which has a political value transcending that of personal and limited romances like that of Leni and Richard. Rather than the withdrawal associated with Roger and Jessica's relationship ("They are in love. Fuck the war"), which expresses a lack of interest in politics, the notion that love can spontaneously unite people, even bringing international conflicts to an end, goes beyond Slothrop's motivating love for Katje in proposing this particular emotion's potential to humanise society. Yet, to whatever extent we think Pynchon might like to see Leni's fantasy realised, it is explicitly presented as nothing more than a daydream, another instance of escapism. Spontaneous revolution is discredited as Pynchon draws attention to the forces lined up against those on the activist Left, reemphasising his point that love alone is not enough, that effective action must be based on a solid awareness of realities fostered via thought and dialogue.

Rich in countercultural allusions, the Weimar episode offers us further avenues of investigation regarding the novel's relationship with New Left practices and ideologies. In the later years of the 1960s, communist influence began to make itself felt within New Left groups. As major chronicler of the sixties Left Todd Gitlin explains, in its formative years, SDS initially distanced itself from communism, viewing it as an outdated ideology "glued to electoral politics, glued to the Democratic Party," and unable to "hear the music of direct action" – although the organisation was critical of the limitations imposed on free speech by Cold War anti-communist hysteria.[39] Despite this, Fidel Castro's Cuba was attractive to many in SDS, as it was to Richard Fariña, who described a trip to the country in *Been Down So Long It Looks Like Up To Me*, for which, as noted earlier, Pynchon wrote an introduction. From the mid 1960s onwards SDS became more amenable to communism, reversing its official line and allowing Marxist-Leninists into its 1965 convention. Other New Left groups emerging in the mid to late sixties were more closely linked to communism from their foundation. These include the Weather Underground, which grew out of SDS, and the Black Panther Party, whose connection with Pynchon's work is explored in the fourth chapter of this study. Although Pynchon is normally considered politically left-wing, his perspective on communism specifically has remained fairly obscure, there being relatively few direct references to the subject in his novels or journalism. Thus the Weimar episode of *Gravity's Rainbow*, featuring a group of communist revolutionaries who idolise the Marxist political martyr and notorious communist leader Rosa Luxemburg (also known as "Red Rosa"), offers a rare insight into Pynchon's view of this most left-wing ideology and its role in the trajectory of the New Left.

The first thing to note is that communism in this episode receives a very favourable treatment compared to that given to Marxism (and particularly Karl Marx as a historical figure) in this novel and in Pynchon's later work. In Chapter 4 of this book, I argue that in a section appearing towards the end of *Gravity's Rainbow* Pynchon expresses distrust regarding one particular aspect of Marxist theory, dialectical materialism, which posits an inevitable communist revolution. Moreover, when Marx is mentioned directly in *Gravity's Rainbow* he is called a "sly old racist" (*GR* 317) by the narrator, who lambasts his shallow appreciation of the realities of colonial regimes. More recently, Pynchon's attitude to Marx may have mellowed somewhat, the narratorial tone of *Against the Day* being far less acerbic when Marx's name comes up, but nevertheless the message is negative as his theory of monetary capital is deemed irrelevant to maintaining freedom in the American West (*ATD* 405). Despite this, in *Gravity's Rainbow* via the character of Leni (nicknamed Lenin by her husband), Rosa Luxemburg, a committed Marxist, is put forward as an ideal presidential candidate for Germany, someone to stave off war and prevent the rise of Hitler to power.

Differences between Luxemburg and Marx on issues of theory and approach help to explain the distinct treatment they receive at Pynchon's hands. Luxemburg, for example, claimed that there were certain oversimplified conceptions in Marx's depiction of capitalist processes which neglected the "context, the struggle and the relations" between world societies in favour of a "bloodless theoretical fiction."[40] In an attempt to rectify this, Luxemburg contributed to Marxist thought a more considered evaluation of the role of colonies in global capitalism, a subject which had previously received scant attention.[41] Furthermore, she "did not consider that the victory of socialism was inevitable," and her distrust of dogma and of predicted futures (in which, as we will see in Chapter 4, she concurs with Pynchon) meant she was able to criticise and question Marx effectively.[42] Rosa was well known for her political passion and commitment to action, qualities which contributed to her assassination in 1919 by the right-wing *Freikorps*, a group assisting the government in putting down the Spartacist revolt (an attempt on the part of the Left to gain control over events following the German revolution of 1918–19) of which Luxemburg was an instigator. Luxemburg also wrote prolifically, creating a wealth of texts that could be "thought about, expanded on, translated into action by the people." She stridently attacks capitalism throughout her works, as Pynchon does most forcefully in *Against the Day*, one aspect of her criticism being the connections between militarism and profiteering, connections which underlie much of *Gravity's Rainbow*'s commentary on the misdeeds of international corporations during the Second World War.[43] (Moreover, in this novel populated with women who embody "right thinking" while many of the men are motivated by little more than lust and greed, Pynchon's decision to incorporate a *female* revolutionary leader into his narrative is probably not coincidental.)

Just how well acquainted Pynchon was with Luxemburg's life and writings in the early seventies cannot be discerned from *Gravity's Rainbow*, but the convergences listed earlier reinforce the interpretation that the sections of the novel devoted to Leni's experience of the Weimar republic offer a degree of support for a communist revolutionary position. I have argued that through its depiction of Leni and her comrades, *Gravity's Rainbow* links communism with both an unrealistic revolutionary idealism and street violence. The latter two qualities of the 1960s youth movements were certainly among the most significant in the eventual triumph of the conservative backlash. As Mark Rudd, previously of the Weathermen, puts it: "We couldn't have done the FBI's work better for them had we been paid agents … We were just stupid kids too in love with our ideas to realize they weren't real…. That's the essence of the downside of idealism."[44] But communism is partially redeemed in the episode via the mention of Rosa Luxemburg, a woman who, in contrast to the New Left, took a decidedly realist position on revolution and expressed a non-celebratory view of violence as a "last resort" in the fight against oppression.[45]

"Do It with Gusto and Joy": The Yippie Alternative

One point on which Luxemburg's revolutionary approach coincides with late 1960s New Left conceits is her view of the value of infusing political actions with positive energy. Speaking of activism, Luxemburg asserts that "you must do it with gusto and joy, not as if it were a boring intermezzo, because the public always feels the spirit of the combatants, and the joy of battle lends the arguments a clear resonance and ensures moral superiority."[46] As I have stated in the introduction, a recurrent feature of the 1960s counterculture was its valorisation of personal pleasure, and as Todd Gitlin explains, during the late sixties an "[e]xpressive politics" developed: the idea that "[d]emonstrators should refuse to sit still; politics should shake, rattle, and roll, move body and soul ... not only to win demands, but *to feel good*.... Its faith was that a politics of universal expression would make the right things happen – *and* be its own reward."[47] One group committed to combining fun with political protest (as their name suggests) were the "Yippies." Founded in 1967 by a group of colourful counterculture veterans including Abbie Hoffman, Jerry Rubin, and Paul Krassner, the Youth International Party utilised street theatre and high-profile pranksterism to have their political say. Nominating a pig as a presidential candidate, showering dollar bills onto the floor of the New York Stock Exchange, and throwing pies at political and media figures were just some of the Yippies' outlandish and satirical political acts. Grabbing a large slice of media attention in the years when Pynchon was writing *Gravity's Rainbow*, the Yippies also appear to have a significant contextual relevance to the novel, which elucidates a final dimension of its anachronistic framing of New Left politics.

In the context of a mainstream New Left which increasingly rejected its earlier non-violence and emphasis on altruistic love, the positive creativity of Yippie-style subversion marked it out as in some degree a continuation of and development from that original ethos. Given Pynchon's apparent preference for the theories and methods of the early counterculture, the group is thus likely to have held a certain appeal for Pynchon. (It must be noted, however, that the Yippies did not uniformly or dogmatically reject violent means, having more of an "anything goes" kind of mentality.) Supporting the notion of a pro-Yippie Pynchon is Molly Hite's article, "'Fun Actually Was Becoming Quite Subversive': Herbert Marcuse, the Yippies, and the Value System of *Gravity's Rainbow*," in which some of the interconnections between the novel and the Yippie movement are explored. With reference to the organisation's emphasis on subversive fun, which for her derives from the philosophies of Herbert Marcuse as expressed particularly in *Eros and Civilization*, Hite argues that *Gravity's Rainbow* "takes it for granted."[48] Her argument is convincing, and could well be applied to Pynchon's entire *oeuvre*, since the comic or simply silly moments dotted throughout all of Pynchon's narratives (the songs being a particularly striking example) often express an underlying social or political commentary, while at the same time functioning to subvert reader expectations of a "serious" author's work. Leo Bersani also perceives Yippie connotations in this novel, noting that Pynchon's work both "recapitulates the saintly assumptions of Rubinesque subversion" and implies that

> profound social change will not result from head-on assaults (terror is ineffective and unacceptable, revolution is unthinkable in the West, and even revolutionary regimes have shown themselves to be changes of personnel unaccompanied by changes in assumptions about the legitimacy of power), but rather from a kind of aggressively seductive subversion of the *seriousness* with which networks of power conduct their business.[49]

I would agree with Bersani in that such an approach to subversive politics is considered viable in Pynchon's work, although it is by no means the only alternative put forward. However, I would question his contention that Pynchon's representation of "Rubinesque subversion" is "ambiguous," and his subsequent point that, for Pynchon, "[t]he counter-culture style of the sixties can provide nothing more than the (always appealing) historical inspiration for more complex models of nonoppositional resistance."[50] In this Bersani underestimates the relevance of sixties tactics and strategies to Pynchon's political thought as expressed through each of his novels.

Both Hite's and Bersani's readings of a Yippie context in *Gravity's Rainbow* are further borne out by a number of scenes in the novel which do not feature in their respective accounts, in which characters strike back against agents of oppression in comic style. Slothrop's pie-ing of his aggressive pursuer Major Marvy from a hot-air balloon, for instance, reproduces classic slapstick comedy conventions in a spirit of left-wing rebellion. Further food-related political antics occur when Roger Mexico, Pig Bodine, and others invent and request a variety of disgusting dishes, successfully disrupting the complacent atmosphere at a dinner party hosted by an employee of the Krupp firm, a real company central to weapons production in Hitler's Germany. As Steven Weisenburger notes, the language employed in this scene demonstrates "a delightful absence of repression and sublimation" as well as "a bluntness that even verges on political aggression"[51] – a commentary which links the scene strongly both to the University of California's Free Speech Movement of 1964, in which Jerry Rubin claimed to have been "reborn,"[52] and, reconfirming Hite's analysis, to the Yippie and more broadly countercultural belief in the political power of Eros. Nor is it insignificant in this context that a kazoo is being played throughout most of the scene: in his Yippie manifesto Rubin calls for "[t]housands of kazoos, drums, tambourines, triangles, pots and pans, trumpets, street fairs, firecrackers" to be put into effect in disrupting the presidential election of 1968.[53]

Moreover, that the Pynchon of *Gravity's Rainbow* views Yippie activism in an unambiguously positive light, seeing it, in fact, as the embodiment of redemptive possibility for the failed counterculture, is suggested by a more detailed analysis of the Krupp dinner party scene. The episode is saturated with the anti-corporate sentiment that runs throughout the novel, and, most importantly for our present discussion, contains an interpretation of the causes of the disintegration of the oppositional "Counterforce" – a fictional group various critics have linked to the 1960s counterculture.[54] According to the narrator, the Counterforce succumbed, primarily, to greed. In a passage which recalls Vanya's commentary on the creation of capitalist pornographies as tools of manipulation as well as Situationist theories of the "society of the spectacle," the narrator claims that what we consider our "Ego" is controlled by "the Man," and that although we are aware that our attraction to "the massive presence of money" compromises our power to subvert existing power hierarchies, "we let it go on. As long as we can see them, stare at them, those massively moneyed, once in a while. As long as they allow us a glimpse, however rarely. We need that. And how they know it – how often, under what conditions" (*GR* 712–13).[55] The Counterforce have not been able to "disarm, de-penis and dismantle the Man" (*GR* 712) because they have failed to comprehend the extent of their own collusion with capitalism. Rather strangely, an albatross-related extended metaphor is employed to reinforce this critique: the Man's "corporate emblem is a white albatross" (*GR* 712–13) and Slothrop, who the narrator contends is present "in spirit" at this dinner party which has come to represent *in toto* the upper echelons of the corporate capitalist system, has ended up as a "plucked albatross," reduced to mere "feathers" characterised by a "complete absence of hostility" (*GR* 712). This implies the stripping of Slothrop's power from him by the agents of capitalist power who have pursued him throughout the novel. Furthermore, the Counterforce are lampooned for not having a firmer grip on the particular categories of "Albatross Nosology" (*GR* 712) (the classification of diseases affecting albatrosses), suggesting their critical inability to recognise points of weakness within the establishment. Whatever the Coleridgean implications of this, the intention is to highlight again the damaging lack of awareness of oppositional figures.[56]

Roger Mexico is also present at Krupp's, and he meditates consciously on his own collusion with the corporate circus, mulling over an "interesting question, which is worse: living on as Their pet, or death?" (*GR* 713). Since the failure of the Counterforce, of which Mexico was a member, the route of active resistance is apparently no longer available – what remains is but a choice between forms of passivity. The establishment even, it seems, has the power to deprive him of love, tempting Jessica back to her lieutenant fiancé Jeremy, who, according to Mexico, "*is* the War," representing "every assertion the fucking War has ever made – that we are meant for work and government, for austerity: and these shall take priority over love, dreams, the spirit, the senses and the other second-class trivia that are found among the idle and mindless hours of the day" (*GR* 177). In the post-radical "evenings of Thermidor" what remains is "the failed Counterforce, the glamorous ex-rebels, half-suspected but still enjoying official immunity and sly love, camera-worthy wherever they carry on ... doomed pet freaks" (*GR* 713).[57] (In fact, Pynchon's depiction of a number of Counterforce veterans at the Krupp party recalls Tom Wolfe's notorious *New York Magazine* essay of June 1970, "Radical Chic: That Party at Lenny's," a diatribe on the embrace of social climbing by various members of the Black Panther Party, as evinced by their attendance at a party hosted by the famous composer Leonard Bernstein, at which they were served hors d'oeuvres by Latin American servants while accepting generous contributions to their cause.[58]) Yet such pessimism regarding revolutionary prospects is significantly undercut by the successes of the scene immediately following, in which, as mentioned earlier, Mexico and Bodine's spontaneous initiation of the "repulsive stratagem" of calling loudly for myriad imagined dishes involving various bodily excretions induces much "well-bred gagging" (*GR* 715), and finally sends guests fleeing from the room. In thus staging a conspicuous rejection of both the culture of consumption itself and the hospitality of those who profit therefrom, in undermining the capitalist spectacle and replacing it with their own, infused with Yippie-like theatricality and humour, the Counterforce regain the revolutionary edge they had lost, and Mexico escapes the binary choice of co-optation or death.

What is offered here is thus an effective alternative to (potentially) violent street protest. Yippie-style subversion of the norms of behaviour – what might be termed "guerrilla pranksterism" – has similar consciousness-raising properties to marching and demonstrating, but allows acts of rebellion to occur in a less-organised, unstructured fashion. Circumventing the expectations of the authorities and refusing to play on their terms, such stratagems both delegitimise official power and limit the potential for police brutality or arrest. With no official leader for the authorities to target (as in the case of the assassinated Rosa Luxemburg), and with less emphasis on large-scale protests within which individual policemen can express personal grievances against the student Left (as in the case of the fictional Peter Sachsa), the risk of getting oneself killed in the act of rebellion is significantly diminished. As Jerry Rubin put it: "Pigs cannot relate to anarchy.... [They] think that we are organized like their pig department. We are not, and that's why we are going to win. A hierarchical, top-down organization is no match for the free and loose energy of the people."[59] The tendency of Pynchon's narratives to vaunt such anarchic principles is a very relevant aspect of his relationship with the New Left, and is explored in more depth in the chapter that follows, in relation to another important approach to revolutionising American society, that of the psychedelic movement.[60]

CHAPTER 3

The Psychedelic Movement, Fantasy, and Anarchism in The Crying of Lot 49 *and* Against the Day*

As the New Left was forming in the early years of the 1960s, an equally influential and revolutionary movement was emerging onto the countercultural scene: the psychedelic movement. Initiated by the experiments of Dr. Timothy Leary and his colleague Dr. Richard Alpert with the recently synthesised lysergic acid diethylamide (LSD), what was originally a small-scale spiritual movement based around Leary and his commune in Millbrook, New York, became in the later years of the decade a hugely controversial mass phenomenon and major component of the hippie counterculture. Albeit similarly aimed at garnering a greater degree of freedom within human society by countering oppressive forces, the practical approach the psychedelic movement took was in many ways diametrically opposed to that of groups like SDS or SNCC. Rejecting conventional politics, Leary proposed a "politics of ecstasy," its mission to expand and liberate consciousness across the United States.[1] In its emphasis on the importance of spiritual engagement with reality, of exploring the potentialities of the individual creative self, and of cultural and lifestyle change, the psychedelic revolution can be seen as an updated version of the Beat movement, and indeed several Beats, and Allen Ginsberg in particular, embraced psychedelics. (Note, however, that Kerouac did not see things this way; for him there was no potential in LSD: according to Leary, Kerouac remained "an old-style bohemian without a hippie bone in his body," he "opened the neural doors to the future, looked ahead, and didn't see his place in it."[2])

Where the literature of the Beats, in its formal radicalism as well as in its content, suggested the liberating potential of a life lived in frantic motion, with free camaraderie and experiential vibrancy, Leary and his scientific circle pointed towards a very similar, "IT"-like freedom by offering up guidance on the use of psychoactive compounds. The parallel emphasis on liberation from oppressive structures and on the attainment of *communitas* is made clear in Leary's definition of ecstasy:

> ECSTASY: The experience of attaining freedom from limitations, either self-imposed or external; a state of exalted delight in which normal understanding is felt to be surpassed. From the Greek "ex-stasis." By definition, ecstasy is an ongoing on/off process. It requires a continual sequence of "dropping out." On those occasions when many individuals share the ecstatic experience at the same time, they create a brief-lived "counter-culture."[3]

However, while in this sense the psychedelic movement confirmed the Beats' adventuresome and exploratory philosophy, it rejected, as Pynchon partially does, their literalised migratory logic; for Leary "[e]xternal migration as a way of finding a place where you can drop out and turn on and then tune in to the environment is no longer possible" (*PE* 356).[4] Instead, "[t]he only way out is in" (*PE* 354). As a guided experience, approached with care and with a definite political goal in mind, the use of LSD as a tool of liberation also circumvents some of the other pitfalls Pynchon seems to associate in his early work with Kerouac's more hedonistic and apolitical celebration of the quest after extreme and prolonged anti-structural ecstasy in *On the Road*.

Consciousness expansion via LSD thus offered a revolutionary alternative to simple spatial escape on the one hand, and more traditional New Left-style activism on the other. Whether and to what extent Pynchon demonstrates an attraction towards this alternative in his work is the major focus of this chapter. To this end I return again to *The Crying of Lot 49*, which, apart from incorporating an LSD-using character into its narrative, seems to contain commentaries on Leary's particular methods, approaches, and media persona. (Bear in mind that since *The Crying of Lot 49* was published in 1966, Pynchon's attitudes towards the psychedelic movement as legible within the novel would have been influenced by the ideas of Leary – the recognised figurehead of the psychedelic movement during its earlier years – rather than those of Ken Kesey and the Merry Pranksters, who were only just beginning to contest his leadership of the movement at this time.) In the interest of providing a sense of the continuities and alterations in Pynchon's political thought on this issue between his earlier and later production, I also draw on *Against the Day*. In analysing this example of Pynchon's more mature work, I elaborate on the wider political implications for the author's work of the psychedelic movement's valorisation of the human mind and its capacity to overstep the narrow boundaries of rationalised, quotidian experience.

LSD, Leary, and *The Crying of Lot 49*

As a well-respected Harvard professor of psychology, Dr. Leary originally became aware of the power of psychedelics after eating the *teonanacatl* or "God's Flesh" mushroom while on holiday with friends in Mexico during the summer of 1960.[5] Perceiving the therapeutic possibilities of such compounds, and also fascinated by the religious connotations of his experience, Leary, alongside Richard Alpert, soon began conducting experiments at Harvard using the mushroom's active component, psilocybin. Before long Aldous Huxley, author of *The Doors of Perception* (1954), a famous account of his experiences with the hallucinogenic mescalin, introduced Leary to the much stronger psychedelic, LSD. Huxley thought that psychedelics might help solve some of the great problems of mankind and was hopeful that Leary's professional standing would help them be accepted into the mainstream of scientific study. Endowed with an open, inquisitive, intensely scientific mind, Leary soon began to see LSD as Huxley did – as having great potential not only in psychotherapies, but in broader society. Like key theorists of the counterculture Ronald Laing and Norman O. Brown, Leary began to consider the dominant Western mindset – what he termed "man's possessive and manipulatory symbolic mind" (*PE* 219) – as unhealthy and self-destructive, and the cure, for him, was LSD.[6]

LSD worked by expanding consciousness. As Huxley had recounted years earlier, psychedelics seemed to open a perceptual portal or "reducing valve" that normally limited for practical purposes the amount of sense data one could be aware of.[7] They allowed an individual

> [t]o be shaken out of the ruts of ordinary perception, to be shown for a few timeless hours the outer and the inner world, not as they appear to an animal obsessed with survival or to a human being obsessed with words and notions, but as they are apprehended, directly and unconditionally, by Mind at Large.[8]

Huxley considered this "an experience of inestimable value to everyone and especially to the intellectual."[9] By allowing the human mind access to dimensions of awareness normally obscure to us, LSD enlightened users, allowing them to see the world and their place within it more clearly, freed from the fears and paranoias propagated by the military-industrial complex which generated the type of docile, unquestioning acceptance of the norm Leary termed "robot behavior" (*PE* 215), and largely perceived on the Left as typical, as we have seen, of American society during the 1950s. "Turn on, tune in, drop out" was the infamous formula Leary used to describe the process of individual growth and change LSD facilitated.[10]

Put simply, to turn on was to take the drug, to tune in was to allow it to expand one's awareness, and to drop out was to act on such expanded consciousness in order "to detach [oneself] from involvement in secular, external social games" which trap people within the "insane and destructive enterprise" of American society (*PE* 215). It is important to note that dropping out did not necessarily imply leaving one's job or family; the community could not be shunned. Also, Leary did not consider dropping out as something easy to achieve or maintain. Rather, repeated cycles of turning on, tuning in, and dropping out were required to keep from slipping back into everyday routines and patterns of thought. In fact, although LSD provided an easier route to *initial* consciousness expansion than Eastern religious practices like yoga or meditation, Leary described the process of dropping out as "the hardest yoga of all" (*PE* 226).

Against detractors who claimed that LSD in fact promoted a similar form of passivity to that already rife within the suburbs and cities of America, Leary defended the drug's revolutionary promise as well as its spiritual relevance, claiming in a 1966 interview for *Playboy* magazine that LSD "spurs a driving hunger to communicate in new forms, in better ways, to express a more harmonious message, to live a better life," and that in fact "[t]he LSD cult has already wrought revolutionary changes in American culture" (*PE* 141) – something that was surely true, at least within the bounds of the counterculture. Leary actually went as far as to consider LSD the only remaining viable trigger to revolutionary action because "before you can take any posture in relationship to this society, you have to sanitize yourself internally" (*PE* 215), and given the advanced stage of the disease ravaging the Western mind, LSD was the only thing strong enough. In line with this, Leary claimed that LSD as a revolutionary tool was far superior to the traditional political means of the New Left, since political action did not necessitate the consciousness expansion of the protestors in the same way. As he said, "if all … the left-wing college students in the world had Cadillacs and full control of society, they would still be involved in an anthill social system unless they opened themselves up first" (*PE* 140). According to Todd Gitlin, Beat poets like Ginsberg and Gary Snyder who became countercultural figures in the 1960s called for the combination of New Left and psychedelic perspectives in a "confluence of politics (on behalf of the outside and the future) and psychedelia (on behalf of the inside and the present)."[11]

Leary's perspective on LSD was intensely influential on the early psychedelic movement. The drug was difficult to obtain at this time, so many had their first trips via Leary's experiments or at his Millbrook commune, experiences which were therefore coloured by his serious, religious view of the drug.[12] The years of the "acid tests" organised by Kesey and the Pranksters, where the drug was primarily an aid to having a good time and was distributed indiscriminately via a vat of "electric" kool-aid, were yet to come.[13] But despite the relative sobriety of Leary's experiments with LSD, controversy surrounding them grew rapidly during the early sixties. Although Leary and his colleagues had some success in using psychedelics to rehabilitate alcoholics and criminals, conservative America's early enthusiasm for the new drug soon waned as it was rumoured that its use was spreading among the student population at Harvard. Before long, Leary's experiments were causing "a hysterical outcry," and his promotion of internal freedom was "becoming a major religious and civil rights controversy," as he himself explained in a lecture delivered on 30 August 1963.[14] That same year, Leary was dismissed from his Harvard post, the official reason given being that he had missed classes.[15] Undeterred, in 1964 he published *The Psychedelic Experience: A Manual Based on the Tibetan Book of the Dead*, a guidebook for users of LSD. Between 1963 and 1968, Leary lived in his self-created Millbrook commune and continued his work with the International Foundation for Internal Freedom (IF-IF), which carried out research on LSD, published the scholarly journal *The Psychedelic Review*, and trained guides for the psychedelic experience. However, the federal government had already begun cracking down on the use of the drug, and it became illegal in October 1966.

Within *The Crying of Lot 49* the controversial psychedelic alternative is presented to the reader most directly via the experiences of Oedipa's husband, Wendell "Mucho" Maas. Initially a bundle of nerves prone to nightmares and sordid affairs with teenage basketball players, Mucho is transformed through the LSD prescribed for him by Oedipa's psychiatrist, Dr. Hilarius, who is carrying out a study into the effects of the drug on married couples in suburbia. Mucho's reaction is unquestionably positive. Relating his expanded perceptions to Oedipa, his eyes "brimming" and a Leary-esque "radiant smile" on his face (*L49* 99, 98), Mucho appears to embody the "ecstatic wonder, ecstatic intuition, ecstatic, accurate movement" of what Leary considered "man's natural state" (*PE* 69). Mucho has certainly turned on, tuned in, and dropped out, and he has dropped out in the positive sense Leary intended, not from society as a whole, but from the "social roles and dramas which are unloving, contracting and which distract us from the discovery of our atomic, cellular, somatic and sensory divinity" (*PE* 36). LSD has enabled Mucho to remedy the loneliness, emptiness, and nihilism that had lately characterised his life – thus he no longer needs extramarital affairs, he now understands and believes in the music he airs as a DJ for the KCUF radio station, and he is no longer haunted by nightmare visions of the sign reading N.A.D.A. (standing for National Automobile Dealers' Association, and meaning "nothing" in Spanish) that used to swing ominously against the clear blue sky at his former workplace. It seems to be, as he describes it, "a flipping miracle" (*L49* 99).

Yet Mucho's apparently successful escape into the realm of "internal freedom" is deliberately positioned within the novel so as to invite comparison to Oedipa's very different endeavour to confront, comprehend, and transcend the "exitlessness" and "absence of surprise to life" that troubles contemporary America (*L49* 118), the alienation described in Chapter 1. Although both characters are seeking freedom via lifestyle change and consciousness expansion, the methods each has chosen are very different, and the ease and rapidity with which Mucho seems to cast off the oppressive aspects of his life contrasts sharply to the numerous practical and psychological difficulties against which Oedipa pits herself as she battles towards an understanding of the shady historical postal service known as the Trystero. The level of insight Oedipa does achieve is garnered by a combination of unwavering curiosity, determination, and a kind of literary critical practice. While Mucho is instantly liberated, Oedipa's approach is full of the "slow, frustrating and hard work" that McClintic Sphere advocated in *V.*, and thus, one might assume, it would be favoured by the author. For McClintic such labour is the only way to avoid what he terms the "cool/crazy flipflop": a negative choice between simple acquiescence in the victory of the oppressors and all-out war (*V.* 365); many critics agree that this perspective, to a considerable degree, is also Pynchon's own.[16] Struggling in this way, Oedipa makes significant progress towards liberating herself from the habits of thought and action that had been blighting her, and the prospect of her joining an underground community of rebels also opens up, but by the end of the novel Oedipa's access to this alternative still hangs in the balance, requiring a further risk to self from the men with "cruel faces" who fill the auction room and the "descending angel" of an auctioneer who will finally, she hopes, confirm or deny her (*L49* 126–7). Pynchon has to date expressed no explicit, final judgement on the value of LSD either in his fiction or journalism, although it is known that during the 1960s he enjoyed smoking the milder psychoactive marijuana, which he describes as a "useful substance" (*SL* 8) in his introduction to *Slow Learner*.[17] But in setting up this contrast between Oedipa and her husband, the author poses a series of questions to the reader: Are psychedelics a viable way of effecting a revolution in American society, do they offer a real route to freedom? Are the levels of consciousness expansion reached by these two routes equal? Is it both easier and better to escape oppression through the use of psychedelic drugs than through concerted action and hard work?

An analysis of the conversation during which Mucho reveals his drug use to Oedipa sheds further light on the possible answers to these questions. The dialogue consists of Mucho extolling the virtues of LSD, and also offering some to Oedipa, while she recoils in shock and panics that her husband has changed beyond recognition. Confronted by his "patient, motherly look," her irritation and alienation are so extreme that she has to control her impulse to "hit him in the mouth" (*L49* 99). The reader, identified with the subject position of the protagonist, is at first inclined to sympathise with Oedipa as she excoriates the drug as dangerous and as having destroyed Mucho's individual personality. Cyrus R. K. Patell's contention that Mucho on LSD represents just another form of alienation seems potentially valid.[18] To some extent, Oedipa's anger over Mucho's serenity seems natural because it has been produced by unnatural means. But on further consideration, the logic of Oedipa's position starts to break down.

The conversation occurs on the same day as a previous exchange between Oedipa and Mucho, the interview Oedipa gives him as a reporter for his radio station, after an episode in which Dr. Hilarius, suffering from a paranoid delusion, holds her hostage. During this interview, which takes place only a few hours before Mucho's revelation described earlier, Oedipa appears relaxed and does not seem to notice anything different about her husband apart from his bizarre insistence on pronouncing "Oedipa Maas" as "Edna Mosh," "allowing for the distortion" (*L49* 96) as the interview is beamed back to the radio station – a dig, perhaps, at the media's propensity for misrepresentation. Oedipa later goes to the radio station herself, where she meets Mucho's boss, who tells her that the DJ is behaving strangely and "coming on like a whole roomful of people" (*L49* 99). Her response here is still calm and defensive of her husband: "It's your imagination … You've been smoking those cigarettes without the printing on them again" (*L49* 97). Thus primed to find Mucho's behaviour unusual, Oedipa goes to meet him. Unsurprisingly then, she starts to feel anxious as soon as he begins describing his new sensitivity to music. Oedipa's anxiety turns to panic as Mucho elaborates on his ability, on LSD, to "break down chords, and timbres, and words too into all the basic frequencies and harmonics, with all their different loudnesses, and listen to them, each pure tone, but all at once" (*L49* 98) – a formulation which recalls Leary's description of how, "when you turn on with LSD, the organ of Corti in your inner ear becomes a trembling membrane seething with tattoos of sound waves ... You hear one note of a Bach sonata, and it hangs there, glittering, pulsating, for an endless length of time, while you slowly orbit around it" (*PE* 125). Once it is revealed that it is Mucho, not his boss, who has been getting high, Oedipa demonstrates her ignorance of the drug by worrying about whether Mucho is addicted (LSD is non-addictive). Thus Oedipa's reaction is revealed as primarily a combination of a lack of knowledge and her now-habitual paranoid relationship with reality. In this light, it seems cruel of Oedipa to deny Mucho the release he has obtained via LSD. If he has, as Oedipa puts it, "dissipated" (*L49* 100), it is only because so much of what he manifested as his former personality was negative.

However, there is something in Pynchon's rendering of Oedipa in this scene which prevents the reader from discarding her perspective entirely. At the end of the scene, for example, the touch of comedy in Oedipa's urge to punch the smug-looking Mucho returns in the description of how, taking leave of each other at the radio station, "they kissed goodbye, all of them" (*L49* 100). This does something to soften potential criticism of Oedipa's panicked overreaction, and also increases the pathos of the final image we get of her in this chapter, sitting despondently "with her forehead resting on the steering wheel" (*L49* 100). Refusing to endorse either Mucho's or Oedipa's subject position entirely, the passage deliberately works to strand the reader in between. Pynchon makes us question both the uncritical acceptance of the value of LSD by a new user, and the hysterical panic of someone who is totally unfamiliar with it, a postmodern technique which reflects a broader countercultural philosophy at work in Pynchon's novels stressing the danger of putting too much trust in any one source of information.

As discussed in Chapter 1, the incommunicable is represented in the *Crying of Lot 49* as potentially destructive: the example given being the experience of the alcoholic sailor, whose apparent insight into alternative dimensions of reality only serves to isolate him from society, whose "quantity of hallucination ... the world would bear no further trace of" if he died (*L49* 88). Likewise, in this exchange between Mucho and Oedipa the incommunicability of the psychedelic experience to a non-user is highlighted as an important drawback in its use as a trigger for social revolution, suggesting that it might only serve to divide society even more deeply than at present. However, the use of psychedelics for consciousness expansion is by no means entirely discredited, as it is suggested that if the barrier of ignorance regarding psychedelics could be brought down, those who remain the prisoners of paranoia and neurosis might find a cure.

Another dimension of Pynchon's mid-sixties attitude towards the psychedelic movement can be brought into view by exploring *The Crying of Lot 49*'s representation of the aforementioned LSD-dispensing shrink Dr. Hilarius, almost certainly a deliberate analogy for Timothy Leary. In his essay on post-Beat Pynchon "A Re-Cognition of Her Errand into the Wilderness," Pierre-Yves Petillon also notes this analogy, going as far as to claim that those Europeans who had spent any time at all in America and had read *The Psychedelic Experience* were quick to recognise Hilarius as "obviously Timothy Leary scarcely transmogrified."[19] But while such a connection should be triggered by the very fact that he is conducting psychotherapies involving the administration of "LSD-25, mescaline, psilocybin, and related drugs" (*L49* 10) in the 1960s, Hilarius is actually far from being Leary "scarcely transmogrified." In fact I would argue that in this novel Pynchon presents us with Hilarius as a deliberately distorted version of Leary in order to satirise media sensationalisation, government vilification, and public ignorance of what he might have considered the "real" Leary. As discussed, much public hysteria surrounded Leary's experiments with LSD at Harvard, although they were conducted on willing volunteers, in carefully controlled environments, and with trained guides. Headlines like "LSD: The Exploding Threat of the Mind Drug That Got Out of Control" were rife in the mid sixties news media, and Oedipa's panic in the face of psychedelics was characteristic of her social milieu.[20] Demonised by the press and the federal government alike, Leary's subversive reputation eventually grew to the point where President Nixon described him as "the most dangerous man in America." Misrepresentative reportage on popular oppositional figures is a manifestation of the repression inherent in the system, and it is something Pynchon battles against in several of his novels. His representation of Leary via the character of Dr. Hilarius is thus, I argue, part of an attempt to counter such repressive tactics. Supporting this hypothesis are a number of direct discrepancies between the character of Hilarius and Leary as he presented himself publicly through his published work and in interviews up until the publication of *The Crying of Lot 49* in 1966.

In particular, Hilarius's madness seems to reflect conservative American perception of Leary as mentally unstable in his very experimentation with psychoactive compounds and in his perceived popularisation of their use. In an article published in *Esquire* in September 1963, for instance, writer and social critic Martin Mayer attacked Leary and Alpert on several counts, accusing them of being "extremely irrational" and "socially withdrawn," of having "delusions of grandeur," and of seeming "likely to wind up in places where they can be closely observed."[21] In fact, Leary comes across as extremely sane and clear-minded in his early interviews, despite his later eccentricities. Writing in the *Harvard Crimson* student newsletter in autumn 1965, Stephen Bello describes Leary as maintaining an "essentially conservative demeanor," and as a "surprisingly staid fellow," whose "tweediness" surely disappointed the hip crowd he had recently addressed.[22] In *Lot 49* Hilarius is ravaged by guilt over his complicity in Nazi experiments using all kinds of methods – "new drugs" (*L49* 95) is even listed – to induce insanity in Jewish prisoners during the Second World War. His unfounded belief that a host of Israelis are hunting him down, seeking revenge for his involvement in such torture, results in the hostage situation mentioned earlier. Although Pynchon would surely have been aware that terrible experiments such as these actually took place in Nazi Germany, that he does not take Hilarius's guilt very seriously is indicated by the fact that his preferred method of tormenting his victims was "face-pulling." It seems that Hilarius is doing satiric penance in this novel, his remorse reflecting that which Leary "should" feel in supposedly risking the sanity of the American youth who volunteered to be part of his LSD experiments, in "psychosis peddling" (*PE* 72) as Martin Mayer put it. In numerous interviews Leary defended the drug from such allegations, stating and restating the statistics which showed LSD use to be safe under the kinds of controlled conditions in which he ran his experiments.

Hilarius's irresponsibility is further underscored through his attempts to persuade Oedipa, despite her clear antipathy to the idea, to take part in his LSD study on suburban housewives, as well as through a suggestion made at the beginning of the novel that he has in fact tried to give Oedipa the drug without her knowledge. (Oedipa does not take the pills Hilarius has prescribed her because she is not convinced that "they're only tranquillizers" (*L49* 10), suspecting her psychotherapist of resorting to covert means to obtain more volunteers for his study.) Yet, as his biographer John Higgs confirms, "before LSD became illegal, Leary's public stance stressed controlled and responsible use of the drug."[23] Leary condemned reports of federal government experimentation with LSD on troops in Vietnam, in which the drug was given to unprepared subjects, warning of the serious danger this could have for those involved and terming such practice "psychological rape" (*PE* 148). Other significant differences include the fact that Hilarius claims never to have taken LSD himself, whereas Leary took the drug hundreds of times and considered this essential to good practice

(*PE* 100, 149). Also, while Hilarius attempts, however unsuccessfully, to emulate Freud's therapeutic methodology, Leary disapproved of him, preferring Eastern psychology which he considered superior to its Western equivalent.[24] One further point relates to Hilarius's possession of a gun and his attempt to shoot his imagined Israeli persecutors from his office. Leary felt similarly under attack during numerous police raids on his Millbrook community, yet he always professed pacifism and claims in a 1995 interview with Paul Krassner never to have owned a gun.[25]

The satire which inheres in such diametrically opposed characteristics of Hilarius and Leary seems to suggest that Pynchon was sympathetic towards Leary as a persecuted countercultural figure, and towards his pre-1966 philosophy of the controlled use of LSD.[26] Further evidence of this is provided if we consider that *The Crying of Lot 49* may contain an extended metaphor for an acid trip. The reader's suspicion in this regard is initially piqued by the suggestion that Hilarius has laced some of Oedipa's prescribed pills with LSD. Although she has not taken these, there are plenty of opportunities within the action for Oedipa to be spiked, perhaps as part of Pierce's posthumous manipulation, from the suspiciously strong Kirsch in the fondue at the Tupperware party she attends, to the dandelion wine offered by Genghis Cohen. Several elements of the narrative support the idea that an LSD trip is one of the several layered structural principles of the novel, most essentially the surreal nature of Oedipa's experiences and Pynchon's repeated descriptions of the "revelations" she is exposed to – a term Leary often used to describe the psychedelic experience and its religious-mystical nature. Furthermore, the duration of the action – forty-nine days – which has tended to be referred by critics to the forty-nine days preceding the Christian Pentecost, could, as Pierre-Yves Petillon has pointed out, equally relate to the forty-nine days between death and rebirth through which *The Tibetan Book of the Dead* – on which Leary and Alpert's book *The Psychedelic Experience* is based – claims to guide the user.[27] Pynchon, in fact, mentions the "Book of the Dead" (*L49* 20) at a particularly hierophanic moment in the novel.[28] Leary's *The Psychedelic Experience* interprets the death and rebirth addressed in *The Tibetan Book of the Dead* as symbolic, likening it to the transformation in state of mind which comes about on taking LSD. Oedipa's progression in the novel fits with these models, as she moves from the death of an old self towards the birth of a new one.

Oedipa's particular experiences also demonstrate a considerable convergence with the descriptions found in *The Psychedelic Experience*, particularly those sections detailing the types of hallucinations that might be had by someone who is struggling to regain their everyday ego – the kind of response we would expect if Oedipa had ingested LSD without her knowledge. On her night-time odyssey through San Francisco, "a night that possesses all the aura of dream and hallucinogenic experience,"[29] Oedipa is inundated by a mixture of memories, fantasies, and dreams, or what Leary calls a "kaleidoscopic vision of game-reality" ("game reality" is what we would consider to be everyday reality), characteristic of the sixth and lowest level of Second Bardo LSD experience.[30] In the Third Bardo state, the period of re-entry into everyday ego-reality to which one is expected to descend after the Second Bardo, "[m]ind-controlling manipulative figures and demons of hideous aspects may be hallucinated."[31] Of course, Pierce Inverarity and the Trystero spring to mind. This state is also characterised by feelings of stupidity, of isolation, of one's surroundings seeming static and lifeless, and of restless movement. Moreover, towards the end of the novel Oedipa begins to experience various physical symptoms, including nausea and pain, to which Leary admits LSD users may be prone.[32]

If we accept this interpretation, the fact that Oedipa's overall experience has both positive and negative aspects implies an ambivalence towards the action of psychedelics on Pynchon's part. On the one hand, Oedipa's confusion, disorientation, and pain act as a warning that LSD trips can be unpleasant and that, as Leary recommended, they should not be attempted in unfamiliar or unsettling surroundings, especially without a guide. On the other hand, the experience is somewhat fruitful for Oedipa, helping her in the process of her "sensitisation," allowing her to perceive the symbols of the W.A.S.T.E. organisation and, towards the end of the novel, the physical presences of whole communities of other American outsiders she had previously turned a blind eye to. The subversive presence of the Trystero within doctored postage stamps, very similar in form to acid tabs, might work to reinforce the previous point, while also helping to explain Pynchon's perennial fascination with stamps, which are often associated with access to alternate realities and spiritual insight. However, awareness, in this novel, does not automatically lead to the kind of understanding that can motivate social engagement. Mucho's psychedelic experience shows him a very personal and apparently apolitical pathway out of oppression; Oedipa, whose unsolicited visions are more bewildering than enlightening, has much work to do in unearthing the meaning of her unusual perceptions, and in initiating a positive course of action. In whichever way we look at Oedipa's trajectory towards rebirth, it is a determination fuelled by belief in the intellect that allows Oedipa to grow and progress, and this heroic rationality is certainly celebrated within the novel – after all, it generates and directs the narrative. It is telling that Mucho's easy slippage out of oppression is, in contrast, quickly passed over. (In fact, when Mucho reappears in Pynchon's later novel *Vineland* – a novel which, it should be noted, recounts a number of positive acid trips – he too has rejected LSD. Having become a notorious dealer of the substance, a career choice which led him to become hooked on cocaine and suffer a "nasal breakdown," Mucho proclaims, as Ken Kesey came to, that "the new trip, the only true trip, is The Natch, and being on it" (*VL* 310–11).)

The conclusion to which this analysis leads is that Pynchon at the time of writing *The Crying of Lot 49* probably considered psychedelics potentially helpful in achieving the countercultural aims of internal freedom and, in turn, social change, but saw drawbacks in the unguided use of the drug and in the incommunicability of the experience it offers. Later on, he may have become aware of further causes to distrust a drug that proliferated as the counterculture grew – the violent crimes associated with it, the possibility that its use helped to accelerate the counterculture's accession to a more aggressive stance – as Todd Gitlin points out, "LSD percolated through the New Left, especially its inventive California wing, at just the same time as the surge in militancy," heightening, to some degree, the "willful suspension of disbelief" which allowed protestors to risk their lives in violent struggles.[33] Hesitant to ally himself too closely with those celebrating LSD as some kind of magical catch-all cure for the ills of society, Pynchon yet, I submit, feeds something of Leary's philosophy through into his novels, employing a writing practice which allows him to provide, in the reader's encounter with the novel, some of the more valuable elements of the psychedelic experience. A writer rather than a purveyor of hallucinogens, Pynchon nevertheless develops and promotes within his novels a parallel political methodology aimed primarily, like the psychedelic movement (as well as numerous other countercultural movements), at consciousness expansion.

In its undeveloped form, as legible in *The Crying of Lot 49*, this method consists of providing an alternate model for the reader to follow towards heightened awareness: the conscious efforts Oedipa makes to gather and interpret evidence on the Trystero. In fact, as a result of the equivalent epistemological status of Oedipa and the reader (much commented on critically), the novel does not so much offer this model up as force us into it, in what is undoubtedly a deliberate move – many of Oedipa's interpretations, like our own, pertain to literary objects. As Frank Kermode has suggested, "[w]hat Oedipa is doing is very like reading a book."[34] Whether on LSD or not, the primary role Oedipa plays is that of the literary critic, not only because the original source of information regarding the Trystero is the play *The Courier's Tragedy*, but also because she employs a kind of literary critical skill in interpreting and forming meaningful connections between the traces of the underground communities she finds strewn across the urban landscape. In this light the narrator's description of Oedipa as "unfit perhaps for marches and sit ins, but just a whiz at pursuing strange words in Jacobean texts" (*L49* 72) takes on a new significance, beyond its superficial intention of poking fun at the apoliticality of traditional literary studies. Arguing against Melissa Lam in her assertion that Oedipa combines "specialized academic training" with a "lack of revolutionary vigor" – "a defunct combination in the rebelliously charged environment of the 60s," I suggest that Oedipa's critical practice – applied to the postmodern environment mirrored in postmodern literary texts such as *Lot 49* itself – is proposed as a viable form of political engagement.[35] In this mid sixties novel Pynchon suggests an alternative route to revolution through the development of intellectual curiosity and interpretative skills; in this his work offers a form of training towards the kind of relationship with reality Pynchon believes conducive to escaping oppression.

It is important to note that this celebration of the rational intellect – operating on the basis of humanist principles – is by no means at odds with Leary's philosophy, despite his assertion that "man's manipulatory and symbolic mind" was at the heart of what was wrong with his society. Like other counterculture thinkers, Leary made a distinction between true rationalism and a perverted version of the same – what Theodore Roszak described as "objective consciousness" in *The Making of a Counterculture*. According to Roszak, objective consciousness is a historical phenomenon which has twisted logical thought to industrial-utilitarian ends. Its adoption has three important implications: "(1) the alienative dichotomy; (2) the invidious hierarchy; (3) the mechanistic imperative."[36] In other words, objective consciousness establishes as a basic truth the essentially false notion of an unbridgeable divide between subject and object, which in turn generates a hierarchy between the two, with the subject privileged. The product of the Enlightenment and the force behind technocratic expansionist capitalism, in privileging the subject this mentality seemingly validates the oppression of one individual or group by another, as well as the domination of nature by mankind, with intensely destructive consequences.[37] Those who preach such "Gospels of Reason, denouncing all that was once Magic," are the target of explicit criticism in *Mason & Dixon*, a novel set in Enlightenment times which, the narrator notes, "are unfriendly toward Worlds alternative to this one" (*MD* 359). In response to the continued prevalence of such modes of reasoning in contemporary society, the many within the counterculture "preached a new mindfulness, a conscientious reconsideration of the rational."[38] The irrationality or antirationality of the counterculture, sometimes self-proclaimed, sometimes a label given by external detractors, can only be understood as an attempt to subvert the perceived sickness of mainstream logic. Leary himself was, of course, a scientist, and relied on rational argument to present his findings to the wider academic community, as well as to the public. He hoped for the triumph of "intellect divorced from old-fashioned neurosis, freed from egocentricity, from semantic reification" (*PE* 188). The liberated, enquiring mind is an ideal for Leary – and so too for Pynchon.

Capitalist Spectacles and Other Worlds: Fantasy as a Political Tool in *Against the Day*

In his later work Pynchon's attempt to expand the consciousnesses of his readers becomes more concretely emulative of Leary's political technique: through his more positive, affirmative use of *fantasy* Pynchon achieves an analogously psychedelic result, while avoiding some of the drawbacks of ingesting psychoactive chemicals, as well as the hedonistic trap Leary and his followers fell into in the late sixties. (Not to mention such inordinate reprisals as the twenty-year jail sentence Leary received for possession of ten dollars worth of marijuana.) In place of the at best semi-conscious, possibly unchannelled ecstasy the psychedelic revolution offered, it is a more deliberate, guided yet still largely independent exercise of the individual imagination that Pynchon, in his fantastical narratives, advocates as an important technique for developing patterns of thought less beholden to the societal norm. In the context of this approach, Jeffrey S. Baker's observation that *Gravity's Rainbow* is "experientially educative for anyone who wants to learn what it would be like to live in the precarious and dynamic flux of a truly democratic culture" is even truer of *Against the Day*.[39] Imaginative experience combined with analytical logic potentially offers benefits comparable or superior to those of psychedelic experience, allowing the subject internal escape from the rigid hierarchies and fixed structures of popular thought, into a world which allows a degree of independence, a world in which all forms are – at least in part – created by the subject themselves. I am suggesting here that Pynchon tries to create an ecstatic experience of sorts in his reader, using the fantastical nature of his novels to tip them out of the grooves of their everyday patterns of thought, to send them on an imaginative journey, to displace them. In doing so, I further propose, Pynchon has a political end in mind: the expansion of the imaginative faculties in tandem with critical skills are, for Pynchon, a specific precursor to political action. And in having this project at its core, Pynchon's work thus challenges prevalent notions of the self-absorption and political irrelevance of postmodern fiction, confirming that such writing can base itself, Linda Hutcheon's arguments to the contrary, on a "theory of agency" potentially capable of enabling real-life political engagement.[40]

That fantasy has a political value in Pynchon's work has been previously suggested by Sam Thomas in his recent study *Pynchon and the Political*. Discussing *Mason & Dixon*, Thomas draws on Ernst Bloch in arguing that fantasy can be "a legitimate (albeit oblique) form of political inquiry," since "it is in the nature of fantasy to be self-aware or self-critical. It is in the nature of fantasy to *doubt*.... Fantasy casts doubts about itself but it also casts doubts about the instruments of reason."[41] Graham Benton takes this a step further, suggesting that "the resistance of realism by fantasy is reproduced as a resistance of the forces of rationalization and totalizing empirical systems" in *Against the Day*.[42] But Thomas seems to ignore (and Benton underemphasises) the fact that fantasy can also be a means of uncritical escapism, channelling subversive desires into innocuous imaginings, making their conversion into purposive action less probable. Indeed, the temptation to imaginatively abscond from the manifold frustrations of life as lived into a realm of illusory powerfulness is a major theme in Pynchon's fiction. Speaking of *Vineland*, Patricia A. Bergh has observed that fantasy in that novel "is infinitely preferable to reality because in a fantasy state, the dreamer is in control of content, direction, and outcome, and never is obliged to confront any anomalies."[43] But Bergh's further contention that in *Vineland* "[t]he naif has been extinguished as cynicism and scepticism have moved into his/her place" is only partially correct.[44] American culture may have become cynical on certain issues by *Vineland*'s mid eighties – particularly, perhaps, regarding the possibility of transforming society on a more egalitarian model – but there remains a vast propensity to self-delusion and easy escapism. Returning to the sixties, in his 1966 article "A Journey into the Mind of Watts," Pynchon describes escapism, relating it directly to LSD use, as especially afflicting the white population:

> The white kid digs hallucination simply because he is conditioned to believe so much in escape, escape as an integral part of life, because the white L. A.

Scene makes accessible to him so many different forms of it. But a Watts kid, brought up in a pocket of reality, looks perhaps not so much for escape as just for some calm, some relaxation. And beer or wine is good enough for that. (J 80)

By combining fantastical narrative with postmodern literary techniques and political commentaries which advocate or require self-awareness of the reader (the former include Pynchon's careful ambiguity, his use of ellipsis, his habit of leaving narratives unresolved, and his incorporation of secret histories and obscure references), Pynchon's novels deliberately counteract such temptation to escape, while at the same time promoting speculation and curiosity regarding alternative realities. In envisaging such alternatives, be they utopian, dystopian, or merely different, fantasy is an innately countercultural literary form.

In *The Crying of Lot 49*, the fantastical is treated with relative ambivalence, its presence interpreted by Oedipa as threatening evidence of her own mental instability, her entrapment within "the orbiting ecstasy of a true paranoia" (*L49* 126). Fantasy is sharply differentiated from reality in Oedipa's mind – the Trystero can either be real or imagined, and if it *is* a fantasy, she is desperate to be talked out of it. As noted in Chapter 1, she tends to cling to her stable ego-identity as Pynchon underscores the potential repercussions of liminal experience for the (post)modern subject. Dr. Hilarius has a different perspective, trying "fiercely" to persuade Oedipa that she should "cherish" her fantasies, arguing that our imaginative experience somehow constitutes our individual identity, and that "when you lose it you go over by that much to the others. You begin to cease to be" (*L49* 95, 96). Yet he too is unwilling to risk his ego in pursuit of the visionary. LSD's potential to blur the distinction between oneself and others, to overcome the subject-object divide and proffer something akin to an experience of *communitas* in its stead, is not attractive to Hilarius, who prefers "to remain in relative paranoia, where at least I know who I am and who the others are" (*L49* 94). Such tension between practical considerations and the *communitas* ideal, between control and ego loss, is better resolved in the fiction of Pynchon's mid-late career, and the fantasy-reality dichotomy Oedipa perceives is ever more forcefully undermined.

This development works in tandem with the greater openness towards Eastern religious meditative practices, particularly those associated with Buddhism and Hinduism, that we find in post-*V.* Pynchon. As noted in Chapter 1, in *V.* Pynchon aligned Ester's experience of ego loss while undergoing rhinoplasty with the entropic forces promoting stasis and passivity rather than positive activity. However, from *The Crying of Lot 49* onwards critics have recognised a deepening interest in Buddhism in Pynchon's writing, and in the novels of his late phase a complete reversal of his earlier attitude is visible.[45] Thus in *Mason & Dixon*, for instance, Eastern forms of temporary ego loss are associated with right action in the political sphere. In the first pages of the novel, the Reverend Cherrycoke experiences "One of those moments Hindoos and Chinamen are ever said to be having, entire loss of Self, perfect union with All" (*MD* 10) while meditating on his name, which, rather than something belonging to himself, is used by the authorities to jail him after he is arrested for posting up unsigned broadsides in the streets, "Accounts of certain Crimes I had observ'd, committed by the Stronger against the Weaker, – enclosures, evictions, Assize verdicts, Activities of the Military, – giving the Names of as many of the Perpetrators as I was sure of, yet keeping back what I foolishly imagin'd my own" (*MD* 9). (This activity recalls the scrawling of anonymous graffiti over the walls of Weimar-era Berlin's communist districts in *Gravity's Rainbow*, which, as discussed in the previous chapter, seem to express a "folk-consciousness" and if analysed and thought about can be "translated into action by the people" (*GR* 155). In both cases the authors of such messages function as analogues to Pynchon himself as author – with a wry nod to his decision to keep textual expression uncontaminated by public persona – something which is especially clear in the later text, where Cherrycoke not only narrates most of the narrative, but bases it on his own written account of his experiences with the astronomers.) Notably, the superficially undifferentiated valorisation of elements of Buddhism and Hinduism we find in *Mason & Dixon* is very similar to that found in Leary's psychedelic philosophy as well as within the counterculture more broadly considered. Such a rapprochement with Eastern religious meditative practice sheds further light on Pynchon's reasons for endorsing visionary and imaginative experience as a political tool in his later work.

In expounding on the particular ways in which the political project outlined earlier is developed within Pynchon's later writing practice I now turn to *Against the Day*, where I believe this project reaches its most mature realisation to date, albeit in close competition with *Mason & Dixon*, whose action incorporates myriad surreal episodes, Mason's mystical and mysterious encounter with the pickled, glowing, and listening Ear of Robert Jenkins being just one instance among many, the more recently published *Inherent Vice* being in many respects an inferior example. Settings and events in *Against the Day* are among the most wondrously fantastical Pynchon has yet produced, and the novel's vast scope allows for both the extended action of the interpretative faculties of the reader and the incorporation of numerous alternative histories; the novel is directly geared towards the positive, concrete realisation that there are multiple levels of human experience. While in *The Crying of Lot 49* alternative worlds are merely glimpsed hierophanically, and the possibility that the Trystero is hoax or hallucination is given equal weight to the possibility that it really exists, in *Against the Day* much of the action takes place within alternative realities described as if objectively real. There is also a greater sense of justice and of positive forces at work: there is more of the good trip in Pynchon's later novels. All in all, the reading experience created harbours possibilities for positive consciousness expansion comparable to those of the psychedelic experience as described by Leary and others: *Against the Day* might be termed Pynchon's most psychedelic novel. In addition, in its focus on anarchism, *Against the Day* goes further than its predecessors in exposing the end goals or political models towards which the writer, through his writing practice, hopes to help lead us.

As part of its attempt to thrust the reader out of everyday "reality," the novel works specifically to problematise the "real." Although each of the several narrative strands exists on a different experiential plane with relation to the world that we usually consider real – the sections dealing with the Traverse family taking place on the plane closest to everyday reality – the fluidity of action between each strand denies the exclusivity of each level. Examples of movement or communication between layers abound: Yashmeen, who is able to enter the Fourth Dimension, walks clean through a wall; Lew jumps into the centre of an explosion and wakes up in a parallel world; "Trespassers" appear from the future; the Chums of Chance enter the "visible" world as a result of the energy released by the event at Tunguska. The categories of "reality" and of "fiction" are upset by the doubly fictional Chums, who are clearly defined as boys' adventure book characters, yet interact with "non-fictional" characters (if they can be so described) and take part in real historical events. And as the imaginary and the factual merge, so do the spiritual and the geographical. This idea is embodied in the "Sfinciuno Itinerary," a map detailing the route to Shambhala, the "hidden city" (*ATD* 279) of Buddhist legend. The map's author, we are told, "imagined the Earth not only as a three-dimensional sphere, but, beyond that, as an *imaginary surface*, the optical arrangements for whose eventual projection onto the two-dimensional page proved to be very queer indeed" (*ATD* 280). A "metafictional reflection on the novel itself," the Itinerary illustrates Pynchon's own ideology and writing practice.[46] As characters shift between levels of "reality," so does the reader. In this way Pynchon suggests to us the potential multiplicity of perceivable realities.

Furthermore, as part of its repudiation of the pseudo-scientific validity of objective consciousness, numerous mathematical and scientific theories are described within the novel which claim (varying degrees of) objective validity for the existence of parallel worlds or dimensions. This is not to say that the scientific is definitely privileged; there are also many spiritual or mystical confirmations of alterative realities. Typical in its combination of the two is Professor Vanderjuice's argument that, based on Zermelo's Axiom of Choice, it is possible in theory to cut a mass the size of a pea into pieces which could be reassembled to form a sphere the size of the sun, hence "those Indian mystics and Tibetan lamas and so forth were right all along, the world we think we know can be dissected and reassembled into any number of worlds, each as real as 'this' one" (*ATD* 1212). In attempting to validate scientifically the idea that parallel worlds may exist beyond the reach of our everyday conscious mind, and that they may be just as real as the environment we usually inhabit, Pynchon again emulates Leary, who claimed that the states of consciousness entered into by the subject following ingestion of LSD constituted "*a direct awareness of the energy processes which physicists and biochemists and physiologists and neurologists and psychologists and psychiatrists measure*" (*PE* 21; italics in the original).

Light and its potentialities are another target of scientific musing in *Against the Day*. The twisting and manipulation of light, acting to hide or reveal sections of the cosmos we cannot normally perceive, occurs repeatedly in the novel and light-related notions of invisibility, doubling, and the like provide another means of troubling the "real." The enigmatic material "Iceland spar," whose name is also the title of one of the novel's longest sections, crops up in various places and is linked to doubling and bilocation. Used in magicians' tricks, mysterious instruments of destruction (the "Q" weapon), and encrypted "paramorphoscopes" (optical devices like the Sfinciuno Itinerary whose use "reveals worlds which are set to this side of the one we have taken, until now, to be the only world given us" (*ATD* 280)), Iceland spar is described early in the novel as "the sub-structure of reality" and the "doubling of the Creation" (*ATD* 149). Its presence in pure form in Iceland means that "this is not *only* the geographical Iceland here, it is also one of several convergences among the worlds, found now and then lying behind the apparent" (*ATD* 149), and its use in paramorphoscopes allows them to "reveal the architecture of dream, of all that escapes the network of ordinary latitude and longitude" (*ATD* 281).

Such suggestions of other worlds invest *Against the Day* with an aura of wonder, and surprise is not in short supply; here, more than anywhere else in Pynchon's fiction, one "steps through the looking glass into a realm governed by magical forces rather than logical ones."[47] Yet there are complications. Invisibility as a *human* condition is sometimes a blessing, sometimes a misfortune in the novel. Applied to characters who are close enough to enlightenment to be able to discern the limits of the given world and in some cases pass beyond them, as in the case of the shamans, it is also the condition of the downtrodden, of those suffering deliberate exclusion from the gaze of the capitalist mainstream. As Thomas puts it, in Pynchon the invisible "carries with it both the full force of radical freedom and the arbitrary horror of being wiped out plain and simple, of repression, abduction, terror and death."[48] These two aspects of the experience of invisibility are, of course, far from mutually exclusive. Such ambiguity in the category of the invisible is again, I suggest, part of a warning elaborated throughout Pynchon's *oeuvre* against allowing imaginative or visionary experience to become an end in itself, dissociated from a critical, interpretative practice aimed at alleviating suffering and escaping oppression.

This warning is expressed more directly in *Against the Day* via commentaries around Kit Traverse's obsession with Vectorist mathematics, in which he immerses himself in reaction to the murder of his father, Webb. As Professor Vanderjuice points out, mathematicians seem to be able to cope better with such disturbing situations, but "it's as likely to be a form of escaping reality, and sooner or later comes the payback" (*ATD* 366). Kit, unable to fully assimilate this perspective at the time, only later comes to realise that Vectorism,

> in which [he] once thought he had glimpsed transcendence, a coexisting world of imaginaries, the "spirit realm" that Yale legend Lee De Forest once imagined he was journeying through, had not shown Kit, after all, a way to escape the world governed by real numbers. His father had been murdered by men whose allegiance, loudly and often as they might invoke Jesus Christ and his kingdom, was to that real axis and nothing beyond it. (*ATD* 759)

In fact, Kit's pursuit of a mathematical beyond had played even more directly into the hands of his father's assassins than this passage suggests; he later discovers that Scarsdale Vibe, the corporate benefactor who had funded his education, had also ordered Webb's execution. Armed with this information, Kit determines to act on the "real axis" and take revenge. (Although, as it turns out, Kit is again distracted from this task by the lure of transcendence, now taking the form of the Buddhist hidden land known as Shambhala. While this time Kit's quest is less illusioned and his approach to enlightenment confers certain powers upon him, Pynchon emphasises the importance of maintaining relationships with others, of love even: as mentioned earlier, when Kit walks through an invisible doorway in Lwów he emerges in Paris to be reunited with his estranged wife, Dally.) Considering now the more specific political concerns such commentaries reveal, I suggest that throughout *Against the Day* Pynchon points again, as he did via the discussion of capitalist "pornographies" in *Gravity's Rainbow*, to the complicity of capitalism in generating within the populace escapist drives such as that to which Kit falls prey, drives which prevent them from acting effectively against the system's manifold injustices.[49] Souring the mix even further are the novel's intimations that our quotidian reality is in large part an escapist fantasy itself, generated to their profit by those who hold political and cultural power. The promotion of this fantasy is bound up within the novel with ideas of light and its manipulation.

Arriving in the Chicago of 1893 at the very beginning of the novel, the "Chums of Chance" – themselves, as discussed, straddling at least two experiential planes – encounter a stark contrast between the "daylit fiction" of the World's Columbian Exposition's "White City," symbol of the American consumer-capitalist "given world," and its "dark conjugate," the working city slaving away behind the scenes, invisible to the distraction-seeking fair goers (*ATD* 11). The Chums in their airship have a different perspective to the pleasure seekers exploring the international exhibits in their bright pavilions, however. Their viewpoint is literally heightened, and they are therefore able to perceive the mechanisms of the Fair's illusions. As they drift over the slaughterhouses of the Chicago stockyards they are in fact unable to locate the White City amongst the "tall smokestacks unceasingly vomiting black grease-smoke, the effluvia of butchery unremitting" (*ATD* 11). Driving home the inhumane perversity of such systems, Pynchon explains how the Chums,

> who, out on adventures past, had often witnessed the vast herds of cattle adrift in ever-changing cloudlike patterns across the Western plains, here saw that unshaped freedom being rationalized into movement only in straight lines and at right angles and a progressive reduction of choices, until the final turn through the final gate that led to the killing-floor. (*ATD* 11)

This is one of those passages whose more intense lyricism seems to reveal it as directly expressive of Pynchon's sentiment. Clearly imaging the entropic drift of human experience to the one definable, objectively explicable world we find ourselves allowed within contemporary rationalist culture; it vividly renders the death that a privileged profit-based logic portends for our counter-entropic imaginative faculties.

Unlike other fictions within the novel, the "daylit fiction" of the White City is not present as a trigger for the imagination, but instead it reveals how fiction may be used as an agent of misdirection. The World's Fair essentially exemplifies the warped view of reality that American imperial capitalism often succeeds in marketing to its people, a correlate to the "cheered land" Oedipa feels she inhabits in *Lot 49*, a hyper-illuminated, hyper-sanitised illusion which distracts us from and allows us to neglect the too-distressing realities of the suffering capitalist exploitation causes. The exotic exhibits which make up the Fair – including Zulus re-enacting their ancestors' massacre of British troops at Isandhlwana, Pygmies singing Christian hymns, and Brazilian "Indians" re-emerging after being swallowed by giant anacondas – are an affront to the countries they represent in either trivialising or masking the ravages of imperialism to which many of them were subjected. The connections between light, illusion, profit, and power drawn in this, the opening scene of the novel, are repeatedly reasserted. They are vocalised perhaps most bluntly by the professional magician Luca Zombini, who, discussing the need to manipulate light in magic tricks by way of mirrors and velvet, states that "[i]t's all about the light, you control the light, you control the effect" (*ATD* 399). The very title of this novel attests to Pynchon's opposition to such subtle propaganda, to this dominant reality, the false daylight of the capitalist "day."

Such concepts recall the French Marxist Guy Debord's theorisation of the mediation of the lives of modern citizens by "the spectacle" (the illusory products of mass media and capitalist consumerism) in his 1967 study *The Society of the Spectacle*. This text was theoretically central to the European revolutionary organisation known as the "Situationist International," which shared many of its values and criticisms of modern society with the American counterculture. Debord's arguments concerned the complicity between capitalism's particular socio-economic form and the creation of false consciousness. *The Society of the Spectacle* contends that "[i]n societies where modern conditions of production prevail, all of life presents itself as an immense accumulation of *spectacles*. Everything that was lived directly has moved away into a representation."[50] Moreover, "[t]he spectacle's form and content are identically the total justification of the existing system's conditions and goals," and, reflecting the arguments of SDS in the *Port Huron Statement* as well as the Beat emphasis on mobility and transformation, the ruling class suppresses the notion of reversible, historical time, preferring to "link its fate with the preservation of this reified history, with the permanence of a new immobility *within history*."[51] According to Debord, the spectacle is "the *main production* of present-day society," by which the economy dominates social life.[52] Pynchon's familiarity with the Situationists is signalled by the epigraph to *Inherent Vice*, which, as mentioned earlier, is a famous Situationist slogan utilised in the French student protests of May 1968: "Under the paving-stones, the beach!" ("*Sous les pavés, la plage!*"). The image in this slogan of the dull paving-stones of the "spectacle" superimposed upon the dazzling sand of the beach asserts the superior beauty of the truly real, and also recalls the psychedelic movement's belief that our perceptive apparatus is arranged for the sake of practicality so as to limit the richness of sensory data available to our conscious minds. In Situationist theory as in Pynchon, this limiting action takes on a much more political dimension. At least in part, it is suggested, human consciousness in Western societies is deliberately restricted, subordinated to the needs of the economy.

Pynchon's Countercultural Anarchism

The social forces working to oppose consciousness expansion and generate instead paranoia, confusion, and apathy were embodied in *The Crying of Lot 49* by the arch-capitalist Pierce Inverarity, and opposed, as discussed, by Oedipa, who functions to a considerable degree as a revolutionary role model for the reader. In *Against the Day* Pynchon moves away from this paradigm and the imposition of authorial authority that it implies, instead offering up multiple potential models, a series of characters who each move in their own fashion towards greater freedom from the illusions described earlier. The Chums of Chance collectively provide one such model, their path of personal development mimicking in several regards the typical trajectory of those young Americans who made up the sixties counterculture. When the reader first encounters the Chums they are recognised as scarcely exaggerated caricatures of the stock characters of the boys' adventure stories popular during the late nineteenth and early twentieth centuries, expressive of an inanely cheerful acceptance of the status quo. Boys' adventure stories were of course an extremely escapist form of literature, and the Chums are thus, within the novel's logic, and more deeply than they initially realise, agents of the ruling elite.

This elite is figured directly by the "Higher Authority" (*ATD* 479) whose instructions, given anonymously, are received intermittently via the airship's Tesla transmitter; in accepting the missions the voice dictates, in embarking on their distracting and adventuresome fictions, the boys contribute to the reinforcement of the placid and unquestioning attitude of the general public. That the Chums' fictionalised exploits serve to aid capitalism and neutralise threats to its power is further clarified by the fact that one of the gang's first escapades is that of helping Chthonica, Princess of Plutonia (Plutonia being a realm hidden within the interior of the earth), whose court is under attack from a legion of gnomes. Described as exerting "Circe-like" an "all-but-irresistible fascination" (*ATD* 131) upon the Chums, the Princess's title connects her to the plutocracy, the target of anarchist diatribes throughout *Against the Day*. But this particular adventure is suddenly curtailed as Pynchon undercuts readers' ingrained eagerness to immerse themselves in the equally Circe-like fantasy outlined here, referring us for the remainder of the story to the non-existent title *The Chums of Chance in the Bowels of the Earth*.

Despite this early collusion with the mechanisms of power, as the novel progresses the Chums grow increasingly suspicious of the invisible superiors who are issuing their orders. In fact, over time they develop a political cynicism, coming to see themselves as the "proletariat" in the eyes of the hierarchy of power above them, "the fools that do their 'dirty work' for next to nothing" (*ATD* 447). Furthermore, after a long period spent on the ground as students of the Harmonica Marching Band Academy, they also come to a more general realisation of the self-sacrifice involved in escapism. As the time they are spending in the Academy lengthens, they begin to question their status, wondering whether they might in fact be

> surrogates recruited to stay behind on the ground, allowing the "real" Chums to take to the Sky and so escape some unbearable situation? None of them may really ever have been up in a skyship, ever walked the exotic streets or been charmed by the natives of any far-off duty station. They may only have once been readers of the Chums of Chance Series of boys' books, authorized somehow to serve as volunteer decoys. (*ATD* 476)

Having come to this realisation, the Chums retake control of their own creative and imaginative potential, returning to their life of adventure with a heightened awareness: "disabused of any faith in their [enemies'] miracle-working abilities," they are "somehow better able to avoid them, to warn others of possible mischief, even now and then to take steps in opposition" (*ATD* 478). Eventually the Chums declare themselves an independent organisation, working on a fundamentally anarchist principle, and undertake political engagement on the ground, helping their erstwhile enemies on the Russian airship the *Bol'shaia Igra* to get aid to those in need during the Second World War.

Consciousness expansion is achieved in the Chums' narrative by way of an increasingly self-motivated and self-directed practice of adventuring which gradually undermines the group's initial insulation from reality. As in his earlier novels *V.* and *The Crying of Lot 49*, in his later work Pynchon retains a post-Beat sensibility, proposing motion in space as a basic means of opening the mind, and endorses an explorative and venturesome approach to reality. But in recounting the Chums' slow process of liberation, something which takes them almost the entirety of this 1,220-page novel, Pynchon also suggests, much as Leary does in his description of the continual process of dropping out as "the hardest yoga of all," that raising one's awareness in a truly useful way can only be a gradual process. By going up in their airship (by "getting high" so to speak) the Chums achieve an instantly broader perspective on the world, but only after numerous trippy adventures, which typically call the familiar co-ordinates of time and space into question, do they come to conceive of their heightened state as potentially valuable in helping others and improving society.

Imaginative opening characterises the narratives of many other characters who move towards valuable political action in *Against the Day*, and that this is often achieved via visionary experience is further evidence of the continuing influence of the psychedelic movement on Pynchon's later work. Lew Basnight, for example, moves towards an engagement with "the right side" (*ATD* 202) – explicitly that of the anarchist workers battling for fair pay and conditions against their capitalist employers – via a mysterious therapy involving induced delirium. This therapy allows Lew to obtain release from his depression over a forgotten crime he has allegedly committed, a reference perhaps to so-called white liberal guilt, another paralysing mechanism of the dominant culture.[53] Having been rejected by all the people who once loved him as a result of this terrible unknown misdemeanour, Lew somehow ends up leaving his everyday world behind and entering into a strange dream-like reality of labyrinthine hotels and topsy-turvy economics (the bell-boy tips *him*), an *Alice in Wonderland*-style pastiche of the fantastical. That the therapy offered in this place is described as "a productive sort of delirium" (*ATD* 46) reconfirms the supposition that, for Pynchon, some types of visionary experience can be useful while others are not. It is not clear whether Lew's delirium is generated through psychedelic drugs or by other means, yet it is productive because it allows him to psychologically transcend his suffering, seemingly influencing his later transfiguration and the development of his extraordinary gifts for observation and invisibility. Recalling to mind the meditation on the Chicago stockyards' killing floors, as well as Huxley's description of psychedelics liberating one from "the ruts of ordinary perception," the man providing Lew's therapy explains to him that "[m]ost people ... are dutiful and dumb as oxen. Delirium literally means going out of a furrow you've been plowing" (*ATD* 46).[54] Lew's therapeutic experience delivers him onto a new track which, as noted, leads to a progressively more intense political engagement with anarchism.

Another narrative strand within *Against the Day* that demonstrates both the importance of imagination to Pynchon's political philosophy as well as his later attitude towards psychedelics is that of Frank Traverse and his peyote-fuelled flights over the plains of Mexico. Frank has a total of three visionary experiences in the novel. The first comes courtesy of the Tamahuare Indian El Espinero's supply of "Hikuli," more commonly known as peyote cactus (peyote being the source of mescalin, inspiration for Huxley's *The Doors of Perception* and an object of Leary's early experiments). El Espinero offers Frank this hallucinogenic succulent in order to give him, as a man who has "fallen into the habit of seeing dead things better than live ones," some "practice in seeing" (*ATD* 442). After taking the drug, Frank describes how he "was taken out of himself, not just out of his body by way of some spectacular vomiting but out of whatever else he thought he was, out of his mind, his country and family, out of his soul" (*ATD* 442–3). What Frank is recounting here is an experience of total ego loss akin to that depicted in *The Psychedelic Experience*. Guided by a young Indian girl, Frank flies across the "starlit country" torn by "arroyos filled with a liquid, quivering darkness" (*ATD* 443). That his trip is much more enjoyable than Oedipa's night-time odyssey is the result of the Indian's knowledge and guidance: finding himself in an maze-like network of subterranean caverns and starting to panic, he is reassured by the girl in a way strongly reminiscent of the specific instructions for dealing with negative visions given in *The Psychedelic Experience*, designed to be read by trained guides: "do not be afraid. They want you to be afraid, but you do not have to give them what they want. You have the power not to be afraid. Find it, and when you do, try to remember where it is" (*ATD* 443).[55]

But while Frank's experience is beautiful, the narrator explains that "it would someday be relegated ... to the register of experiences he had been unable to find any use for" (*ATD* 444). Later in the novel, however, Frank meets El Espinero again, and is quick to enquire after the cacti. In the second of his visions, Frank travels through an elaborate alternative reality, a forgotten metropolis, which is linked to a dark history of persecution. It is a world which seems to relate to a previous life of Frank's, a characteristic that recalls Leary's description of the potential for LSD to take us back down the chain of our previous lives. As Leary put it: "The psychedelic experience is the Hindu-Buddha reincarnation theory experimentally confirmed in your own nervous system" (*PE* 27). On this occasion Frank seems more open to the experience as potentially useful, so that the following day, when he encounters the "real world" correlate to the envisioned city in the ruins of a lost civilisation, he realises that this was "what El Espinero had wanted him to see – what, in his morose and case-hardened immunity to anything extraliteral, he had to begin to see, and remember he saw, if he was to have even an outside chance of saving his soul" (*ATD* 1041). What the vision finally helps him to perceive is that

> the history of all this terrible continent, clear to the Pacific Ocean and the Arctic ice, was this same history of exile and migration, the white man moving in on the Indian, the eastern corporations moving in on the white man, and their incursions with drills and dynamite into the deep seams of the sacred mountains, the sacred land. (*ATD* 1042)

Again, visionary experience provides a holistic perspective and reveals patterns of exploitation and suffering usually hidden from view.

Frank's third hallucination is triggered not by Hikuli, but by staring into a tree full of fireflies, whose dance enables him to enter a trance-like state. The resultant vision takes him back to the same apocalyptic city he saw previously, and he feels directed towards "a part of the city hidden from most of its inhabitants" (*ATD* 1117). Passing beneath an archway – one of several appearing within the novel which facilitate passage between the worlds – Frank emerges onto the recent scene of a savage bloodletting, with corpses littering the streets. On awakening Frank is told of the triumphal coup effected in Mexico City by General Huerta, the enemy of the anarchists Frank has recently been fighting alongside. In this light Frank's final vision assumes a particular relevance, rendering vividly salient the tragic nature of the battle for power. This time such visionary experience has a definite value, as it generates in Frank a full awareness of the danger he is in, allowing him to escape Mexico alive. It also directs him towards love and towards a more personally relevant political engagement: returning to North America, Frank becomes involved in the struggle of striking miners holed up in a tent colony in Ludlow, Trinidad. (Frank's father, Webb Traverse, was martyred to the cause of the miners earlier on in the novel.) Stray, the woman who throughout previous parts of the novel had been signalled as Frank's "true love" – Pynchon's later work being considerably more sentimental than his earlier – is there when he arrives, dodging bullets and trying to help the miners with medicine and provisions. By involving himself in the strike Frank helps to avenge his father's death and, in the process, finally forms a solid alliance with Stray.

By the end of the novel Frank's former "immunity to anything extraliteral" has been successfully broken down, and his narrative ultimately reconfirms Pynchon's alignment with Leary's basic ideology as expressed in his early publications and interviews. It suggests that the development of a critical perspective can be achieved via a kind of visionary training, which is especially effective when guided by one more experienced in the art of consciousness expansion, in this case the Tamahuare elder El Espinero. Again, only once interpretation is applied can the visions yield valuable insights. But as in *The Crying of Lot 49*, preference is shown in this novel for visionary experience which is *not* produced by the use of psychoactive drugs, their necessity having been transcended. As we have seen, for the Chums of Chance and Lew Basnight imaginative opening functions as precursor to an anarchist political engagement. For Frank, already an anarchist, experiences of the extraliteral trigger the development of a more personally relevant political practice. Thus, by way of such narratives, Pynchon implies that opening one's mind to alternative experiences leads one naturally to the adoption of a politics at once more liberal (in the original sense of the word) and less abstract.

In order to truly demonstrate the variety of the pathways to consciousness expansion Pynchon lays before the reader of this novel, one further brief example is required. Alongside adventuring and involvement in the social underworld, sexual experimentation is one of the key practices which impel Yashmeen, Reef, and Cyprian towards political action, a practice which, underscoring the connections in Pynchon's work between love and politics explored in the second chapter of this study, works to expand each one's capacity to love unconditionally and indiscriminately. Such taboo-breaking activity can be described as critical as it interrogates the oppressive moral codes of the dominant social structure. It also functions as another route out of the capitalist "spectacle," offering a means of gratification divorced from the capitalist marketplace. Again, such positive escape proves unifying: it is the strong bond which develops between the three adults and Yashmeen's unborn child, symbol of their union, which motivates their quest into Eastern Europe in an attempt to deactivate the "Interdikt," a superweapon primed to release devastating quantities of light, that has been discovered stretched across the Balkan landscape.[56]

Again, then, in *Against the Day* visionary or psychedelic experience is, for Pynchon, only one way of opening the mind to hidden corners of experience, reading his challenging novels being another, but by no means the only, alternative.

Having elucidated somewhat Pynchon's mature stance on consciousness expansion, what remains is to consider the significance of the fact – in the countercultural context of this study – that, as observed earlier, in *Against the Day* Pynchon's most enlightened characters all move the same way, towards an engagement with anarchism. As I have argued, Pynchon's writing practice seems to be directed towards expanding the consciousnesses of his readership and developing within us a critical perspective on the given world. If the development of such a mindset in Pynchon's characters leads them towards anarchism, does that necessarily mean that anarchism is the ideology towards which Pynchon hopes to guide *us*?

In one regard anarchism is present within *Against the Day* as an alternative history, part of Pynchon's ongoing clarification and demystification of what has been historically misunderstood. Usually thought of today as a kind of celebration of chaos within which the individual claims the ultimate liberty to enact violent disorder, the historical reality of anarchism is very different. A declaration like that of the early anarchist theorist Pierre-Joseph Proudhon, who claims in 1840 that "[a]s man seeks justice in equality, so society seeks order in anarchy," reveals the modern, colloquial use of the term as an inversion of its original meaning.[57] Historically, anarchists have envisaged a society which is fundamentally anti-authoritarian, but not chaotic. In fact, the theory points to a kind of ideal midpoint between unconstrained chaos and reified structure. Anarchism rejects the state, both Proudhon and Mikhail Bakunin (another influential anarchist theoretician) sharing with Pynchon premonitions of an increasingly totalitarian society devoid of free thought and ruled by bureaucracy, and perceives bourgeois democracy as an illusion which the populace swallows due to a lack of education.[58] But although anarchism would forego state power, it does not, excepting in its individualist minority, generally reject social organisation. Its preference is for ad hoc formations resistant to centralisation; as Bakunin explains, "I want society, and collective or social property, to be organized from the bottom up through free association and not from the top down by authority of any kind."[59] Anarchism is, in truth, libertarian and egalitarian: it "aims at the liberation of peoples from political domination and economic exploitation."[60]

That Pynchon would support anarchism as a basic ethos seems virtually unquestionable if we accept the central premise of this book, that the author's fundamental concern is with the oppression and exploitation of the masses by the powerful capitalist few and with methods for escaping or combating this. Indeed, recent critical work on Pynchon's anarchism, sparked by the deep interest the author displays in anarchic social models and anarchist history in this vast novel, confirms the congruence of the author's ideals and those of this particular political paradigm. For Graham Benton, who has produced the most exhaustive analysis of anarchy in Pynchon yet published, anarchism acts as a "utopic horizon" across the novels.[61] The present analysis complements that of Benton, my specific focus being to reveal the relationship between Pynchon's anarchism and his experience of the sixties counterculture in general, and its investment in "openness" – both in terms of open-mindedness and willingness to participate socially – in particular. I suggest that Pynchon's attachment to the anti-structural ideals of the sixties would presuppose an affinity with anarchist principles: in all essential regards anarchist thought mirrors the ideology of the hippies and counterculture movement more broadly. As Ruth Kinna states, contemporary anarchism, as distinguished from the first great anarchist wave which occurred in the early twentieth century, "can be traced to 1968 when … student rebellion put anarchism back on the political agenda."[62]

Innately anti-dogmatic, anarchism is a tough concept to pin down, and one of the causes of its contemporary misrepresentation is the multiplicity of its factions. *Against the Day*, which deals with the period from 1893 to the early 1920s, focuses on the first wave of the phenomenon, which encompassed varied points of view right from the outset. Perhaps in an attempt to delineate correspondences and divergences in the ideologies and methodologies of such factions, the novel makes itself home to myriad anarchist organisations representing the full spectrum of anarchism from the individualism of the old Wild West through to the anarcho-syndicalism of the miners. We come across anarchists from the Balkans, Mexico, Chicago, Colorado, Italy, and Barcelona; there are anarchist preachers, bombers, and mathematicians; there is even an anarchist spa complete with anarchist golf. Not all brands of anarchism are, however, valued equally by Pynchon. Individualism, which the anarchist communist Peter Kropotkin described as "the full liberation of the individual from all social and moral bonds," and which is perhaps most responsible for the view of anarchism as claiming a licence for destructive unrestraint, was a common form of anarchism in the United States in the days before the closing of the frontiers and is treated with a certain nostalgia in the novel.[63] The narrator reminisces about "how wild, how much better than 'wild' it'd been not all that many years ago ... waking up each day never knowing how you'd end it ... any ailment, or animal wild or broke, or a bullet from any direction might be enough to propel you into the beyond" (*ATD* 404–5). A stark contrast to the empty hedonism which, as described in *V.*, was later to become society's only access to excitement.

This frontier life was also, according to Pynchon, one of direct, unsublimated violence, "[w]here you didn't yet keep [a pistol] away in the drawer of some Chicago-built office desk, but always close to your person" (*ATD* 405). As I argue throughout this study, such violence has a tacit place in Pynchon's political philosophy. But as I made clear in Chapter 2, it is not a political ideal, and neither is individualist anarchism. *Against the Day*'s descriptions of unconstrained frontier liberty work primarily, I suggest, as a foil to the dearth of personal freedom in contemporary America. In fact, Pynchon may even invest somewhat in Scarsdale Vibe's argument that this "fish-market anarchy of all battling all" was what in fact led to the development of "the rational systems of control whose blessings," so Vibe contends, "we enjoy at present" (*ATD* 38). By and large, individualist anarchism represents for Pynchon nothing more nor less than a system in which there remain the spaces of freedom needed for the development of better social forms, spaces that, as discussed earlier, the imposition of capitalist structures of control have virtually eliminated. In line with this, Ewball Oust claims that the prevalent individualism of Mexico means it has infinitely better chances of seeing a people's revolution than does the United States:

> these folks down here at least still have a chance – one that the *norteamericanos* lost long ago. For you-all, it's way too late anymore. You've delivered yourselves into the hands of capitalists and Christers, and anybody wants to change any of that steps across 'at *frontera*, they're drygulched on the spot. (*ATD* 722–3)

Another form of anarchism which seems to represent more of a compromise with the present than an ideal for Pynchon is that which employs terrorist tactics through the use of bombs. Throughout the novel certain characters defend anarchist "Propaganda by the Deed" – a term first coined in 1876 by the Italian anarchist Errico Malatesta.[64] Cyprian, for example, considers "bomb-chucking" (*ATD* 807) socialists as representing perhaps the only hope for Russia. Others, meanwhile, attack the practice. A relevant episode occurs when Reef meets his "anarchistic and dynamite-crazy" (*ATD* 952) friend Flaco in Nice. Sitting in a café discussing anarchist terrorism, Reef argues that it's "[o]ne thing to try and keep to an honorable deal with your dead ... another to just go spreading death any way you can" (*ATD* 953). A moment later a bomb explodes within the café. Reef and Flaco survive, but Reef's point has been proven: the bomber could easily have killed fellow anarchists, and the fact that both Flaco and Reef go in to help the wounded bourgeoisie confirms their disapproval. Anarchist-sympathiser Ewball Oust has a similar perspective: "There's plenty of folks who deserve being blown up, to be sure ... but they've got to be gone after in a professional way, anything else is being just like them, slaughterin the innocent" (*ATD* 1034).[65] Rather than setting bombs more or less at random, Ewball suggests identifying and destroying particular individuals whose role in committing indiscriminate violence has been definitively established. This approach is vindicated through Pynchon's representation of the assassination of Scarsdale Vibe as a form of karmic rebalancing. However, Stray Briggs, who Ewball has been trying to convince with these arguments, considers targeted murder nihilistic. Her own, equally anarchist approach is to help those suffering the worst effects of capitalist oppression by providing them with medical aid and provisions. This more positive approach is also taken up by the Chums of Chance, as previously mentioned, and it is supported, furthermore, by the story of Webb Traverse. Webb, whose obsession with dynamiting railway lines gives him the nickname "the Kieselguhr Kid," is devoured by his own anger to the point where he alienates his family. Anger, Pynchon suggests, can be valuable, yet it is unstable and it might be easily directed against the wrong people.

More ideal (and idealistic) forms of anarchism appearing in the novel include that practised at the spa Yashmeen, Reef, and Cyprian visit at Yz-les-Bains, France. Here the reader encounters a social anarchism whose functioning principle one of its practitioners, Ratty McHugh, describes as follows: "We work for one another, I suppose. No ranks, no titles, chain of command ... no structure, really" (*ATD* 1047). Things are planned "[b]y knowing what has to be done. Which is usually obvious common sense" (*ATD* 1047). And although the group members still carry guns, they apparently rarely engage in acts of terrorism, preferring instead "more of a coevolutionary role, helping along what's already in progress," namely "[t]he replacement of governments by other, more practical arrangements ... some in existence, other beginning to emerge, when possible working across national boundaries" (*ATD* 1048). This brand of anarchism approaches more closely to what Wolfe Tone O'Rooney, in conversation with Reef and the jazz musician "Dope" Breedlove, describes as "perfect Anarchist organization" (*ATD* 417). For O'Rooney this is represented by the "amazing social coherence" (*ATD* 417) he perceives amongst the members of "Dope"'s jazz band, the quality of spontaneous synchronicity Pynchon repeatedly returns to as an ideal throughout his novels.[66] Such anarchism is also that of the native Mexican tribal societies described in *Against the Day*, within which "[n]o matter how far any of them may wander, the single greater organism remains intact, coherent, connected" (*ATD* 1116).

James J. Farrell has suggested that "[c]ountercultural politics … was the politics of anarchism" because the counterculture "empowered people to live well with self-government."[67] Although this can be said of virtually all the radical factions of the sixties, it seems especially true of commune culture. That Pynchon makes similar connections between anarchism and the counterculture, even in his more contemporary work, is demonstrated by his manner of depicting the anarchist commune at Yz-les-Bains. Exhibiting clear markers of hippie-dom such as long hair (on men), beards, sandals, involvement in polyamorous relationships, and an enthusiasm for hashish, the group anachronistically signals the 1960s as the latest historical moment in which the anarchist impulse towards freedom made itself felt, the most recent example of a pattern which has recurred throughout history. The centrality of consciousness expansion, the real subject of this chapter, to such anarchist revolutions, is suggested by Michael Lerner's observation that the words of the "Hippies" who "spoke in embarrassingly utopian terms of changing people's minds" were, "[d]rug-induced or not," in fact

> indistinguishable from those of anarchists as dissimilar as Tolstoy and Bakunin who thought that the revolution had to be in men's minds. "There will be a qualitative transformation, a new living, life-giving revelation, a new heaven and a new earth, a young and mighty world," Bakunin wrote, a vision that the songs of the counter-culture described precisely.[68]

Pynchon's enthusiasm for anarchism in this late novel thus substantiates the thesis of his continuing alignment with the ideals of the counterculture and of the psychedelic movement as expression thereof.

When O'Rooney describes his perception of the jazz band's coherence to "Dope" Breedlove, he claims that it is "as if you all shared the same brain" (*ATD* 417). Anarchism aims at closer, more spontaneous interactions between people, at the breaking down of unnecessary boundaries so as to achieve a greater social harmony. In my earlier analyses of Pynchon's valorisation of anti-structural *communitas* in the Beat movement and of the role of love in the New Left, such harmony is revealed as central to Pynchon's political philosophy. It is also at the core of the psychedelic movement, for which drug-induced consciousness expansion could uncover an overarching unity in the workings of the universe. As Tom Wolfe explains in *The Electric Kool-Aid Acid Test*, "[u]nder LSD, if it really went right, *Ego* and *Non-Ego* started to merge. Countless things that seemed separate started to merge, too ... and you [could] *feel* it, the entire harmonics of the universe from the most massive to the smallest and most personal – *presque vu!* – all flowing together in this very moment."[69] In *The Psychedelic Experience* Leary similarly claims that through ingesting LSD one can achieve a feeling of "[e]cstatic, orgiastic, undulating unity," the sense of being "[m]erged with all life."[70] The psychedelic movement thus offered a kind of spiritual or pseudo-scientific validity to the anarchist dream of human oneness.

Yet in his treatment of anarchism, Pynchon remains staunchly realistic in his recognition of the tenuousness of its changes for substantial success. Partially, it is suggested, anarchism (and equally, it must be inferred, the sixties counterculture) has not yet established itself as a functional socio-economic system on any permanent, large-scale basis because of its own emphasis on leaderlessness and spontaneity. This is demonstrated in *Against the Day* by the plight of the Quaternionist anarchists Kit Traverse encounters at Göttingen. "[D]efining the axes of space as imaginary and leaving Time to be the *real* term" (*ATD* 599) the Quaternionists' mathematical challenge to the status quo forms a parallel to Pynchon's literary one. Within his novels Pynchon too destabilises the co-ordinates of space, while time, though also often subverted, tends to retain more solidity as necessary to an understanding of the progression of historical events and their relevance to the present situation. But in the conceptual battle between mathematical factions, the innovative Quaternionists have been defeated by their enemies the Vectorists, led by Josiah Willard Gibbs and Oliver Heaviside, representatives of the closed-minded establishment. Opinions in the novel differ as to the root cause of this failure. One of the Quaternionists claims that it is the transient, disorganised quality of anarchist groups which necessitated their failure, complaining that

> Anarchists always lose out, while the Gibbs-Heaviside Bolsheviks, their eyes ever upon the long-term, grimly pursued their aims, protected inside their belief that they are the inevitable future, the *xyz* people, the party of a single Established Coördinate System, present everywhere in the Universe, governing absolutely. We were only the *ijk* lot, drifters who set up their working tents for as long as the problem might demand, then struck camp again and moved on, always ad hoc and local, what do you expect? (*ATD* 599)

Although the Vectorists are here described as "Bolsheviks," their sense of security in the retention of power also makes them a metaphorical equivalent of corporate capitalists; Pynchon thus suggests the relative impermeability to change (and so to anarchist subversion) of centrally organised societies. But this is perhaps not the only cause of the Quaternionists' ineffectuality. Another speaker opines:

> Actually Quaternions failed because they perverted what the Vectorists thought they know [sic] of God's intention – that space be simple, three-dimensional, and real, and if there must be a fourth term, an imaginary, that it be assigned to Time. But Quaternions came in and turned that all end for end … simply inadmissible. Of course the Vectorists went to war. Nothing they knew of Time allowed it to be that simple, any more than they could allow space to be compromised by impossible numbers, earthly space they had fought over uncounted generations to penetrate, to occupy, to defend. (*ATD* 599)

In other words, the simple radicalism of the Quaternionists' theory, their subversion of certain cherished certitudes, brought upon them a backlash which they could not survive. But such difficulties do not equate to futility, or, as Seán Molloy suggests, cause Pynchon to reject the politics of resistance – much the opposite.[71] However, in the light of such insights, and given the fundamentality of the "ad hoc and local" to its ethos, it seems the only hope for anarchism lies in opening the minds of the populace to its suggestions, redeeming them from the category of "the inadmissible," and thus derailing the opposition.

Via Pynchon's commentaries on anarchism and the psychedelic movement, two core elements of the philosophy of the counterculture – criticism of the capitalist system and the impulse towards positive escape – are revealed not only as still present in Pynchon's *Against the Day*, but as more intensely and thoroughly explored therein. An early interest in the concept of "internal freedom" propounded by Leary appears to have contributed to Pynchon's creation of reading experiences aimed ever more self-consciously at encouraging the rejection or interrogation of accepted truth, advocating instead imaginative opening and the acceptance that there may be alternatives to capitalism in terms of social organisation. Synthesising his own version of the psychedelic experience in *Against the Day*, Pynchon incorporates overlapping and interacting layers of reality whose validity is attested to by scientists and mystics alike. The imperative to combine the amplification of one's awareness with a critical, interpretative practice that is so central to saving Oedipa's sanity in *The Crying of Lot 49* is substantially reconfirmed in *Against the Day*, which is more surefooted in its guidance of the reader, through such development, towards the particular politics of anarchism. This novel, like the others, is also formally anarchist, or, to return to the terminology of Chapter 1, anti-structural. As Benton observes, "Pynchon's formal techniques – which favor heterogeneity over uniformity, spontaneity over conformity, and fragmentation over consolidation – align with an anarchist aesthetic."[72] Critics have naturally and correctly shied away from labelling Pynchon a socialist or a Marxist, but he is undoubtedly an anarchist.

---

[*] A version of Chapter 3 was previously published as "LSD, Leary and the Political Role of Fantasy in Thomas Pynchon's The Crying of Lot 49 and Against the Day" in Zofia Kolbuszewska ed., *Thomas Pynchon and the (De)vices of Global (Post)modernity*, 114–133 (Lublin: Wydawnictwo KUL, 2012). Author: Joanna Freer. Reprinted with permission.

CHAPTER 4

The Black Panther Party, Revolutionary Suicide, and Gravity's Rainbow*

The cultural revolution of the 1960s, as we have seen, owed much to the pioneers of the Beat generation. But the counterculture's politically activist factions took more significant inspiration from the civil rights movement, which had begun in earnest in the mid fifties. Student groups like SNCC and SDS were active in the civil rights cause; SDS argued that "the permeating and victimizing fact of human degradation, symbolized by the Southern struggle against racial bigotry, compelled most of us from silence to activism."[1] On an ideological level, consciousness of the racial hypocrisy into which white America was indoctrinated fostered a wider realisation of the general irrationality of the socio-economic system. On a methodological level too, the civil rights movement was influential on the early New Left, which adopted similar forms of pacifist activism, including sit-ins, marches, and boycotts. Meanwhile, African American culture was valorised as many young whites (like their Beat predecessors) came to see black experience as potentially more genuine than their own. Hence Charles A. Reich, in his influential commentary on the sixties *The Greening of America*, describes black communities as making "a substantial contribution to the origins of the new consciousness" that bloomed among radical white youth, merely by providing an oppositional "model to emulate."[2]

The dramatic conflicts of the civil rights movement undoubtedly played a role in generating the similar awareness of white American hypocrisy and racism, and a concurrent interest in black culture, that we find in Pynchon's fiction. As noted in Chapter 1, recorded jazz and Mailer's *The White Negro* sit alongside Kerouac's *On the Road* in the triad of "centrifugal lures" Pynchon credits in his introduction to *Slow Learner* with counterbalancing the power of tradition. Racial discrimination and persecution was a key issue in Pynchon's short story "The Secret Integration" (1964), which deals centrally with the problems of desegregation in the American suburbs. An earlier story, "Under the Rose" (1961), expresses Pynchon's burgeoning interest in exploitative colonial regimes, being a spy story set against the late nineteenth-century backdrop of "the race to carve up Africa" (*SL* 107). This fascination with African history continues into his first novel, *V.*, of which a prominent section is devoted to postcolonial critique of the atrocities the German imperial regime carried out upon the native Herero and Hottentot populations inhabiting the South West. While in *The Crying of Lot 49* the theme of race appears to recede somewhat into the background of the piece, a number of clues suggest that the Trystero may be intended to represent Black Power activists at least as much as other activist groups.[3] In the last novel of his early phase, *Gravity's Rainbow*, the theme of race rises to the surface again as Pynchon refocuses on the bloody history of the Herero under German imperial rule. Striking scenes of racist violence are employed in this novel, as in others, to throw into stark relief the exploitative logic of the American plutocracy and its colonial ancestors. This theme is, of course, picked up later in Pynchon's career in *Mason & Dixon*, where the global institution of slavery is repeatedly attacked for "the inhuman ill-usage, the careless abundance of pain inflicted, [and] the unpric'd Coercion" it entails, particular reference being made to slavery's relationship with capitalism and the desire for "yearly Profits beyond the projecting even of proud Satan" (*MD* 412).

Pynchon's scant non-fiction of the period yields further evidence of his commitment to exploring racial injustice and its causes. Particularly relevant is the 1966 article "A Journey into the Mind of Watts," published in *The New York Times Magazine*. In this article Pynchon demonstrates a great deal of sympathy for the black population of Watts, who he describes as caught in a vicious cycle of poverty and violence. Unlike other commentators on the riots of 1965, who tended to focus blame on one element of the situation – be it the LAPD, the emasculation of black men, or even James Baldwin's novel *The Fire Next Time* – Pynchon aims to delineate a whole complex of influences behind the uprising, sketching a truly depressing state of affairs in which the oppressors are as trapped as the oppressed.[4] Thus if blame is to be found it is with the basic operating principles of the American social system, a conclusion characteristic of countercultural anti-capitalist critique.

U.S. persecution of non-white cultures both at home and overseas (we may think of the Vietnamese as a prime example) was often dramatised by the counterculture as part of a rather simplistically conceived more general global subjugation of predominantly non-white "culture[s] that valued unity and integration" by a white "culture valuing analysis and differentiation," to use Pynchon's own terminology.[5] Admiration for cultures of unity was linked to the counterculture's criticism of "objective consciousness," the perverted rationalism forming the dominant mode of consciousness in Western societies theorised by Roszak and described, in relation to Timothy Leary's more open logic, in the previous chapter.[6] In line with the romantic primitivism of much of the counterculture, tribal societies, perceived as untouched by objective consciousness, were especially idealised. Perhaps surprisingly, Pynchon seems to invest wholeheartedly in this idea in his early and mid career writing – in *Gravity's Rainbow* the native African Herero community is portrayed as enjoying an undisturbed subject-object relationship which is epitomised by the story of the woman who buries herself up to her neck in the ground as part of a fertility ritual, feeling "power flood in through every gate" as she becomes "a seed in the Earth" (*GR* 316). Even in later works this logic still basically holds; although in *Mason & Dixon* Pynchon does not portray Native American societies as entirely guiltless (suggesting their involvement in slaveholding, for instance (*MD* 616)), he represents them as victims of the same kind of "white Brutality" perceived by Mason and Dixon at Cape Town (*MD* 306), describes the interconnectedness of native tribes through family bonds as far surpassing that of white communities (*MD* 343), and posits an awareness of the value of unity in certain native groups who, according to Cherrycoke, "believe that eating the flesh, and particularly drinking the blood, of those one has defeated in battle, will transfer the 'Virtues'" and engender "a mystical Union between the Antagonists" (*MD* 386), such cannibalism not being decried but taken as a challenge to limited Western ideas of the sacred. Moreover, the astronomers' professional activities explicitly mark them out as agents of an analytical culture, a culture that seeks to create and enforce divisions which will inevitably result, according to the Chinese Captain Zhang, representative of a more unitive cultural tradition, in "War and Devastation" (*MD* 615).

Postcolonial critique may have been central to Pynchon's work since the very beginning of his career as a writer, but race has been a neglected theme in Pynchon criticism. David Witzling's 2008 publication *Everybody's America: Thomas Pynchon, Race, and the Cultures of Postmodernism* is an exception to this, being the only book-length study to date that deals centrally with the issue. The present chapter contributes to this field of study in exploring some important aspects of Pynchon's countercultural sensibility in relation to black protest as expressed through certain sections of *Gravity's Rainbow*. Specifically, my interpretation reveals the author's view of certain figures within the black rights movement, as well as his assessment of its particular position on violence, and thus offers further insight into both Pynchon's attitude towards the violent turn taken by the counterculture more generally in the late 1960s, and his perspective on the forces to blame for its general demise by the early 1970s. The focus of analysis in what follows is *Gravity's Rainbow*'s commentary, discernable amongst the myriad political perspectives and positions in the novel, on the most notorious of the revolutionary black rights groups, the Black Panther Party (BPP).

Panther Theory: Dialectical Materialism and Revolutionary Suicide

Founded in Oakland, California, in 1966 by Huey P. Newton and Bobby Seale, the BPP aimed to protect and gain autonomy for black communities within the United States: its ten-point platform and program demanded among other things freedom, employment, decent housing, and an end to police brutality.[7] The organisation was linked to the Black Power movement, which developed out of a disaffection with the traditional pacifist civil rights activism that seemed to have taken the struggle for black rights as far as it could, but not far enough. Far from desiring integration with the capitalist system as earlier civil rights activists had, the Panthers perceived the capitalist ethos as a key cause of racism in America.[8] Describing themselves as Marxist-Leninists and strongly influenced by contemporary communist leaders such as Mao Tse-tung of China and Fidel Castro of Cuba, the Panthers' ultimate aim was a total communist revolution in American society. "Survival Programs" such as free community breakfast and transport services for prison visitors were at the centre of the BPP's attempts to liberate black citizens from the worst effects of white oppression. Yet the organisation gained fame not through such community programmes but as a result of the particularly sensational images of the Panthers dressed in military-style uniforms and brandishing shotguns that circulated in the national news media. The firearms they carried were a practical application of the teachings of the late Malcolm X, intended to enable self-defence against the unfair treatment African American individuals were receiving at the hands of the LAPD,[9] and the military uniform – black trousers, blue shirts, black leather jackets, topped off with a revolutionary black beret – was intended to underscore the group's professionalism and unity.[10] The BPP appealed to the white student organisations of the late 1960s New Left, both in making "vivid" the idea of revolution, and in their ability to embody simultaneously several currents within the white Left: as Todd Gitlin points out, "[i]n the person of the Panthers ... the anarchist impulse could be fused with the Third World mystique, the aura of violence, and the thrust for revolutionary efficiency."[11] Unfortunately, however, the group's aggressive image and militant stance did little to endear it to either the general public or the federal government, and a huge FBI counter-intelligence operation was targeted at the group, employing tactics of infiltration, murder, and misinformation. This, combined with other factors, meant that by 1971 the organisation had been virtually wiped out.

In this chapter I suggest that the disintegration of the Black Panther Party was profoundly resonant for Pynchon, and that in *Gravity's Rainbow* he examines the causes of its failure as a test case in considering the failure of that "little parenthesis of light" (*IV* 254) that was the sixties. In *Gravity's Rainbow* Pynchon does not mention the Black Panthers by name, as he does in the more recently published *Inherent Vice*. Here, the protagonist Doc Sportello declaims the FBI's attempts to undermine the organisation by generating conflict with other black rights groups (specifically Ron Karenga's cultural nationalist organisation, US) (*IV* 75). *Gravity's Rainbow*'s analogy between the fictional black rocket corps known as the "Schwarzkommando" and the Black Panther Party has attracted previous critical attention, particularly from David Witzling in his aforementioned study. Yet that Pynchon was thinking of the Panthers while writing his 1973 novel has so far been a matter, essentially, of speculation. Like everything else in this novel, the Schwarzkommando are multi-referential; their narrative certainly encodes a number of commentaries on the particular exigencies of the Second World War Europe they inhabit, larger global themes and issues such as the legitimacy of leadership in religious and political contexts, as well as the contemporary sociopolitical situation of late 1960s and early 1970s America in which Pynchon was writing. Yet towards the end of *Gravity's Rainbow* there lies a passage, previously neglected in criticism, which establishes virtually beyond doubt the presence of the BPP within the novel. It is a conversation which occurs between the Russian Marxist Vaslav Tchitcherine and the German corporate spy Wimpe.[12] Their dialogue revolves around the value of revolutionary suicide as a form of political activism, a concept peculiar to the Black Panther Party and anachronistic in the Second World War context of *Gravity's Rainbow*. Moreover, they debate "Marxist dialectics" (*GR* 701) – by which we understand dialectical materialism – a concept which the Panthers adopted and which became an integral part of their political theory.[13] The passage thus acts as a commentary on both the ideology and methodology of the BPP, as well as on Marxism more generally.

Revolutionary suicide was arguably Huey P. Newton's best-publicised concept and, given his role as co-founder, leader, and "chief theoretician" of the BPP, is to be considered part of the official party line.[14] Often misinterpreted as evincing a "death wish,"[15] revolutionary suicide is essentially the willingness to risk death in the struggle against oppression and to improve the lot of one's community. Newton was vocal in advocating this idea at the height of the Panthers' influence, before publishing a formal written theorisation in his autobiography of the same name.[16] Drawing on Émile Durkheim's study *Suicide* and another by Dr. Herbert Hendin on black suicide rates in America, Newton distinguishes two types of suicide. The first is "*reactionary* suicide," which he describes as "the reaction of a man who takes his own life in response to social conditions that overwhelm him and condemn him to helplessness" (*RS* 4) – conditions such as those, Newton argues, confronted by black people in contemporary American society. He claims that "a spiritual death" has been the result of the current state of affairs, and that the belief is widespread that nothing can be done against the monolithic power of the American government. Newton's concept of "*revolutionary* suicide," on the other hand, does maintain hope that change can be effected because "[a]lthough I risk the likelihood of death, there is at least the possibility, if not the probability, of changing intolerable conditions" (*RS* 6).

The conversation which is the focus of our present analysis begins with Tchitcherine bringing up what the narrator describes as "political narcotics," otherwise known as "[o]piates of the people" (*GR* 701). This is of course an allusion to Marx's famous statement that religion "is the opium of the people."[17] The use of the plural "opiates" indicates that we are not merely discussing religion here, but all means by which people might distance themselves from what others would consider real. Tchitcherine argues that "Marxist dialectics" is the "antidote" to such opiates, a means of logically cutting through veils of illusion (or we might call it "spectacle," following a Situationist model) and getting at the truth of the situation. Wimpe's counterargument is that Marxist dialectics is just another of the political narcotics in question, offering a means for one group to gain power over another. Having momentarily silenced Tchitcherine with this point, a cynical Wimpe smiles an "old, old smile to chill even the living fire in Earth's core" and goes on to "lay it right out for the young fool":

> "The basic problem," he proposes, "has always been getting other people to die for you. What's worth enough for a man to give up his life? That's where religion had the edge, for centuries. Religion was always about death. It was used not as an opiate so much as a technique – it got people to die for one

particular set of beliefs about death. Perverse, natürlich, but who are you to judge? It was a good pitch while it worked. But ever since it became impossible to die for death, we have had a secular version – yours. Die to help History grow to its predestined shape. Die knowing your act will bring a good end a bit closer. Revolutionary suicide, fine. But look: if History's changes *are* inevitable, why not *not* die? Vaslav? If it's going to happen anyway, what does it matter?" (*GR* 701)

Tchitcherine's argument reflects Newton's standpoint on dialectical materialism. Specifically, Newton argued that dialectical materialism was the most rational and effective system of thought possible in its linking of the Kantian concept of "rationale," or pure reason, with the established rules for the empirical observation of phenomena. In a "historic" speech delivered at Boston College in November 1970,[18] Newton explained that,

> If, like Marx, we integrate these two concepts or these two ways of thinking, not only are we in touch with the world outside us but we can also explain the constant state of transformation. Therefore, we can also make some predictions about the outcome of certain social phenomena that is not only in constant change but also in conflict.[19]

Dialectical materialism was a means of reliably predicting future events for Newton, including the revolution to come. In the same speech, he argued that improvements in technology would lead to a "technocracy" in America. Technological innovations would cause the *Lumpenproletariat*, those jobless outcasts from the American social system, to swell massively. From the thesis of technological development, through the antithesis of a growing force of discontented unemployed, Newton reaches the synthesis: the revolution of the *Lumpenproletariat*.[20] From the perspective of the early twenty-first century, the flaw in Newton's logic here is clear: he failed to consider the various ways in which the technocracy might seek to prevent or remedy the situation, perhaps by creating new jobs for those made redundant by the introduction of advanced machinery or by appeasing the masses through the development of welfare provisions.

I submit that Pynchon mistrusted the logic of dialectical materialism from the start in its very presumption of a predictable future. Shortly after the exchange cited earlier, Pynchon's narrator suggests that fear plays a major role in people's desire for the predictable, describing how Tchitcherine only came to believe in "the dialectical ballet of force, counterforce, collision, and new order" once "the War came and Death appeared across the ring" (*GR* 704). Confronted with the very real possibility of personal annihilation, Tchitcherine turned to "a Theory of History – of all pathetic cold comforts – to try and make sense of it"

(*GR* 704). And Pynchon also seems to disdain the notion that revolution is the archetype of historical synthesis. One of the major representatives of revolutionary zeal in the novel, the "Counterforce" (a group whose dates, 1966–71, match those of the BPP, and who talk about "The Man" in a very similar way (*GR* 712)), conspicuously fail to achieve its objectives; at this historical juncture Pynchon's novel, unsurprisingly, represents revolution as a highly unlikely eventuality. This logically makes it all the more imperative that revolutionary movements perceive the difficulty of achieving their goal, thus putting the onus on each individual to help make it happen. As Pynchon suggests throughout his works, the focus must be on sharpening our awareness of the concrete, practical situation we are faced with, rather than turning to easy or escapist solutions.

Through the Wimpe-Tchitcherine dialogue, then, two problems with dialectical materialism's representation of revolution as predictable and inevitable are demonstrated. The first is encapsulated in Wimpe's formulation that "if History's changes *are* inevitable, why not *not* die?" Self-sacrifice becomes hard to defend in the context of a predictable future. In the specific case of the Panthers, Wimpe's comment reveals their two core ideological concepts, revolutionary suicide and dialectical materialism, to be essentially conflictual. The confusion caused by attempting to combine these concepts is evident in Newton's Boston College speech, in which he argues that although the Panthers "are using the method of dialectical materialism we don't expect to find anything the same even one minute later because 'one minute later' is history."[21] Newton intended to show by this that the party was strongly aware of the constantly shifting parameters of the historical situation in its use of the dialectical materialist method, and would therefore not sink into complacent inactivity. I would argue that this confusion of aims demonstrates that the strength of Newton's commitment to revolutionary suicide, to purposive action of this kind, was superior to his commitment to the dialectical method. But his attempt to retain, within the dialectical method, both the idea that the world is in a state of constant flux, and the predictive element, exposes the central problem with the modern use of dialectics.

Modern dialecticians have, in fact, perverted dialectics from a method of rational argument (in which an awareness of the ever-changing flux of life was valuable) into a method of prediction. Clearly, a method for predicting the future on the basis of fixed material variables cannot function when such variables are allowed to change from one minute to the next. In making dialectics predictive, modern thinkers have turned a search for truth which, in its dualism, worked against rhetoric and control, into a theory by mastering which one can claim a logically valid power of foresight. The apparently incontestable authority this can lend to revolutionary leaders is the second problem with the dialectical method Pynchon highlights. Josef Stalin, to take a powerful example, in elaborating his "diamat" interpretation of dialectical materialism, gained thereby some of the command he used to maintain his despotic rule over the Soviet Union. And we can only suppose that in making predictive dialectical materialism central to their ideology, the Panther leaders also hoped to gain a level of command over their people. It would make sense that, in a society dominated by scientific rationalism, the need was felt for a theory seen as serious, logical, and having universal application. By using dialectical materialism, Newton perhaps aimed to confer such qualities onto a group considered by the general public as irrationally given to violence and having narrowly race-oriented interests. But employed in this way, the theory clearly goes against the utopian, egalitarian ethos Newton developed in his doctrine of revolutionary suicide. Instead, it allies itself with the innately masculinist, authoritative self-image the BPP initially aimed to promote through wearing uniforms, reading from law books, and carrying firearms. As noted earlier, this aggressive attitude – although adopted to facilitate self-defence – contributed to the Panthers' downfall.

The potentially pernicious nature of the dialectical materialist approach receives further attention in a scene which appears much earlier in the novel, in which Pynchon's narrator launches into a diatribe against Marx, describing him as a "sly old racist" (*GR* 317). This attack occurs in the midst of a discussion of the colonial persecution of the native Herero population in German South-West Africa, and of the mysteriously falling birth rate which attended it. Amid a vision of a colony left as "[j]ust a big hunk of desert" a mirage of Marx appears, "skipping away with his teeth together and his eyebrows up trying to make believe it's nothing but Cheap Labor and Overseas Markets" (*GR* 317). The rationale of the narrator's attack on Marx in this section most probably stems from his treatment of colonial regimes as a necessary evil on the road to communist revolution. In an article published in the *New-York Daily Tribune* in 1853, Marx discussed the British regime in India, taking pains to point out its brutality and destructive nearsightedness, but ending with a quotation from Goethe which reads: "Sollte diese Qual uns quälen / Da sie unsre Lust vermehrt?" ("Should this torture then torment us / Since it brings us greater pleasure?").[22] Marx's argument is essentially that colonialism is an integral part of capitalism and since capitalism must reach its predestined shape before the communist revolution can occur, then its evils are something that must be endured. Rosa Luxemburg's criticism of Marx, her claim that he offered up a "bloodless theoretical fiction" which overlooked the "context, the struggle and the relations," is exemplified in this article: the dialectical materialist method leads Marx to an oversimplistic view of what colonies actually are (much more than "Cheap Labor and Overseas Markets"), which in turn allows him to effectively sanction the imperialist exploitation he claims to abhor.[23] A third problem with dialectical materialism is thus demonstrated: its materialist and predictive aspects allow even highly intelligent thinkers to find justifications for human suffering.[24]

My analysis thus confirms Lawrence Wolfey's observation that Pynchon rejects Marxism because "its materialism ignores the fact that the world is a projection of spirit, and its much touted dialectical method is merely a cover for a perverted millennialism, itself an excuse for totalitarian structures."[25] This explains why Weissmann, probably the most negative character in the novel, has a "dialectical Tarot" whose product, created via some "Marxist-Leninist magicians," is "a new kind of demon" (*GR* 748). *Against the Day* contains further evidence of an anti-materialist Pynchon in its attraction towards "the beyond" in various guises and in its approving nod to the Otzovist strain of Marxism.[26] Pynchon's viewpoint on Marxism has most probably been influenced by his experience of the New Left's increasing embrace of communist doctrine towards the end of the sixties. As I argued in Chapter 2, Leni Pökler's role in *Gravity's Rainbow* suggests that Pynchon associates communism with both a naive idealism and reckless street violence.

However, while the author would seem to agree with Wimpe that Marxist dialectics often functions as an opiate of the people, *Gravity's Rainbow* does not promote the idea that self-sacrifice for a revolutionary cause is entirely worthless, or that cynicism is a preferable mental stance. Tchitcherine may be a "young fool" for one with such mercenary motivations as the corporate spy Wimpe, but he is not entirely so for Pynchon. Newton argues, in a formulation reminiscent of the speeches of Dr. King, that "the revolutionary suicide is a 'fool,' a fool for the revolution in the way that Paul meant when he spoke of being 'a fool for Christ.' That foolishness can move the mountain of oppression; it is our great leap and our commitment to the dead and the unborn" (*RS* 333). Tchitcherine's logic may betray an overoptimistic idealism (a naivety Newton celebrates in this quotation), but Wimpe's earth-chilling wisdom is that of the selfish, cold-hearted oppressors. While maintaining a clear-eyed sense of the practical difficulties of effecting any revolution, it seems evident that

Pynchon's sympathies, if not his faith, would lie with the idealist in such a contest.

That Pynchon's interest in the Panthers attached itself primarily to the concept of revolutionary suicide is manifested by its thematic recurrence in *Gravity's Rainbow*, particularly in the Schwarzkommando sections discussed later in this chapter. The egalitarian ethos behind the concept of revolutionary suicide is something I suggest resonates with attitudes towards political revolt expressed in many of Pynchon's works. Even its violence can be justified in the terms with which Pynchon defends the actions of rioters in "A Journey into the Mind of Watts." Here Pynchon considers the overt violence of the retaliatory act preferable to the sublimated violence of the American corporate state, although his general attitude towards violence is one of distaste. In a relevant article, Kathryn Hume has similarly suggested that "if only out of despair over a lack of effective peaceful alternatives" Pynchon seems to support political aggression in *Against the Day*.[27] Yet her thesis of an increasingly aggressive Pynchon overlooks the Watts article, focussing instead for an example of this sentiment in embryonic form on the "minor character" Father Rapier's suggestion in *Gravity's Rainbow* that "They" (who Hume defines as "the Elect, plutocratic owners of technologies and industries") must be killed, because "[o]nce the technical means of control have reached a certain size, a certain degree of *being connected* one to another, the chances for freedom are over for good."[28] This chapter thus extends Hume's analysis, suggesting that political violence was a definite (albeit unfavoured) contender for Pynchon on the spectrum of political alternatives well before the publication of *Gravity's Rainbow*.

In "A Journey," Pynchon contends that in Watts "violence is never far from you: because you are a man, because you have been put down, because for every action there is an equal and opposite reaction" (J 82). In this environment forces clash in comprehensible ways, as if according to physical laws. But for the "innocent, optimistic child-bureaucrats" who inhabit the "well-behaved unreality" of the corrupted corporate power system, violence becomes "an evil and an illness, possibly because it threatens property and status they cannot help cherishing" (J 84). Expressing their lust for power through mediated acts of aggression, the "child-bureaucrats" could never count as "men." So when Wimpe, true to his name, denies that he could bring himself to sacrifice his life for any cause, he represents the cowardly hypocrisy of "Whitey, who knows how to get everything he wants, no longer has fisticuffs available as a technique, and sees no reason why everybody shouldn't go the Niceguy route" (J 84).

Motivated by a very similar sense of exitless oppression, Newton's revolutionary suicide can be seen as an organised, institutionalised manifestation of the kind of violence Pynchon tacitly sanctions in Watts, its aim being always to prevent further violent acts in the future. Grasping at the only leverage remaining to a group bereft of economic power, the revolutionary suicide contends with the charade of political choice Herbert Marcuse, spokesman for the New Left, describes in *One-Dimensional Man* (1964). The complex of values behind the theory represents a condensation of what Pynchon appears to have respected in the basic philosophy of the counterculture, namely its deep sense of continuity and identity between people, its championing of the ideal of *communitas* or non-possessive, altruistic love. As Newton explains in the epilogue to *Revolutionary Suicide*: "There is an old African saying, 'I am we.' If you met an African in ancient times and asked him who he was, he would reply, 'I am we.' This is revolutionary suicide: I, we, all of us are the one and the multitude" (*RS* 332). In this sense, revolutionary suicide converges with the truly heroic act. However, although its core ethos is undeniably to be respected, Pynchon's commentary does not suggest unqualified support for Newton's theory.

Like Marcuse, Pynchon may well question the ultimate value of such desperate action. In *Counterrevolution and Revolt* (1972) Marcuse argues that,

> Martyrs have rarely helped a political cause, and "revolutionary suicide" remains suicide. And yet, it would be self-righteous indifference to say that the revolutionary ought to live rather than die for the revolution – an insult to the Communards of all times.... But then, the desperate act may have the same result – perhaps a worse result. One is thrown back to the inhuman calculus which an inhuman society imposes: weighing the number of victims and the quantity of their sacrifice against the expected (and reasonably expectable) achievements.[29]

Risking one's life for the good of one's people demonstrates a commitment to the community greater, even more idealistic, than many white exponents of the counterculture were willing to take on, despite their emphasis on unity. In 1973 it is unclear whether Pynchon would actually have supported the idea of one individual sacrificing their life for the benefit of the group, but later in his career he voices his position on this a little more plainly, emphasising that such sacrifice must be based on strict necessity rather than on bravado. In *Against the Day*, for example, Frank, Stray, and her son Jesse flee the miners' strike which is being broken up by the owners' hired militia. To stay in the encampment would mean certain death, but Jesse objects to their escape on the grounds that "[c]owards run away." Frank, having achieved a certain wisdom via some hard-won life experience, responds: "Sometimes they're just not brave enough to run" (*ATD* 1140).

Unfortunately, the doctrine of revolutionary suicide failed to reach the people in the pure form described earlier. A perspective on how theory failed to coincide with practice can be found, again, in the Wimpe-Tchitcherine dialogue. As the dialogue progresses, Wimpe's criticism of dialectical materialism subtly merges into a criticism of revolutionary suicide. This must be read as referring, anachronistically, directly to the Black Panthers' unique combination of the two concepts, because, although Wimpe's critique here is directed against a Marxist opponent, revolutionary suicide is not a concept that appears within traditional Marxism in any form. Wimpe's criticism culminates with the formula: "Die knowing your act will bring a good end a bit closer. Revolutionary suicide, fine" (*GR* 701). This could be reformulated as: "Commit revolutionary suicide to help prove the theory of dialectical materialism." In its heroic sense, revolutionary suicide could be seen as a pure dialectical act, risking everything to push the dialectic forward towards the hoped for revolution. As such, it would work against the problems of dialectical materialism, privileging practice over theory, faith over logic, and leaving no room for the self-interested individual to accumulate authority. But Wimpe's argument suggests that within the Black Panther Party, the use of dialectical materialism in fact undermined the concept of revolutionary suicide. In having Wimpe merge the two concepts in such a way, the novel implies that by combining revolutionary suicide with a dialectical materialism whose goal was to garner power and authority for the leadership, the Panthers unwittingly set up the former to be perceived by the general public as just another way of "getting other people to die for you." In the following section, I will attempt to shed further light on Pynchon's exposition, through the medium of *Gravity's Rainbow*, both of how the Panther project came to be misinterpreted by the general public, and of how the Panthers proved unable, in various ways, to live up to the ethos behind the doctrine of revolutionary suicide.

The Schwarzkommando Narrative: A Lesson in Revolutionary Leadership

As noted earlier, the commentary on the Black Panther Party we see developing in this novel is further elaborated through the Schwarzkommando plot line, which deals with the attempts of a militant faction of "Zone-

Herero" to right the wrongs committed against them in their homeland of South-West Africa. Predominantly first-generation descendants of the small percentage of Herero who survived the German imperial regime in Südwest, they have arrived in Europe by a variety of routes, whether brought back as "specimens of a possibly doomed race" by Rhenish missionaries, as servants to the soldiers who had put down their uprising, or, more recently, as part of a Nazi scheme to create "black juntas, shadow-states for the eventual takeover of British and French colonies in black Africa" (*GR* 315). In 1945, these Herero survivors have escaped such dubious benefactors and have somehow coalesced to form a community inhabiting a network of mineshafts close to the Mittelwerke, the wartime centre of German V-2 rocket production.

Unfortunately, and significantly, the Zone-Herero no longer enjoy the apparently undisturbed unity of their ancestors, the natural balance of whose tribal societies is symbolised by the mandala the Schwarzkommando retain as a symbol. An ideological split amongst the Zone-Herero community has led to the formation of two opposed but coexisting factions: standing against the Schwarzkommando are the "Empty Ones." The Empty Ones are deliberately working towards the final death of the Herero race through a regimen of enforced abortion and abstinence from heterosexual sex. In this way they pay tribute to their forefathers, whose birth rate fell seemingly involuntarily as they faced loss of livelihood, freedom, and life itself at the hands of the German colonisers. In apparent contrast to the Empty Ones' deliberate enactment of a pseudo-Freudian death wish, the Schwarzkommando, led by Oberst Enzian, have formed an independent army corps and are on the attack. Their aim is to reconstruct a rocket from pieces of exploded V-2s scavenged from around the Zone. The ultimate target of this rocket is unclear; its firing will be primarily a symbolic act through which Enzian hopes to work some magic and facilitate a spiritual-tribal homecoming of sorts. He believes that while the rocket itself is bound to (Western, linear) time, its launch will allow his people to return to "the Center again, the Center without time, the journey without hysteresis, where every departure is a return to the same place, the only place" (*GR* 319).

The Schwarzkommando have received various critical interpretations, but I would agree with Frederick Ashe in his assertion that "[a]s an African population forcibly imported to be exploited by a white nation, then hysterically oppressed when its usefulness runs out and it gains a measure of autonomy, the Schwarzkommando obviously pertain more to the United States than to the Germany Pynchon fictionalizes."[30] The relevance of the group to discussions of a civil rights context in *Gravity's Rainbow* is at least twofold. Perhaps most directly, its presence as a black-only unit recalls Second World War controversies over segregation within the U.S. armed forces, a key issue in revealing the hypocrisy of America's ongoing role as defender of the "free world" and in feeding the sense of domestic injustice which was so important in uniting the African American population behind the civil rights cause in the 1950s. Yet for readers of 1973, Black Power, ubiquitous in the American news media throughout the late 1960s and early 1970s, would have been a more immediate cultural referent for the Schwarzkommando. Indeed, Ashe makes this connection in his article. As mentioned previously, David Witzling notes the more particular analogy between the Schwarzkommando and the Black Panther Party. The Schwarzkommando narrative can be read, I suggest, as a sort of countercultural cautionary tale offering theories on the causes of the failure of the youth movements of the 1960s, and the BPP in particular, to ultimately transform American society – an appropriate subtitle might be: "How Not To Run a Revolution."

Revolutionary suicide reappears in connection to the Schwarzkommando through insistent suggestions that Enzian is planning to fire himself in the V-2 rocket he will construct. He seems to believe that committing suicide in this way will improve the rocket launch's chances of effecting the hoped for return to "the Center." Given the novel's examination of the subject, it seems legitimate to consider whether Enzian's prospective self-sacrifice fits the rubric for revolutionary suicide detailed by Newton. At first, it appears that it does. Enzian, at least, seems to believe that this ritualised martyrdom offers him (in Newton's words) "the possibility, if not the probability, of changing intolerable conditions" for his community. Yet the tone of the commentary which Pynchon builds around this event is overwhelmingly negative, and it becomes clear that Enzian's death will actually be much more reactionary than revolutionary. Indeed, the very fact that in the rocket launch Enzian will certainly die excludes his sacrifice from the category of revolutionary suicide. As Judson L. Jeffries emphasises, for Newton, "to take one's own life or to quit one's station willfully is a cop out – the ultimate expression of Reactionary Suicide."[31] To quote Newton: "[w]e have such a strong desire to live with hope and human dignity that existence without them is impossible. When reactionary forces crush us, we must move against these forces, even at the risk of death" (*RS* 5). The point is to *risk* death, not to seek it. Enzian, the narrator implies, is being seduced towards death, a situation turned to tragi-comic effect in the song "Sold on Suicide" (*GR* 320). This seduction has been achieved in part via the machinations of the sinister Ombindi, leader of the Empty Ones, another Zone-Herero faction advocating complete tribal suicide. Such internal racism is, in fact, echoed to some extent in Tchitcherine's support for revolutionary suicide, given that he is on a mission to kill Enzian, his half-brother, despite a number of essential similarities between the pair.

Gravity's Rainbow presents the reader with reactionary suicide masquerading as revolutionary suicide, and in doing so the novel questions the practicality of Newton's doctrine and its resistance to misinterpretation. Because taking one's own life goes directly against the spirit of the theory, to name it "suicide," albeit "revolutionary," is deeply problematic. Furthermore, in demonstrating that Enzian's suicide would play nicely into the hands of those wishing for his personal destruction and/or that of his community, Pynchon suggests that the theory might surreptitiously channel unconscious self-hatred. But Pynchon's Schwarzkommando narrative contains more than a critique of revolutionary suicide in practice – it also incorporates a commentary on the problematics of revolutionary leadership, both with specific reference to the Black Panther Party, and to other 1960s protest movements, given that the Schwarzkommando also represent oppositional groups more generally.

Enzian is a failure as leader of the Schwarzkommando, who fade out of the novel before their dubious revolutionary premise is tested – much as the BPP faded out of American history in the early 1970s, without having achieved its aims. Through the character of Enzian, Pynchon suggests that oppositional leaders can fail to lead effectively, to inspire their communities, due to an excessive self-interest and lack of connection to those they have undertaken to lead. Enzian does not have the requisite "I am we" mentality, instead the reader finds repeated references to the unattenuated strength of his individual ego, instances of disharmony between himself and his community, and an accumulation of fears and doubts as the day of the rocket launch approaches. Following an attack by the Empty Ones upon his pregnant cousin, Christian, one of Enzian's closest allies, rages against his leader's self-centredness: "you don't care about me, you don't care about my sister, she's dying out there and you just keep plugging her into your equations – you – play this holy-father routine and inside that ego you don't even hate us, you don't care, you're not even *connected* any more –" (*GR* 525). Later, talking about the consequences of his relationship with Captain Weissmann ("Whiteman" in German), who brought him to Europe from Africa as his homosexual lover, Enzian imagines himself looking out over the "Rocket state" he now belongs to, and explains that he has become an "estranged figure at a certain elevation and distance ... who has lost everything else but this vantage" (*GR* 660). A few days before the rocket launch, Enzian finally seems to realise the depths of this estrangement, as he wonders "[w]ho will believe that in his heart he wants to belong to them out there, the vast Humility sleepless, dying, in pain tonight across the Zone?" (*GR* 731). Indeed, the Zone-Herero seem to have become overtly hostile to their stony-faced leader, causing Enzian to feel that "[h]is people are going to demolish him if they can" (*GR* 731).[32] Given Enzian's personal doubts and Ombindi's sinister enthusiasm (Ombindi describes suicide as "the most erotic thing there is ... embrac[ing] all the Deviations in one single act" (*GR* 319)), it should have become clear to even the most optimistic of readers by the end of the novel that Enzian's suicide will not help the Schwarzkommando recreate an autonomous community on the model of Herero tribal society.

A similar disconnection within the Black Panther leadership has been put forward by Huey P. Newton himself as one of the major factors contributing to the decline of the group, and it may be that Pynchon intends a deliberate analogy between Enzian and the figure to whom Newton's criticism attached itself in particular, Eldridge Cleaver. Cleaver was an ex-con who had been recruited to the Party in 1967. As a result of the apparently FBI-led imprisonment of Newton and Seale, Cleaver rose through the ranks at a critical time in the development of the organisation. Described in a *Los Angeles Times* obituary as "the era's embodiment of black militancy," Cleaver was accused by Newton of almost singlehandedly destroying the BPP, and was formally expelled from the group in 1971.[33] For Newton, Eldridge "talked only empty rhetoric about 'dealing blows' and triggering sensational actions" (*RS* 135). He spent most of his time appearing on TV and radio shows, and loved media attention. He "would not support the survival programs, refusing to see that they were a necessary part of the revolutionary process, a means of bringing the people closer to the transformation of society" (*RS* 331). All in all, he "lived in a fantasy world" (*RS* 135) in which the realities of the community's needs were ignored:

> Long before Eldridge's actual defection from the Party he had taken the first steps of his journey into spiritual exile by failing to identify with the people. He shunned the political intimacy that human beings demand of their leaders. When he fled the country, his exile became a physical reality. Eldridge had cut himself off from the revolutionary's greatest source of strength – unity with the people, a shared sense of purpose and ideals. His flight was a suicidal gesture, and his continuing exile in Algeria is a

symbol of his defection from the community on all levels – geographical, psychological, and spiritual. (*RS* 331)

In Cleaver, a lack of identification with the people lurks behind the actions of a leader whose apparent attempts to help ultimately express a desire to escape real responsibility while creating a myth of self, and this is also largely true of Enzian, although his negative characteristics have so far been neglected in criticism. Thanks to his apparent nobility, dignity, and overall charisma (not necessarily a positive quality in this era of Weberian routinisation), Enzian garners considerable reader sympathy.[34] Cleaver too was charismatic, and despite Newton's misgivings met approval with other youth movements of the 1960s, even, for some, achieving the status of "folk hero."[35] Very little criticism of individual Panthers or of their particular strategies was offered up by contemporary revolutionary groups, rather, as Todd Gitlin has pointed out, "[a]t a time when the hierarchy of sacrifice certified revolutionary virtue, the Panthers were irresistible allies."[36] I suggest that Pynchon aims to redress the balance somewhat in *Gravity's Rainbow*.

Pynchon also calls into question, as we have seen, the oversimplistic equation of martyrdom with "revolutionary virtue." Of particular importance to the commentary offered via the Schwarzkommando narrative on the Black Panthers and the protest movements of the late 1960s more generally is the question of violence. It was violence, and the concurrent serious risk of harm to self, which characterised the majority of these movements, distinguishing them from earlier oppositional groups. Student organisations such as SNCC and SDS, initially dedicated to peaceful protest, turned to violence in this period. In its representation of the Panthers' theories, *Gravity's Rainbow* has seemed to offer support for the views of Newton, and although Newton, in co-founding the BPP, initiated the idea of presenting a militant front and carrying firearms, he was quick to realise that "weapons and uniforms set [the Panthers] apart from the community" (*RS* 329). The most essential and destructive element of Cleaver's philosophy, according to Newton, was his obstinate clinging to the notion that revolution "could take place only through violence, by picking up the gun and storming the barricades" (*RS* 331). For Newton, this "obsessive belief alienated [Cleaver] more and more from the community. By refusing to abandon the position of destruction and despair, he underestimated the enemy and took on the role of the reactionary suicide" (*RS* 331). Newton's statements make it clear that Cleaver's brand of violence was very difference from that advocated within the doctrine of revolutionary suicide. It was a form of violence that, rather than expressing a deep connection with the revolutionary community, actually worked to drive people apart. Involving far more masculinist posturing than desperate struggle, it was a violence which sought to mimic that of the oppressive regime, to accumulate power to the self. Unfortunately, it was this type of violence which spread throughout the radical Left towards the end of the decade, fragmenting the movement and leading to numerous confrontations with police forces, to the formation of groups such as the terrorist Weather Underground, and to tragedies such as the killings at Kent State.

Cleaver's glorification of "the intense moment when combatants stood at the brink of death" (*RS* 330) recalls Enzian's elevation of his own moment of sacrifice to the status of a martyrdom. For Enzian the rocket is a mode of deliverance just as the rifle was for Cleaver. The connection between the Panthers' attachment to firearms and the Schwarzkommando's rocket worship is discussed by Witzling, who further argues that Pynchon's treatment of the latter suggests a belief that technologies like advanced weaponry are "bound to continue serving an existing hegemony rather than marginalized groups."[37] Yet while it is true that such weapons, in their ability to divorce subject from object and to make death abstract, better suit the scientific rationalism or "objective consciousness" of the incumbent authorities than oppositional groups, Witzling misses a bigger point here. It is not so much the rocket itself that is a problem for the Schwarzkommando, but the fact that they *worship* it. The rocket, embodying the power of the ruling class, is lusted after by those who wish to challenge and co-opt that power. Moreover, this idolatry is combined with deeply unrealistic ideas about what the firing of the rocket can achieve. For Pynchon weapons can be used as effective tools of rebellion by oppositional groups, but as I suggest throughout this book, the author accepts violence not as a readily adopted means of self-aggrandisement but only as a despised last resort.

Witzling considers Pynchon to be exploring the "self-conscious" use of weaponry by oppressed peoples in *Gravity's Rainbow*'s Schwarzkommando narrative, but what this novel really emphasises is the failure of such appropriations to be adequately self-conscious.[38] The narrator makes it clear that Enzian's misguided notion of effective political activism is in substantial part down to the negative influence of the Western society he lived in for many years as a young man. Through Enzian's personal history, Pynchon thus builds a countercultural critique, commenting on the potential for those who are ostensibly working towards a more egalitarian society to be attracted, despite themselves, towards forms of power generated and valued by cultures of "Analysis and Death" (*GR* 722), forms of power which base themselves on a logic of division and alienation. Such a commentary may, again, have been influenced by Guy Debord's ideas as expressed in *The Society of the Spectacle*. Debord claims that "[j]ust as it presents pseudo-goods to be coveted, [modern society] offers false models of revolution to local revolutionaries."[39] In line with this, the Counterforce find themselves co-opted by "The Man," and the Zone-Hereros' "Tribal Unity" is revealed as merely a pretence, an attempt to "make believe the Christian sickness never touched us, when everyone knows it has infected us all, some to death" (*GR* 320–1).

That Enzian is thinking of his relationship with Weissmann – who represents the abuse of power – when he pictures himself as an "estranged figure" underscores the importance of the role white Western society has played in his estrangement and reiterates points Pynchon makes in this novel and others regarding love's coercive power. The narrator recounts how, leaving behind him the warmer, more balanced community of his South-West African tribe, Enzian was brought to Nazi Germany, the apotheosis of analytical culture, a "Kingdom of Death" (*GR* 722), and indoctrinated by Weissmann and other Nazis into a peculiar logic (or as *Gravity's Rainbow*'s communist revolutionary Vanya would put it, a "pornography") of love which "had to do with masculine technologies, with contracts, with winning and losing. Demanded, in his own case, that he enter the service of the Rocket" (*GR* 324). The connection made here between Enzian's fascination with the rocket and his love for Weissmann is further clarified in a discussion around Weissmann's codename, "Blicero." The reader is told that Weissmann's adoption of Blicero as his SS pseudonym was intended to indicate to Enzian "yet another step to be taken toward the Rocket" (*GR* 322). With its etymological links to death, bleaching, and blankness, "Blicero" sets up a concurrence between whiteness, death, and the rocket, an analogy which has worked to push Enzian "toward a destiny he still cannot see past this sinister cryptography of naming, a sparse pattern but one that harshly will not be denied, that cries and nags him on stumbling as badly as 20 years ago" (*GR* 322). It is this alliance which will engender the nightmarish "Rocket state" which Enzian envisages himself presiding over, a society based on the worship of technology, controlled by corporate interests – essentially Pynchon's dystopian vision of the future. That Enzian is indeed corrupted by the logic of this degraded Western culture is further demonstrated by the specifics of Christian's attack: Christian accuses Enzian of indifference to the humanity of his sister, of merely, analytically, "plugging her into your equations," and describes him as playing the part of a "holy-father," which corresponds to Pynchon's recurrent criticism of the complicity of certain forms of Christianity, particularly Puritanism, in the development of objective consciousness and the oppression of Third World peoples.

That Enzian's self-destructive collusion with forces wishing him ill is essentially unwitting is what redeems him in this novel. The sympathy he attracts as a character is cemented via the pathos of his situation as a hopeful yet misguided revolutionary leader. Enzian's vulnerability to poorly understood outside influences is further underscored when we learn that he is troubled by

> the odd feeling, in moments of reverie or honest despair, that he is speaking lines prepared somewhere far away (not far away in space, but in levels of power), and that his decisions are not his own at all, but the flummeries of an actor impersonating a leader. He has dreamed of being held in the pitiless emprise of something from which he cannot wake ... he is often aboard a ship on a broad river, leading a rebellion which must fail. For reasons of policy, the rebellion is being allowed to go on for a bit. (*GR* 327)

In this passage Pynchon also seems to be making reference to the more overt means by which oppositional groups were dominated during this era, hinting at the epic FBI COINTELPRO with which the Black Panthers were blighted. Pynchon's description of the enemies Enzian knows are listening in to Schwarzkommando radio transmissions could thus be read as a nod to such FBI tactics as phone tapping and using inside informants. A typically countercultural hostility to underhanded governmental interference in revolutionary organisations is expressed as the sinister nature and the superior power of these "faceless, monitoring" enemies is highlighted, and Enzian realises that they seem to be "waiting for the optimum time to move in and destroy without a trace" (*GR* 326). Significantly for Pynchon's commentary on the Black Panthers' use of weapons, Enzian "believes they will wait for the first African rocket to be fully assembled and ready for firing: it will look better if they move against a real threat, real hardware" (*GR* 326). Enzian also sees himself as personally "hunted" (*GR* 327), a potential allusion to FBI assassinations of Panther leaders such as Fred Hampton.

Such treatment of Enzian's leadership failures suggests that Pynchon would not place blame for the misuse of violence in the late 1960s only, or even primarily, with those individuals who adopted or advocated it. Cleaver, like Enzian, had the wrong attitudes and adopted the wrong methods, but apparently believed he was helping those who looked up to him as a leader. But unfortunately, as Weissmann created a destiny for

Enzian, so the United States created one for Cleaver, and in both cases it was a destiny which only gratified and strengthened the system. Or as the narrator puts it in *Vineland*, speaking of the CIA and FBI's manipulation of the "people's miracle" of the 1960s through paranoia and monetary incentives to betrayal: "These people had known their children after all, perfectly" (*VL* 239). That Pynchon's portrait of Enzian focuses in this way on the susceptibility of revolutionary leaders to serious misconceptions regarding the role they are playing, as well as to various kinds of attack from the incumbent powers, fits with the anarchism that runs throughout his novels and his apparent championing of ad hoc, officially leaderless groups like the Yippies. The Schwarzkommando narrative, considered in this context, suggests that oppositional groups like the BPP should not organise themselves on a hierarchical model which mirrors that of the wider society and whose workings and points of weakness are thus more comprehensible to agents of oppression seeking to derail the movement. Moreover, by way of the firearms rocket analogy, *Gravity's Rainbow* works to criticise the Black Panthers' decision to mobilise in manifest form the psychology of threat employed by the oppressive system, which, in its attempt to create a new power hierarchy, worked against the egalitarian ethos of revolutionary suicide. In the case of the Panthers, the problem was compounded by their attempt to garner support via another specifically Western technology, the national news media.

Visual media like photographs or films operate on the same logic of division as guns and missiles – they both permit the separation of person from person, of image from content, allowing for misrepresentation and vilification, as in the case of Timothy Leary examined in the previous chapter. When the Black Panthers appeared on the nation's television screens wearing paramilitary uniform and brandishing loaded firearms, again, the reality of the situation was obscured. Having, as noted, become aware of community relations issues around the Panthers' use of weapons, Newton also eventually came to realise that the Panthers had taken a wrong step in courting the media, complaining in *Revolutionary Suicide* that

> For years the Establishment media presented a sensational picture of us, emphasizing violence and weapons. Colossal events like Sacramento, the *Ramparts* confrontation with the police, the shoot-out of April 6, 1968, were distorted and their significance never understood or analyzed. Furthermore, our ten-point program was ignored and our plans for survival overlooked. The Black Panthers were identified with the gun. (*RS* 330)

In fact, the Panthers were so inextricably bound to their media image in the public mind that there was the widespread belief that they were "media-created."[40] Once in the hands of the media, the threatening image which the Panthers had (un)intentionally helped to disseminate became a tool which the government could use to attack the group. Newton's attempts to steer the Party away from its violent self-image were successfully foiled by the FBI, who worked specifically to exaggerate what appeared as threateningly irrational in the Panthers, even stooping so low as to publish the "Black Panther Coloring Book," featuring image after image of Panther militia shooting pig-like white policemen.[41]

Unlike the Black Panthers, the Schwarzkommando do not have access to the media in the post-war Zone of *Gravity's Rainbow*, but Pynchon builds a commentary around the potential for media misrepresentation of such groups by introducing an alternative story of their "creation." This story suggests that the Schwarzkommando spontaneously materialised after a propaganda film was made about a black SS unit of the same name by agents of the White Visitation psychic-intelligence agency in England. Made by agents in blackface, the film was intended to intimidate the general public in Germany, who, it was assumed, would fear the presence of black troops in their neighbourhood and turn against their own government. In this way Pynchon highlights the media's power to create and propagate a negative, distorted image, an image which then takes on a life of its own. The success of such misrepresentations in spreading specifically racist views is implied in *Gravity's Rainbow* by the comments of the consistently villainous American Major Marvy, who expresses his concern that the Schwarzkommando's rocket-plan is "*awful* dangerous. You can't trust *them* – With *rockets*? They're a childlike race. Brains are smaller" (*GR* 288). Such racist mythology regarding the relative IQs of African Americans and whites had been causing public controversy in the early 1970s.[42] For both the Schwarzkommando and the Panthers, then, the nobility of their attempt to reinstate a lost community is obscured behind a created image which tells a very different story. Thus, it seems, *Gravity's Rainbow* represents an attempt to uncover the mechanisms of misinformation regarding the Black Panthers and to redress some of the central misconceptions formed by the American public as a result.

All in all, those sections of *Gravity's Rainbow* which deal with the Black Panther Party express support for the stated aims of the group, and especially for the ideology articulated by Huey P. Newton, but also a keen awareness of the various ways in which these ideals were betrayed, leading to the failure of the organisation's plans to revolutionise its society. Going beyond the well-known role of the FBI in bringing down the Panthers, the novel draws readers' attention to subtler factors at play within the BPP and in other contemporary revolutionary groups, implying again the author's preference for ad hoc and leaderless opposition, and warning future revolutionaries to maintain a clear unity of means and ends, to question the motives of those who seek to lead and of those who advocate violence, and not to accept political theory or proposals for action without due thought and debate. This is why Pynchon imposes on each of his readers the onus of research and interpretation. As Newton put it, there must be "dialogue, dialectical struggle, or struggle through words" towards "the next advance man will make; that he will put down the club."[43]

---

* A version of Chapter 4 was previously published as "Thomas Pynchon and the Black Panther Party: Revolutionary Suicide in Gravity's Rainbow" in *Journal of American Studies* 47, no. 1 (February 2013): 171–188. Author: Joanna Freer. Copyright © Cambridge University Press 2012. Reprinted with permission.

CHAPTER 5

Feminism Moderate and Radical in The Crying of Lot 49 *and* Vineland
Pynchon and the Women's Movement

Outlined at the end of the preceding chapter, Huey P. Newton's sentiments regarding advances to be made by "man," expressing a conviction that "he" should move away from aggression and violence, are of course very laudable, but during the 1960s many women were starting to resent such emphasis on the male and to assert their right to pursue a distinct set of aims. One of the first women to take such a stand was Betty Friedan, whose investigation into the causes of the peculiar "malaise" of American women in the mid twentieth century, *The Feminine Mystique* (1963) is often considered to have sparked the women's movement. Friedan's study focussed on the post-war return of women to the housewife role, a role that was increasingly rejected in the early 1960s as the introduction of the contraceptive pill brought sexual liberation and as women became politically involved in the first manifestations of the New Left on university campuses. Later in the decade second-wave feminism gathered force as female members of activist groups like SDS began to rebel against the sexist practices of the predominantly male leadership. Organisations dedicated to defending women's rights sprang up across the United States promoting a wide range of agendas. At one end of the spectrum was the moderate reformism of groups like Friedan's National Organization for Women (NOW), which sought legislative changes "to isolate and remove patterns of sex discrimination, to ensure equality of opportunity in employment and education, and equality of civil and political rights and responsibilities on behalf of women."[1] At the other was the extreme social radicalism epitomised by Valerie Solanas's *SCUM Manifesto*, which suggested that women should "overthrow the government, eliminate the money system, institute complete automation, and destroy the male sex."[2]

The women's movement persisted well into the 1970s, involved vast numbers of women with wildly divergent aims and approaches, and achieved major improvements to women's status both in the law and in society. As Todd Gitlin explains, it "broke down so many barriers as to have transformed American social relations ... beyond recognition."[3] Its successes mean that, as Christopher Gair contends, the women's movement is more than a mere "subsection" of the counterculture, and to claim otherwise is to do it a "disservice."[4] However, it does equal disservice to represent the counterculture and the women's movement as distinct phenomena, a practice which is common in historical accounts of the era. It may have been large in scale and lacking in a clear left-wing political consensus, and it may have substantially outlived most other countercultural movements, but women's liberation was, nonetheless, essentially directed against oppression in the name of personal freedom and social equality, pitting itself against a fundamental limiting principle of the dominant culture, and as such should not be rigidly or arbitrarily differentiated from other, less successful protest movements originating in the 1960s. Like the hippie counterculture (and to a lesser extent perhaps all of the other movements considered in this study), it contained those whose interest lay primarily in personal liberation, and those with a broader social revolution in mind. To make a distinction here, as Debra Michals points out, "denies the existence of a feminist counterculture, and in doing so negates the impact of women and women's movements on the social and cultural revolution of the 1960s and 1970s," and also "belies the importance of understanding not only the expansive and varying aspects of the counterculture but, more importantly, the interconnectedness of all these groups."[5]

With these connections in mind, the final chapter of this book offers an analysis of responses to the women's movement discernible in *The Crying of Lot 49, Vineland*, and other novels of Pynchon's late phase. By considering how these novels treat female characters and relevant issues like motherhood, gender, and sexuality in the context of the wider counterculture and the social and political revolutions of the sixties, this chapter reveals further facets of the author's countercultural sensibility relating in particular to the viability of separatism within revolution and to the role of women in activist practice. My interpretation builds on work done in previous chapters towards identifying the sources and sustaining structures of oppression against which Pynchon's fiction rails, drawing again on the core thematic binaries of alienation/community, escape/escapism, and structure/anti-structure as conceptual frameworks for understanding his political philosophy. Finally, the chapter reveals a potential flaw in Pynchon's revolutionary writing project as framed in Chapter 3. This flaw, I argue, ironically results from an apparent lack, when it comes to representing the female body and female sexuality, of the kind of awareness of subtle manipulative forces at work within society, and of the political consequences resulting from a failure to respond to these appropriately, which is repeatedly posited as a prerequisite for effective oppositional action throughout Pynchon's work.

Liberation versus Revolution: *The Feminine Mystique* and *The Crying of Lot 49*

The Crying of Lot 49 was published in 1966, when second-wave feminism was still a relatively new development, and it is the first of Pynchon's novels upon which an imprint of the phenomenon is visible. The early second wave was dominated by the perspectives put forward in Friedan's *The Feminine Mystique*, which had come to print three years before, shortly before Pynchon's first novel, *V.*, and had quickly become a bestseller despite a very limited initial print run. The significance of Friedan's study lay in its revelation, through detailed and extensive sociological research, of a cultural consensus within the United States, first appearing in the post-war period, that located femininity exclusively within the housewife/mother. This consensus, Friedan suggested, worked to channel all women into that limited role via advertising, women's magazine articles, and "educational functionalism."[6] Worrying evidence of increases in alcoholism, addiction to tranquilisers, aggressive sex seeking, and psychosomatic disorders was symptomatic, for Friedan, of women's widespread frustration with the cloistered life of a housewife. She termed such restless female dissatisfaction "the problem that has no name" because, as she claimed, it had been consistently ignored by government bodies, health care workers, and the general public alike. As Daniel Horowitz claims, her critique proved revolutionary, "awaken[ing] hundreds of thousands, if not millions, of women to what they had long felt but been unable to articulate – the way the mystique of suburban motherhood smothered aspirations for a more fulfilling life."[7]

Although there is no direct reference to Friedan in Pynchon's novels, the influence of her work is undeniable in *The Crying of Lot 49*, which, as detailed in previous chapters of this study, charts Oedipa's emergence from the mundanity of her suburban existence in the mist-shrouded Kinneret-Among-The-Pines, California.[8] The very first words of the novel, often highly relevant in Pynchon's work as in that of other writers, seem to position his protagonist as explicitly inhabiting a Friedanian housewife role: "One summer afternoon Mrs Oedipa Maas came home from a

Tupperware party" (*L49* 5). Distinct in both tone and content from what we as readers might expect from Pynchon as a serious, "difficult" writer, the author's choice of phrasing here implies a mockery of the dumbed-down short stories and female-targeted advertisements that filled women's magazines during the era of the mystique and played an important role, according to Friedan, in its promulgation. Reinforcing the notion that *The Crying of Lot 49* is in sympathy with contemporary feminism from the outset, the saccharine simplicity of the opening is immediately undercut by the both the intimation of alcoholism in the suggestion that Oedipa's host had been tempted to put a little too much kirsch in the fondue (Oedipa, on returning, also makes a concerted effort "to feel as drunk as possible" (*L49* 5)), as well as by the tangled mess of Oedipa's thoughts and memories, triggered by her discovery that she is required to help execute the will of Pierce Inverarity. The discordant note of Oedipa's unusual name in the first sentence also, presumably, sets the reader to thinking about Sigmund Freud's notorious "Oedipus complex," with its prescribed and rigidly distinguished roles and desires for males and females; in the fifth chapter of *The Feminine Mystique*, Friedan points out such shortcomings in Freud's treatment of women and in contemporary applications of his theories.[9] Amongst other suggestions of an incipient awareness of feminist cultural analyses in Pynchon's work is the fact that the interrogation of gender norms implied in this first passage becomes a recurrent theme in *The Crying of Lot 49*, later to be further developed in *Vineland*.

That Friedan's *Mystique* is to be a significant intertext for Pynchon's mid sixties novel is an impression sustained throughout the first chapter as the narrator describes Oedipa's trip to the market and preparation of the evening meal, as she gives priority to her husband's worries over her own on his return from work, and as we learn that she has been seeing a psychotherapist for her own unnamed problem, for which she has been prescribed tranquilisers. Oedipa also fits the model in that she is well educated and intelligent, having been "just a whiz at pursuing strange words in Jacobean texts" (*L49* 72) during college, but she does not work. Nor, it seems, does she otherwise use her talents; she reads book reviews in *Scientific American* but never, it is implied, reads the books themselves. Her life in Kinneret, as we saw in Chapter 1, follows a reified pattern; empty and meaningless, it is little more than a "fat deckful of days which seemed ... more or less identical" (*L49* 6). The only point on which Pynchon's protagonist diverges from type is in her childlessness, but this appears to be a felt lack for Oedipa who is haunted by references to the reproductive cycle throughout the novel, and even at one point imagines herself pregnant.[10] Because the novel proceeds to follow Oedipa's departure from Kinneret on a convoluted and bewildering journey which requires her to exercise the powers of analysis she developed at college in the process of following a trail of clues towards the promise of emancipation, it seems, on the face of it, that the humanist and countercultural principles traced in Pynchon's work throughout this study encompass a firm commitment to female liberation. *The Crying of Lot 49* seems to support Friedan's criticism of contemporary gender roles as well as her call for housewives to actively seek a more fulfilling way of life. Commentators who have interpreted the novel in this way include Cathy Davidson, for whom *Lot 49* centres around Oedipa's "struggle for completion" against an "offended patriarchy," and Tracey Sherard, who suggests that Oedipa embraces a new female (and feminist) subjectivity.[11]

Thus Pynchon's 1966 novel ostensibly sets itself forth as a novel offering considerable support from a male author for the burgeoning women's movement. Organised around a relatively strong female protagonist, whose engagement with her environment, though narrated in the third person, is nevertheless the focus of the narrative, the novel diverges markedly from the standards of Pynchon's short stories, first published between 1959 and 1964, in which women tend to appear in limited cameo roles as beautiful enigmatic muses, drunken college sophomores, or bunny-boiling wives.[12] It also, I submit, certainly marks a progression from *V.*, whose female protagonist is never fully present as a real woman, instead remaining splintered, distanced, disturbingly inhuman, and primarily symbolic. Despite Davidson's and Sherard's positive feminist readings of *The Crying of Lot 49*, such an interpretation of *V.*, published a mere three years earlier, is far from critically unsupported. Alice Jardine's short analysis appearing in her study *Gynesis: Configurations of Woman and Modernity*, for instance, claims that "V. is the very substance of the Other sex. The search for V. ... will lead you only to interpretive Nothingness," and that the novel itself is essentially "the disjointed maternal body of the infantile or psychotic's fantasy."[13] Molly Hite concurs, arguing that in *V.* "'the feminine' was a force aligned with deathward-tending natural and historical processes – and against human agency" in her article on feminism in *Vineland*.[14]

In 1984 Pynchon was to apologise for his early sexism with particular reference to the short story "Lowlands" (*SL* 11), and although this apology was not entirely satisfactory for reasons I will go into later, in terms of the evolution of Pynchon's attitudes to women, *The Crying of Lot 49* appears as an attempt to atone for past sins and to demonstrate an acceptance of the equality of women (as real rather than symbolic) with men in terms of fitness as literary subjects. The narrative voice has correspondingly become less gendered, neutral overall but conforming to the gender of its subject in places. On page 8, for example, as the narrator reports the thoughts of Oedipa's husband, Mucho, the voice aligns itself with a typically male perspective – "a woman or car you coveted," while on the following page, reporting Oedipa's thoughts, it expresses a typically female viewpoint – "[y]ou comfort [your husbands] when they wake pouring sweat or crying out in the language of bad dreams." The sense of an appreciation for the female mind as not fundamentally different from the male is underscored by the various biographical parallels between Pynchon and his protagonist Oedipa: close in age, Oedipa, like Pynchon, has passed through college, studying English "at a time of nerves, blandness and retreat among not only her fellow students but also most of the visible structure around and ahead of them" (*L49* 71), a time before the student protest movements of the sixties had begun to unsettle American society.[15]

Like the Beat movement, the women's movement's initial stirrings can be understood as a reaction to the listless years of the Eisenhower presidency, and Betty Friedan's take on the 1950s is very similar to that of Pynchon's narrator, whose assessment reflects the author's own view of the "aimlessness" of the decade as revealed in his *Slow Learner* introduction (*SL* 11). Friedan describes the post-war period as an era in which "[w]e found excuses for not facing the problems we once had the courage to face. The American spirit fell into a strange sleep; men as well as women, scared liberals, disillusioned radicals, conservatives bewildered and frustrated by change – the whole nation stopped growing up."[16] This retreat was, according to Friedan, one of the factors behind the development of the mystique of femininity as "the cherished and self-perpetuating core of contemporary American culture"[17]; there was a need, experienced by both men and women, to cocoon oneself amid the familiar comforts and illusions of "traditional" family life, and this impulse was being deliberately translated into an embedded cultural practice by those in positions of power – politicians, psychoanalysts, educators, capitalists – who stood to gain from it.

At the beginning of *The Crying of Lot 49*, Oedipa already has a level of awareness that her own life expresses the pervasive alienation of this newly industrial, suburban era, this unvoiced yet desperate need for distraction and distance from disturbing realities. During a holiday with Pierce in Mexico which occurs before the temporal starting point of the novel, the pair visit an art gallery and Oedipa experiences an epiphany of sorts while viewing one painting in particular, "Bordando el Manto Terrestre," a symbolic representation of the *Wizard of Oz*-like mechanism which maintains the illusion that America is, in fact, the "cheered land" (*L49* 125) Oedipa once took it for. Depicting a chamber at the top of a tower, in which "a number of frail girls" are embroidering a vast tapestry depicting "the world" – a tapestry which is simultaneously spilling out of the windows into "a void" which they are "seeking hopelessly to fill" (*L49* 13), the picture reflects the ubiquitous American escapism described here and in previous chapters, and seems to critique the exploitation of women in its perpetuation, while also being a semi-humorous metaphor for the concrete situation of suburban housewives, who, as Friedan points out, multiply pointless and endless housework and craft tasks in a futile attempt to deny the emptiness of their lives.[18]

Oedipa's viewing of this painting affords her at least a partial disillusionment. She realises that she too is a "captive maiden," that she had "gently conned herself into the curious, Rapunzel-like role of a pensive girl somehow, magically, prisoner among the pines and salt fogs of Kinneret" (*L49* 13, 12). The trip to Mexico had been fundamentally motivated by a need to escape, and Oedipa had hoped that Pierce could be her "knight of deliverance" (*L49* 13), but exactly what she was seeking to escape from eludes her at this point.[19] In one sense, this passage seems to push Oedipa further into Friedan's housewife mould. *The Feminine Mystique* describes the willingness of housewives to engage in self-delusion despite a sense of dissatisfaction, explaining that with "all the forces of her culture tell[ing] her she doesn't have to, will be better off not to, grow up," many prefer to "seek the sanctuary of the home" and simply acquiesce in the "pretty lie of the feminine mystique."[20] Oedipa's confusion over the source of her sense of enclosure, seeing it at one moment as self-inflicted, and at the next as the result of an anonymous external force, is also characteristic. An inquisitive attitude is, of course, inimical to any self-conning process. The passage's style, moreover, referencing the standard romance novel fare of women's popular fiction in the 1950s as well as the traditional fairytale with its analogous representations of idealised feminine passivity, recalls specifically Friedan's criticism of American "functionalism" – a branch of social science that she accused of affixing ill-considered value judgements to certain roles in society. As Friedan explains, "[b]y giving an absolute meaning and a sanctimonious value to the generic term 'woman's role,' functionalism put American women into a kind of deep freeze – like Sleeping Beauties, waiting for a Prince Charming to waken them, while all around the magic circle the world moved on."[21]

But bear in mind that despite such apparent parallels, Oedipa is not, at this point, a housewife – she is yet to marry Mucho. Since Oedipa already feels entrapped by her life in Kinneret while she is only Pierce's girlfriend, the passage potentially indicates a more complex relationship between Pynchon's and Friedan's respective sociological analyses of fifties- and sixties-era America. The logic of the sequence – in line with that of the novel as a whole – emphasises a broader critique of alienation as a phenomenon potentially affecting both married and unmarried women, and men too. Moreover, as Oedipa views "Bordando El Manto Terrestre" from behind her green bubble shades, her central realisation – that perceived reality is subjective, an individual construction, that her Mexico "had only been woven together a couple thousand miles away in her own tower" (*L49* 13) – transcends the gender specific in referencing idealist philosophy. Oedipa may follow Friedan's behavioural model in that she chooses marriage as a palliative measure to deaden her sense of confinement, and this confinement may be expressed through highly gendered imagery, but in the final analysis her problem is not presented as intrinsically related to her biological sex.

Further support for the concept that Pynchon does not, in *The Crying of Lot 49*, actually construct a specifically female-focussed narrative of oppression and liberation is to be found by considering the state of the numerous male characters in the novel. Oedipa is surrounded by men in this novel, and the majority are struggling with their own sense of desolation and lack of identity. Just as Oedipa is shaken by Remedios Varos's vivid depiction of all-consuming emptiness, so is her husband Mucho equally disturbed by the void intimated by the sign at his former workplace reading N.A.D.A.. As mentioned in Chapter 3, recurring nightmares in which Mucho envisaged "[j]ust this creaking metal sign that said nada, nada, against the blue sky" (*L49* 100) troubled his sleep for years before LSD provided him with an alternative world view. He obtained this LSD via Oedipa's psychotherapist Dr. Hilarius, who had been involved in the community hospital's research into the effects of psychedelic drugs on "a large sample of suburban housewives" (*L49* 10), but had at some point, and significantly, "broadened his program to include husbands" (*L49* 99). Prior to this, Mucho had sought release from his nightmares via sexual relationships with underage girls – an equivalent of the aggressive female "sex-seeking" Friedan characterises as a symptom of the problem that has no name.[22] Metzger and Genghis Cohen have taken a very similar approach, while others, such as Pierce Inverarity, the Paranoids, or Randolph Driblette, cling to assumed personas as masks for their emptiness: Pierce runs through a series of impersonations on the phone to Oedipa, the Paranoids' pudding-bowl haircuts and pseudo-British accents are designed to mimic the Beatles, and the end of the run for Driblette's play sees him commit suicide, dressed as his character, by walking into the Pacific Ocean. Alcoholism, acts of sadism or masochism, and pseudo-Buddhist retreat from community are further responses depicted.

In fact, by contrast to the men around her, Oedipa is relatively spirited; once her journey towards potential freedom from the constriction of her former life has begun, she manages to resist the temptation to relapse into easy escapism. Compared to the men, she is not as predisposed to hide from reality and its cruelties, as confirmed by the fact that she would be the "first to admit" (*L49* 6) the dullness of her routine, by the equanimity with which she has confronted Mucho's affairs and with which she faces the prospect of leaving Kinneret to execute Pierce's will, by her practicality and thoughtfulness, even by such little details as her habit of *listening* to the Muzak that accompanies her trips to the market. This difference is fundamentally what enables her to embark on the odyssey she undertakes in the novel with any chance of success. But, as described previously, she has to overcome many doubts and obstacles as she approaches the possibility of a better life symbolised by the Trystero, a group which, it should be noted, seems to encompass within its ambiguity the possibility that it is intended as a analogy to the women's movement.[23] In fact, the intensity of Oedipa's struggle almost drives her mad. Yet in the end, the male characters disappear one by one, while Oedipa, alone, persists.

In *The Feminine Mystique* Friedan set a gender-specific critique of American inequality against the backdrop of a general, and much broader, societal malaise. Such a refocusing was necessary, for Friedan, because while American society was all too conscious of a male identity crisis, it was turning a blind eye to the problems of women. In *The Crying of Lot 49* Pynchon seems to reject this logic in prioritising the general over the gendered, further universalising the problem by having it affect single as well as married people. (Indeed, perhaps the two happiest people in the novel, in a rather bizarre subversion of our expectations, are the college professor Emory Bortz and his wife, Grace, a woman who expresses an exasperated vitality in chasing the children for whom she has apparently given up a promising career.) A novel whose opening suggests a focus on feminist issues becomes an expanded critique of an ill-defined angst afflicting American society as a whole. With the problems of Oedipa all but submerged beneath a flood tide of male insecurities and anxieties, it seems, then, that Pynchon's novel denies both the superior urgency of the "woman question" and the notion that women were suffering more than their male counterparts within a generally oppressive America. On the one hand, it could be argued that this demonstrates a stronger grasp of the kind of global awareness and united front necessary to tackle such deeply rooted alienation. Yet at the same time, it seems to devalue female-specific issues at a time when the sexes were emphatically not treated equally. My analysis of the novel thus diverges somewhat from the positive feminist interpretations mentioned earlier, and particularly that of Cathy N. Davidson, who has argued that Oedipa's nascent proto-feminism allows her to recognise her oppression and become a hero to herself, actively freeing herself from the "men" who constitute the "tower" in which she was trapped.[24] It does not seem to me to be the case that Oedipa is driven by an awareness of her oppression *as a woman*, something none of her internal monologues touch on, but by a much more obscure sense of oppression as an inhabitant of contemporary American society. Nor, I suggest, is Oedipa a hero because "only Oedipa – as a woman – can be a deliverer," but simply because she struggles, putting in the "slow, frustrating and hard work" (*V.* 365) advocated in *V.*[25] As I will argue, Pynchon does perceive a revolutionary value in the female, but he is not quite so quick to write off the entire male sex.

The paradigm of an initial sense of ideological common ground between Pynchon and Friedan giving way to divergence reveals itself again if we consider the two authors' respective attitudes to the role of capitalism in American alienation, be that generalised alienation, as in Pynchon's case, or gender specific in Friedan's. As noted earlier, Friedan apportions a great deal of blame for the prolongation and institutionalisation of the mystique to those who intended to make a healthy profit out of it:

> the perpetuation of housewifery, the growth of the feminine mystique, makes sense (and dollars) when one realizes that women are the chief customers of American business. Somehow, somewhere, someone must have figured out that women will buy more things if they are kept in the underused, nameless-yearning, energy-to-get-rid-of state of being housewives.[26]

In *The Crying of Lot 49* capitalism is linked to a similar stultifying and homogenising impulse, engendering the eerie atmosphere of silence and stagnation which pervades San Narciso, the hub of Pierce Inverarity's extensive property empire. At the local Yoyodyne arms plant, in which Inverarity had invested heavily, employees complain of being undervalued as individuals. The company's contract deprives them of their patent rights, which "stifles your really creative engineer" (*L49* 59), a species nearing extinction according to Stanley Koteks. The sadistically oppressive zeal of a capitalist system which seeks to preserve itself at all costs is embodied within the novel by Inverarity himself, a man reduced to a symbolic fulcrum around which the narrative turns. In his relationship with Yoyodyne he can even be said to represent some condensed form of the military-industrial complex. Jesús Arrabal, the Mexican anarchist, is deeply troubled by this ability to typify capitalism, explaining to Oedipa that Pierce is "too exactly and without flaw the thing we fight" (*L49* 83). Whereas the economically privileged in Mexico are "always, to a finite percentage, redeemed – one of the people" (*L49* 83), Pierce seems to have transcended humanity as he has transcended the limits of his mortality, afflicting and controlling Oedipa from beyond the grave by having her execute his will.

Pierce's apparent control of Oedipa is certainly malicious, and perhaps bespeaks a sense of the jealous authoritarianism of the establishment, the notion that the organs of capitalist democracy grasp more firmly those who seek to escape the system, using whatever methods are available, however inhumane – or it might even suggest that the power of capitalism is so ubiquitous as to be finally inescapable. The critique of capitalism we find in *The Crying of Lot 49* is thus much more expansive than Friedan's criticism of marketing in women's magazines and on television. In *The Feminine Mystique* Friedan did not present herself as a political radical, although she did have socialist sympathies. The book, Horowitz notes, "marked a brief interlude in Friedan's longer term political commitments."[27] Also, as Rachel Bowlby has pointed out, there is a "middle-class, professional focus which is implicit throughout" *The Feminine Mystique*, and this manifests itself, at points, in a patronising attitude towards the working classes.[28] Although she described a relationship between profit and female misery under the reign of the mystique, Friedan contended that the latter

> was not an economic conspiracy directed against women. It was a byproduct of our general confusion lately of means with ends; just something that happened to women when the business of producing and selling and investing in business for profit – which is merely the way our economy is organized to serve man's needs efficiently – began to be confused with the purpose of our nation, the end of life itself.[29]

The solution she proposed for women was integration into the workforce as it stood. Her ideas were reflected in the aims of NOW, founded in 1966, of which Friedan was president. As noted, NOW sought legal reforms but remained relatively traditionalist at a time when others were calling for the complete deconstruction of traditional gendered identities.

Given Pynchon's more intense social radicalism, *The Crying of Lot 49* may thus encode at least a partial critique of the reformism of the early second-wave feminist movement. Pursuing a now familiar mode of criticism, Pynchon may even be suggesting in this novel that the feminism of the early sixties was in some way unwittingly playing into the hands of the capitalist system, given that Oedipa only leaves her housewife role as a result of Pierce's naming of her as executrix, and that we can never be sure whether her journey is self-directed or an unconscious capitulation to Pierce's plans. Underlying these narrative choices might be a suspicion that market imperatives were subtly driving women's return to work, and Pynchon would certainly have considered women who were seeking "liberation" from a newly reconstituted patriarchy by entering the corporate workplace to be misguidedly inserting themselves into a yet more rigidly oppressive structure. In line with this, working men in the novel are represented as more deeply afflicted than Oedipa by the alienating effects of the socio-economic system they inhabit – Mucho's harrowing experience as a second-hand car dealer, hyperaware of his profession's tendency to reduce both its practitioners and its customers to a state of interchangeability, to an "unvarying grey sickness" (*L49* 8), is a case in point. In *The Crying of Lot 49*, men, apparently making up the vast majority of the workforce in San Narciso and its environs, suffer more immediate exploitation by and dependence on the system. If Oedipa *is* being manipulated by Inverarity, it is by way of various men who have been bought off or blackmailed by him, men who are apparently completely under his sway. Oedipa herself, by contrast, can only be worked on at a certain remove, and thus has a greater chance of retaining her autonomy.

Earlier chapters of this study have established Pynchon's basic sympathy with the original values and priorities of New Left organisations, and this analysis suggests that Pynchon's perspective on second-wave feminism within a broader revolutionary context was not dissimilar from that of many male members of the New Left in the mid to late sixties. Various accounts of the era represent the largely male-run Left as consistently neglectful of the *particular* grievances of women, a neglect justified on the basis that to address these issues would distract from the central aim of effecting society-wide revolution. But such arguments sat awkwardly with the sexist attitudes then rife in the movement. In *The Sixties: Years of Hope, Days of Rage*, Todd Gitlin describes this aspect of the New Left, observing that in the early to mid decade many women in groups like SDS began to notice a "discrepancy between their potential and their position in the movement."[30] Generally well educated and capable, they felt discriminated against because of their sex by the male leaders of groups they worked for, men who "sought them out, recruited them, took them seriously, honored their intelligence – then subtly demoted them to girlfriends, wives, note-takers, coffeemakers."[31] Gitlin further explains how, later in the decade, when this sense of discrepancy had consolidated into calls for women's liberation within the movement, such demands were ridiculed by male members. A pivotal moment was the discussion of the issue at the 1967 SDS convention:

> After a debate punctuated by hoots and catcalls, the convention passed a watered-down resolution, which was published in SDS's *New Left Notes*, as Sara Evans points out, "alongside a cartoon of a girl – with earrings, polka-dot minidress, and matching visible panties – holding a sign: 'We Want Our Rights and We Want Them Now.' SDS had blown its last chance."[32]

The result of this debacle and others like it was the emergence of a separate, independent women's movement. Women's anger at their treatment within the New Left, and, indeed, within the wider counterculture, was finally expressed in print towards the end of the decade, a particularly pertinent example being Robin Morgan's essay of 1970, "Goodbye to All That." Here Morgan describes the argument put forward by SDS males, the "simplistic notion that automatic freedom for women – or non-white peoples – will come about ZAP! with the advent of a socialist revolution" as "[b]ullshit" and calls for the building of "an ever stronger independent Women's Liberation Movement, so that sisters in counter-left captivity will have somewhere to turn."[33] Gaining in power and success, the new women's movement withdrew a certain quantity of revolutionary energy from the New Left, contributing in part to the latter's contemporaneous fragmentation and decline. On perceiving this Pynchon may well have shared with prominent male New Left-ers the sense that this was in some ways "the final nail in the coffin of the beloved community."[34] Yet this is not to say that Pynchon's neglect of the particular issues confronting women in *The Crying of Lot 49* equates to sexism on his part – although there are some questionably pro-feminist fetishised and stereotyped depictions of women scattered through his *oeuvre*, Pynchon's mid sixties novel possibly represents the high-water mark in the author's narrative treatment of women, recognising their equality with men in terms of intelligence and ability, as well as their need to take up a more central role in society. It seems more apposite, rather, to point out that such an attitude tallies with

Pynchon's anarchist emphasis on unity and *communitas*. A distaste for political separatism would also further explain *Gravity's Rainbow*'s apparent championing of Huey P. Newton's brand of black rights activism over that of a figure like Eldridge Cleaver.[35] However, in failing to recognise the need to balance long-term group aims with more immediate and individual concerns, Pynchon may be as guilty as the New Left of a damaging lack of revolutionary foresight.

Radical Feminism, Family, and Community in *Vineland*

From New York Radical Women, to Redstockings, to WITCH, the radical feminism which developed in the late 1960s and early 1970s was a deeply varied phenomenon, made up of a multitude of separate groups with diverse aims and opinions. Feminists were divided on issues of gender essentialism, over their relationships with men, over the extent and manner of their engagement with wider revolutionary goals and movements, and on manifold other points. While a growing number abandoned the New Left to join independent feminist groups, there was also a substantial group of "politicos," women who continued to prioritise their involvement in left-wing politics and the anti-war movement.[36] Firmly in the former group was Robin Morgan, who in her article rejected "those simple-minded optimistic dreams of socialist equality all our good socialist brothers want us to believe" on the basis that they could not deliver the "profound changes that would give birth to a genderless society ... Beyond what is male or female ... *Beyond all known standards* ... Beyond, to a species with a new name, that would not dare define itself as Man."[37] In response to this, the politico Genie Plamondon's "Hello to All That," published in *The Berkeley Tribe* less than a month later, directly countered Morgan's aggressive separatism:

> I'm not going to join any women who want a "genderless society" – they can have their own genderless tribe, I'm not down on that – I love to fuck, I love being a woman, I love women, and I love *men* – oh yes I do – Nor am I going to join any woman, any body, who wants to "take over the movement" – bullshit – I align myself with all revolutionary people who are dedicated to serving the people and liberating the planet from *all* oppressive forces.[38]

In 1973, when *Gravity's Rainbow* was published, the women's movement was at the height of its influence, and both this novel and the later *Vineland* reflect their author's experience of such radical feminist perspectives. Focussing on the question of the integration of motherhood and family life with activist practice, this section examines representations of the choices and attitudes of female revolutionary characters within the two novels. Reference is made to the notions of *communitas*, love, altruism, and self-sacrifice which this study has identified as key countercultural values displayed throughout Pynchon's work.

Yet it must first be acknowledged that *Gravity's Rainbow*'s engagement with radical feminism is fairly limited. Many of its women are represented in stereotypical form as deeply connected to nature and the irrational, or appear, as in Pynchon's early stories, in bit-part roles as the voiceless objects of male desire. There is evidence of sensitivity to female-specific issues within a revolutionary context, but this is contained within just a few passages of this vast novel. One of these instances concerns Leni Pökler, the communist activist discussed in the second chapter of this book, a character who quite clearly identifies with radical feminism. The passage in question narrates Leni's response to her lover Peter Sachsa's concern that if the political activities she continues to pursue were to lead to her arrest, her daughter, Ilse, might be left vulnerable. Rejecting this entirely, Leni contends that conventional motherhood is but a mechanism of state control:

> "That's what they – Peter can't you see, they *want* a great swollen tit with some atrophied excuse for a human, bleating around somewhere in its shadows. How can I be *human* for her? Not her *mother*. 'Mother,' that's a civil-service category, Mothers work for *Them!* They're the policemen of the soul." (*GR* 219)

This point of view is anachronistic in its context, being far more characteristic of the kind of questioning of gender roles found within second-wave feminism than of the earlier suffrage movements which Leni, in 1929–30, would have been familiar with. Leni's argument echoes the perspective of Germaine Greer in *The Female Eunuch*, first released in the United States in 1971, who states that "[w]hen children are falsely presented to women as their only significant contribution, the proper expression of their creativity and their lives' work, the children and their mothers suffer for it."[39] It also recalls Shulamith Firestone's assertion of the "tyranny of the biological family" and the need for huge changes in child-rearing and reproductive social practices as put forth in her influential book *The Dialectic of Sex: The Case for Feminist Revolution* (1970).[40] An unambiguous narratorial judgement on Leni's argument follows: "she means it, and she's right" (*GR* 220). *Gravity's Rainbow* thus demonstrates an awareness of feminist arguments around motherhood and endorses Leni's particular point of view. Yet importantly, it is the anti-authoritarian aspect of Leni's argument that is foregrounded in Pynchon's version of revolutionary feminism and its aims; he lays emphasis on the *political* over the *personal*. The passage does not distinguish Leni's rejection of conventional motherhood from her communism; rather, the two are presented as resulting from one and the same revolutionary impulse. Leni's feminism is radical, but it does not demand a separate movement, only a change in certain common ways of thinking about women's roles. Her ideas are representative of the politico faction of second-wave feminists, her point of view is more akin to Genie Plamondon's than Robin Morgan's. Furthermore, although there has been mention of "*male supremacy*" (GR 155) amongst Leni's communist comrades, men are not individually to blame – for Leni, it is not *men* who prefer women "atrophied," it's *the State* – and revolution is her primary aim.[41] Thus in *Gravity's Rainbow*, as in *The Crying of Lot 49*, a fundamental affirmation of women's need for increased liberty and opportunity for fulfilment coexists with a consideration of the social difficulties faced by women which concerns itself not so much with their effect on women's private lives, but with their impact on political change or the ways in which they reveal an oppressive society, as Pynchon continues to defer more to the broadly social than the female specific.

The tentative gesture discernible here towards the narration of alternative parenting models becomes a major structural principle in Pynchon's next novel, *Vineland*. Published in 1990, seventeen years after *Gravity's Rainbow*, it centres around ex-hippie Zoyd Wheeler's life with his daughter Prairie, who was abandoned as a newborn by her mother, Frenesi, a left-wing political activist and member of the oppositional "24fps" film collective turned government informant. Post-natal depression, experienced before there was widespread awareness of the condition or systems to help with it, is presented as the primary cause of Frenesi's decision to leave her child in the care of others. But it is also bound up with a fear of mortality, with an apparently selfish desire to evade the passage of time which maternity renders Frenesi so painfully sensible of: "She had been privileged to live outside of Time, to enter and leave at will, looting and manipulating, weightless, invisible. Now Time had claimed her again, put her under house arrest, taken her passport away. Only an animal with a full set of pain receptors after all" (*VL* 287). Like Leni, Frenesi comes to see herself, as mother, risking becoming merely an "atrophied excuse for a human," reduced to "bleating around" a child that is always given absolute priority. And again, adopting such an intensely self-sacrificing attitude amounts to complying with the wishes of those running society: "'This is just how they want you, an animal, a bitch with swollen udders lying in the dirt, black-faced, surrendered, reduced to this meat, these smells'" (*VL* 287). However, this last statement is not voiced by Frenesi, but by Brock Vond, a federal prosecutor and the novel's definitive right-wing "bad guy," and its simple equation of motherhood with the subhuman differs significantly from Leni's point of view in that it offers up no more enlightened form of mothering as an alternative.[42] Where Leni suggests that by sticking to one's principles and remaining an active contributor in the world one can "be human for" one's child, a belief which helps her to continue her activist practice while simultaneously caring for her daughter, Vond's logic cements Frenesi's determination to divorce herself from all interaction with Prairie, a disconnection which also serves to draw her closer to Vond and the life of a "Cooperative Person" (*VL* 280) he has led her into, in direct betrayal of her earlier countercultural values.

The right of women to reject motherhood was, of course, a central issue in the women's movement. There was widespread (although not universal) support for the use of the birth control pill, and many groups, such as the National Association for the Repeal of Abortion Laws (NARAL), called for legislative changes to make abortion more accessible across the United States. As noted earlier, many second-wave feminists saw pregnancy and child-rearing as a "burden" on women and a major cause of social inequality between the sexes. Particularly relevant to our present discussion are contemporary feminist perspectives like that of Ti-Grace Atkinson, who likened childbearing women to "beasts of burden" in her 1974 book *Amazon Odyssey*, and claimed that because men had historically taken advantage of the fact that only women could give birth, women had been reduced to "the functional – or animal."[43] In an attempt to provide a solution to this imbalance, in *The Dialectic of Sex*, Shulamith Firestone went as far as to suggest that, ideally, "[t]he reproduction of the species by one sex for the benefit of both would be replaced by (at least the option of) artificial reproduction," a view many others shared.[44] Some were even more fundamentally against childbirth: the ranks of the anti-natalist feminists were swollen by the rise of the environmental movement. All in all, there were few voices within the women's movement during this era suggesting that motherhood should be a primary life focus for women. As the feminist social psychologist Bernice E. Lott claimed in a 1973 study,

> It appears to me that a significant number of the most forceful spokeswomen for liberation have essentially very little use for children. When spoken of at all, the tendency is to do so coldly and unsympathetically, and

to project the view that children are nuisances and a major barrier in one's path toward fulfillment in the larger world outside one's home.[45]

Lott includes Shulamith Firestone, Kate Millett, Germaine Greer, and Ti-Grace Atkinson amongst such spokeswomen.

Because these debates were a major focus of public interest in the 1970s and into the eighties, it is unsurprising that Pynchon's narration of the female in his 1990 novel is so centrally concerned with parenting and the family. The kinds of arguments described earlier were beginning to circulate at the time of Prairie's birth in *Vineland*, which occurred in 1970, and Frenesi's trajectory within the novel, as well as that of her abandoned child and first husband, expresses a perspective on such radical feminist agendas and their impact on the attainability of countercultural political and social goals. While the narrator firmly endorses Leni's brand of feminism in *Gravity's Rainbow*, this later novel is almost as definitive in representing the parenting choices made by Frenesi as, essentially, the wrong ones. The emotional intensity with which Zoyd and Prairie feel the absence of Frenesi is a major facet and driver of the narrative. Although Zoyd is presented as a fine father for Prairie, both feel that something is missing from their relationship, something that only Frenesi could provide. Frenesi also comes to yearn for Prairie, imagining where her child might sleep every time she moves into a new apartment with her second husband, Flash. With a name connoting madness, distraction, and folly, Frenesi is presented as wrongheaded and evasive of responsibility in many of her actions, and especially in her erotic attachment to Vond, who, apart from reinforcing her equation of pregnancy and childrearing with a humiliating animality and encouraging her to reject her early political principles and become a government informant, also persuades her to embrace a hedonism and violence in *complete* violation of the values of the early counterculture so prized in Pynchon's work, and to prove her new loyalties by participating in the murder of her lover, the campus revolutionary leader Weed Atman.[46]

It thus appears that while Pynchon supported the idea that women should not allow motherhood to become their sole *raison d'être* in *Gravity's Rainbow*, he does not go as far as to endorse the total dislocation of mothers from the raising of their children in *Vineland*. Taken together, Pynchon's narratives suggest that the rejection of motherhood goes against certain core countercultural values, implying that the anti-maternal element in radical feminism is, in effect, inimical to the achievement of a loving, egalitarian society. Countering this negative impulse within the women's movement is clearly extremely important to Pynchon in 1990, given that Frenesi's journey towards reconnecting with her daughter provides *Vineland*'s basic narrative impetus. In the way of an alternative for mothers, Pynchon's fiction proposes that those who wish to contribute to political change can do so with their children in tow. This is the point Leni Pökler makes, and it is supported in *Vineland* by evidence from Frenesi's family history: both her mother and her grandmother were active on the Left, yet they combined this with childrearing. More recently, *Against the Day*'s Yashmeen gives birth to her first child while on a mission to find and disable the "Interdikt" weapon in an Eastern Europe torn apart by conflict. However, from a feminist perspective there is a certain, possibly troubling ambivalence in Pynchon's work around the potential results of such maternal choices. In the case of Leni, apparently contradicting the narrator's vindication of her parenting choices is the fact that her ongoing defiance does, in the end, put her daughter in danger – in this extreme political situation, Ilse ends up in a concentration camp. In *Vineland*, Frenesi's female line has passed on to her both her original political sympathies, and also, it is claimed, her much commented on predilection for men in uniform, a fetish which is the basis of her attraction to Brock. Yashmeen's child Ljubica, whose birth during a rose harvest is invested with a deliberately quaint romanticism, faces a long trek across dangerous terrain and a progressive "narrowing of choices" (*ATD* 1082) thanks to her parents' decision to enter the Balkans on the brink of the First World War. Although they get out alive, and despite the fact that Ljubica is often stimulated by and engaged with her environment – "From the very first moment her eyes were enormously given to all the world around her" (*ATD* 1066), we are told – the baby is also upset by close-range gunfire. However, rather than expressing a lurking, chauvinistic desire to limit the scope of female revolutionary action, I propose that such examples merely demonstrate the increasing value of the family in Pynchon's later fiction.

Many critics and reviewers have noted the deepening sentimentality of Pynchon's world view over the course of his career. While in his earlier work characters tend to prioritise their own personal quests for meaning or community, and brief and conflicted moments of sentimental affirmation sit uncomfortably, as Nadine Attewell makes clear, with Pynchon's parodic postmodernity, from *Vineland* onwards the basic tenor of the writing is sentimental.[47] This change is especially marked in Pynchon's treatment of familial relationships, and as the years pass, it seems that Pynchon comes to view the family as a social ideal and even as a last bastion of *communitas* in self-interested times, as a blighted but resilient unit of resistance within which, in post-revolutionary America, altruistic, non-possessive love still has a chance to flourish and relationships can function, at least partially, on a principle of anarchistic spontaneous synchronicity. This would explain the almost galling corniness of *Against the Day*'s uncharacteristically tidy denouement, which sees not only Yashmeen feathering a comfortable nest, but a number of other heterosexual couples marrying and starting families, all delivered without any noticeable irony.

Given the importance of the family to Pynchon's post-sixties politics thus defined, his male characters are not exempted from fatherly responsibility, and those who abandon their progeny generally pay a heavy price. In *Mason & Dixon*, for instance, Charles Mason is greatly troubled by the long absences from his wife, Rebekah, and their children necessitated by his career as astronomer-surveyor, and is haunted by Rebekah's ghost following her death. Perhaps his suffering would have been lessened if Mason's father had given him the advice he had wanted to:

> What happens to men sometimes … is that one day all at once they'll understand how much they love their children, as absolutely as a child gives away its own love, and the terrible terms that come with that, and it proves too much to bear, and they'll not want it, any of it, and back away in fear.… Yet if [the father] could but survive the first onrush of fear … he might find a way through … (*MD* 205–6).

Nine years later, in the family drama of *Against the Day*, Mason's situation is paralleled by Webb Traverse's regret over his own abandonment of his extensive brood in order to ensure their safety as he pursues an anarchist bombing campaign. In fact, the deep sense of "emptiness at the core of his body" (*ATD* 107) this separation causes in Webb is, if one accepts my previous analysis, the result of a fundamental misunderstanding. If the pursuit of an anarchist utopia requires Webb to "set aside his feelings" (*ATD* 107) and become cold and unloving towards his offspring, it also destroys the very basis of a functioning anarchist society.[48]

That men are equally capable of caring for a child is repeatedly affirmed in Pynchon's later work. Indeed, the deep connection between fathers and their offspring alluded to by Mason Sr. is affirmed in two particular instances via mention of an eerie, trans-temporal recognition operating within the relationship. In the first instance, which occurs in *Vineland*, an uncanny sense of having met the newborn Prairie before filters through Zoyd's "cheery haze of paternity" (*VL* 285). Sixteen years later, this experience is echoed and intensified in *Against the Day*'s representation of the transvestite Cyprian's first encounter with Ljubica, whose conception he facilitated, during which "[h]is nipples were all at once peculiarly sensitive, and he found himself almost desperate with an unexpected flow of feeling, a desire for her to feed at his breast," accompanied by a sudden certitude: "I knew her once – previously – perhaps in that other life it was she who took care of me – and now here is the balance being restored – " (*ATD* 1067). This emphasis on fatherhood may be partially a result of Pynchon becoming a father himself,[49] and may also reflect the influence of the fathers' rights movements that had evolved in the two decades prior to the publication of *Vineland*, and which in the late eighties and early nineties were "placing the father-child bond at the centre of their efforts."[50] But whatever the motives behind it, it implies an equality in Pynchon's treatment of parenting roles: his novels come to assert that neither women *nor men* must entirely turn their backs on family in pursuit of personal and/or political goals. In fact, the progression I have been describing here reaches its logical conclusion in Pynchon's *Inherent Vice*, as purposive social action and the protection of the family come together in Doc Sportello's attempts to reunite the Harlington family.

In one sense, then, Pynchon's later novels reflect an affinity with the women's movement's questioning of conventional parenting roles, underscoring the importance of the family to his male characters. But his novels also critique excessive self-interest in both women and men, and do not suggest that children should be left in the care of others or might legitimately be something other than the first priority of those responsible for their care. Rather, Pynchon's work implies that within the context of the family (and, as we saw in the previous chapter, ideally within the larger society too), both men and women should be prepared to make sacrifices that benefit the well-being of the entire group. Theoretically, the parent-child bond affirms the power and beauty of nature, allows the family unit to function on an anarchist model, disdains the kind of unfocussed violence which might affect the innocent, and continually undermines scientific rationalism's division of subject from object. Thus Pynchon's work cannot express support for the kind of extreme adaptations to familial arrangements called for by radical feminists of the era.

Gender, Oppression, Rebellion

On the question of parenting Pynchon's later fiction appears to resist associating a nurturing attitude exclusively with the female sex. However, *Vineland* does play host to a discourse of gender essentialist feminism which requires men to take primary responsibility for producing modern society, and for its failure in all respects to match up to the post-revolutionary utopias envisaged by the counterculture. A primary locus of such views within the novel is the Sisterhood of Kunoichi Attentives, a self-funded commune formed of female ninja devotees – "a sort of Esalen institute for lady ass-kickers" (*VL* 107), as it is described in the fictional *Aggro World* magazine. Sister Rochelle, Senior Attentive of the Sisterhood, puts forward an anti-male re-interpretation of the Fall narrative, in which she claims that men were originally absent from the garden of Eden:

> Paradise was female. Eve and her sister, Lilith, were alone in the Garden. A character named Adam was put into the story later, to help make men look more legitimate, but in fact the first man was not Adam – it was the Serpent.... It was sleazy, slippery man ... who invented "good" and "evil," where before women had been content to just be. In among the other confidence games they were running on women at the time, men also convinced us that we were the natural administrators of this thing "morality" they'd just invented. They dragged us all down into this wreck they'd made of the Creation, all subdivided and labeled, handed us the keys to the church, and headed off toward the dance halls and the honky-tonk saloons. (*VL* 166)

For Sister Rochelle, who implicitly rejects Leni's communist emphasis on the state as oppressor, it is men who have made women "policemen of the soul," and the power-hungry rationalist impulse to subdivide and label, the "objective consciousness" discussed in previous chapters, is innately masculine. Her account recalls those radical feminist manifestoes, such as, again, Robin Morgan's "Goodbye to All That," which called for female world leadership on the basis of a deeper innate connection between females and the natural environment. Moreover, although hardly academically rigorous, it evokes recuperations of the Fall narrative and of the rabbinic legend of Lilith made by feminist theologians and members of the women's movement like Judith Plaskow, whose 1972 re-telling, which also focuses on the sisterhood of Eve and Lilith, is similarly casual in tone:

> In the beginning, the Lord God formed Adam and Lilith from the dust of the ground and breathed into their nostrils the breath of life. Created from the same source, both having been formed from the ground, they were equal in all ways. Adam, being a man, didn't like this situation, and he looked for ways to change it. He said, "I'll have my figs now, Lilith," ordering her to wait on him, and he tried to leave to her the daily tasks of life in the garden. But Lilith wasn't one to take any nonsense; she picked herself up, uttered God's holy name, and flew away. ... [51]

Considered in isolation, it is not clear whether Sister Rochelle's comments coincide with the novel's general attitude to men as historical actors, but the plaintive tone lent to the thoughts of another radical woman, Frenesi's mother, Sasha, makes it difficult to completely reject the notion that Pynchon, in this text, does consider the male sex largely, although not entirely, culpable for society's evils:

> The injustices she had seen in the streets and fields, so many, too many times gone unanswered – she began to see them more directly, not as world history or anything too theoretical, but as humans, usually male, living here on the planet, often well within reach, committing these crimes, major and petty, one by one against other living humans. (*VL* 80)

Moreover, particular men are found guilty of smaller-scale brutality as the novel offers support for feminist critiques of the vulnerability of women and girls to male relatives within the contemporary familial power hierarchy. Various instances of domestic abuse are committed by male characters, such as that of DL's mother, Norleen, at the hands of her macho husband, Moody Chastain, in his youth a gang member who liked "driving fast" and "discharging firearms inappropriately" (*VL* 118), later to become a military policeman. There is also an instance of the child abuse of a female: Prairie's teenage friend Ché is harassed into a sexual relationship with her mother's boyfriend, who, as she describes, "transforms into Asshole of the Universe anytime he gets to see a inch of teen skin" (*VL* 329).[52] As Molly Hite claims in her article "Feminist Theory and the Politics of *Vineland*," Pynchon's first post-hiatus novel evinces an awareness of the connections between gender and power that had been absent in his previous works.[53]

Hite's article also demonstrates that *Vineland* directly references two key works of feminist literature which make similar points to those of Sasha and Sister Rochelle, and which further confirm Pynchon's deepening interest in the products and perspectives of the women's movement in the period between *Gravity's Rainbow* and *Vineland*: Sandra Gilbert and Susan Gubar's *The Madwoman in the Attic* (1979) and Eve Sedgwick's *Between Men* (1985).[54] Yet in showing sympathy for such commentaries, Pynchon's work certainly does not write off the entire male sex – one thinks of Zoyd Wheeler as a particularly redemptive figure and foil to the likes of Brock Vond – and, there is also clearly an ironic or even parodic dimension to Sister Rochelle's Fall narrative.[55] Indeed, this is true of the whole idea of the Kunoichi Sisterhood, which functions as unambiguous analogue to the radical feminist group Female Liberation Cell-16, an early separatist feminist organisation whose members rejected conventional femininity and adopted masculine dress, practiced celibacy and masturbation, and trained in karate. In fact, this penchant for the martial arts was "ridiculed" by *Playboy* journalist Morton Hunt in a May 1970 article entitled "Up against the Wall, Male Chauvinist Pig!"[56] as the magazine, of which Pynchon is a confessed reader, espoused an anti-separatist but in some respects pro-feminist agenda which shares several characteristics with Pynchon's own position as revealed in this chapter. Furthermore, Pynchon's representation of the Sisterhood seems to be somewhat in line with the view put forward by Germaine Greer – who, incidentally, granted an interview to *Playboy* in 1972 – on all-female communes. In *The Female Eunuch*, Greer critiqued Judith Brown's late sixties separatist rejection of the politico position and resultant call for independent female communes in Part II of the manifesto *Towards a Women's Liberation Movement*. According to Greer, Brown "did not see that an all-female commune is in no way different from the medieval convents where women who revolted against their social and biological roles could find intellectual and moral fulfilment, from which they exerted no pressure on the status quo at all."[57] Beyond the obvious allusion in the Kunoichi Sisterhood's name, the building which now houses them was once, as the narrator points out, actually a nunnery home to The Sisters of Our Lady of the Cucumber Fields ("Las Hermanas de Nuestra Señora de los Pepinares" (*VL* 107)). Pynchon's distrust of feminist separatism, already legible as a distaste for the female specific in *The Crying of Lot 49*, is thus confirmed in *Vineland*.

As argued earlier, Pynchon's political distaste for separatism reflects his repeated affirmation of the value of community. But perhaps it also derives from a questioning of essentialist notions of gender. Following this logic, Pynchon's critique of male greed and brutality would be aimed not at men per se, but at the gendered attributes society compels them to adopt. Influenced perhaps by feminist analyses of the '70s and '80s such as those of Kate Millet's *Sexual Politics* (1970) or Gayle Rubin's "The Traffic in Women: Notes on the 'Political Economy' of Sex" (1975), *Vineland* often works to destabilise the equation between gender and biological sex, revealing gender as a social construct.[58] Gender in this novel can be free floating and malleable, as Frenesi learns when, one day in the late sixties, she attempts to document a street demonstration for 24fps and finds herself stranded in the no-man's land between a line of riot police and a contingent of angry protestors. Thinking "Oh, I need Superman . . . Tarzan on that vine" (*VL* 116), she is suddenly rescued by a mysterious motorcyclist in full leathers on a red and silver bike. Grasping onto the stranger during their escape, Frenesi assumes a man has saved her, but it is in fact Darryl Louise Chastain ("DL"), who reveals her identity once they have reached safety. DL seems to actively encourage this kind of misapprehension, having adopted a number of characteristically male traits: "In those days DL was just cruising up and down 101 looking for girl motorcycle gangs to terrorize, drinking drugstore vodka out of the bottle, hustling guys named Snake for enough double-cross whites to get her to the next population center offering a suitable risk to her safety" (*VL* 115).

In its depictions of Brock and Frenesi, both of whom enact too completely their prescribed gender roles and thus appear doomed to coexist in a relationship of sadomasochistic violence, *Vineland* advances *The Crying of Lot 49*'s critique of gendering, putting forward a Derridean view of "male" and "female" as potentially "fixed containers, prisons, trapping men no less than women within one place, one role," which is in line with Pynchon's general deconstructivist attitude towards binary oppositions.[59] *Vineland* also points to the implications of this entrapment for the lives of dependents and loved ones. Gender thus appears in Pynchon's later work as another regulatory structure through which the capitalist status quo maintains itself, a structure into which, again, individuals are drawn in escapist flight from a more troubling and unstable reality. Yet once its arbitrariness is acknowledged, the system of gender/sex associations can become a tool of oppositional politics. Via the deliberate manipulation and exploitation of embedded expectations and assumptions, gender can be put to subversive effect, something, of course, many within the women's and gay rights movements during this era recognised. Such a strategy underlies DL's impersonation of the super-feminine Frenesi, which allows her the opportunity to get close to Brock and carry out a sting operation, and the idea that the performance of gender allows one to play the system is given further currency in the very first pages of the novel, where Zoyd transforms himself into a badly put together drag act and throws himself through a roadhouse window in front of the assembled Vineland media so as to obtain government mental disability payouts. The imperative of awareness, a major feature of Pynchon's political philosophy as revealed in this study, reappears again in *Vineland* in the context of gender.

Yet to fully escape gender conventions is shown to be no mean feat, with powerful social forces requiring our adjustment to the norm. Psychosexual conditioning, transparently and concretely corporate sponsored in *Gravity's Rainbow*, is a more opaque phenomenon in *Vineland*, where women are attracted to Vond "for reasons they later could or would not specify" (*VL* 275), and the variously effective gender bending of Zoyd and DL does little to suggest the possible advent of a truly genderless society. DL simply adopts explicitly masculine or feminine guises, and Zoyd's drag act demonstrates how deeply socially ingrained are caricatured ideas of what constitutes male and female. There seems to be no "beyond" to gender conventions in *Vineland*. Or, if there is, unravelling their associations with biological sex is to be a lengthy and involved process. However, disturbing and possibly partially undermining Pynchon's gender commentary is the possibility that the author fundamentally lacks concern that *certain* gendered qualities should be destabilised. It is not clear that a genderless society is at all desirable to Pynchon, an author who at times appears to celebrate a female sexual attractiveness sustained through highly gendered dress and behaviour.

Femininity as Fetish: A Flaw in Pynchon's Revolutionary Strategy

As noted earlier in this chapter, although Pynchon's later work continues to espouse basically pro-feminist values, it also contains stereotyped and fetishised representations of women and the female body. Whether they generally conform to or reject traditional femininity, women in *Vineland*, as in all of Pynchon's novels, are more often than not also objects of desire whose sex appeal is conveyed via (soft) pornographic imagery catering to the male gaze. Thus we are told that after she is rescued by DL, "[w]ith her bare thighs Frenesi gripped the leather hips of her benefactor," before DL, *Charlie's Angels*-style, removes her helmet and "shake[s] out her hair, which lit up in the approaching orange sunset like a comet" (*VL* 117). Later, this fetish is further indulged with details of how "the scent of DL's sweat and pussy excitation diffused out of the leather clothing, mixed with motor smells" (*VL* 118). This tendency to eroticise also comes through in scenes which should require a certain gravity of touch, such as that of the Japanese white slave auction, in which girls are sold into lives of unwilling prostitution. Here, concessions to the injustice of the situation are swamped by the author's love of cartoonish surreality and his extended descriptions of the erotic details of the women's dress. Particularly problematic from a feminist perspective are narratorial insinuations that female characters take a masochistic pleasure in sexual degradation. Thus, in the slave auction scene, DL is sexually aroused as she is auctioned off – "She smiled even with her eyes ... alert now at nipples and clitoris, the price being bid upward deliriously" (*VL* 137). Even more disturbing examples of female masochism are to be found in Pynchon's work, most notable perhaps being the depiction of Lake Traverse as willing slave to the aggressive sexual desires of her husband, Deuce, and his sidekick Sloat in *Against the Day*:

> They kept her naked most of the time. Sometimes they put a pair of leather side hobbles on her to keep her attached to the bed, but enough chain so she could move. Not that they had to, she was always ready to oblige. After

she had given in to the notion of being doubled up on, she found herself going out of her way looking for it ... They took her down to the Four Corners and put her so one of her knees was in Utah, one in Colorado, one elbow in Arizona and the other in New Mexico – with the point of insertion exactly above the mythical crosshairs itself. Then rotated her all four different ways. Her small features pressed into the dirt, the blood-red dirt. (*ATD* 302–3)

While it should be noted that not all of Pynchon's pornography expresses a hetero-normative perspective, these apparently gratuitous representations of female sexual submission in Pynchon's prose, persisting into his most recent production, suggest the need for ongoing reflection on Pynchon's gender politics. If interpreted negatively, such treatment of the female threatens not only to undermine the notion of a basic affinity with women's liberation in Pynchon's work, but indeed to render ambivalent Pynchon's humanism with regard to women.

Of course, it might be objected at this point that feminists are by no means in agreement on the issue of the relationship between pornography and the social oppression of women, on which public debate raged during the twenty years leading up to the publication of *Vineland*. In the early 1970s, an anti-pornography critique was advanced by certain members of the women's movement including Robin Morgan, whose controversial pronouncement was that "[p]ornography is the theory, and rape the practice."[60] Catharine MacKinnon and Andrea Dworkin took a practical approach to the issue, working to reform legislation on pornographic material found degrading to women, which they defined as involving imagery including that in which "women are presented as sexual objects who enjoy pain or humiliation" or "being raped," or "as sexual objects" in "positions of servility or submission or display."[61] Yet on the other side of the debate, liberal feminists formed groups such as the Feminist Anti-Censorship Taskforce, from whose platform commentators such as Barbara Dority declaimed the anti-pornography movement's "blanket condemnation" of certain materials, as well as their "claim to possess the exclusive ability to distinguish 'dehumanizing, objectifying, degrading' materials from 'erotica,'" and suggested that "[i]n making these judgements for everyone, and in vigorously promoting Indianapolis-style anti-pornography ordinances, the feminist movement has taken a sexist, moralistic, censorial, and anti-sex stance."[62]

Moreover, there is some evidence to support the view that Pynchon's intention in writing scenes like those described earlier is at least partly critical, as would indeed be suggested by the author's commentary around

Femininity as Fetish: A Flaw in Pynchon's Revolutionary Strategy   153

"pornographies" in *Gravity's Rainbow*, in which, as discussed in Chapter 2, "pornography" is a term used to connote any subtly exploitative mechanism of capitalist power. In *Inherent Vice*, Pynchon's retrospectively sixties novel, one of the most prominent examples of the erotic objectification of the female body occurs in the narrator's description of the various silk ties owned by Mickey Wolfmann, upon which have been painted the meticulously detailed nude forms of his various (ex)girlfriends, each in a different submissive pose. This is an idea which has stuck with Pynchon over the years, first appearing in *Gravity's Rainbow*, where Slothrop sports a similarly pornographic image of a topless lady on what he claims is a "genuine hand-painted ... Wormwood Scrubs School Tie" (*GR* 190), and again in *Vineland*, where Weed Atman attends Thanatoid get-togethers "in ensembles of vivid chartreuse, teal, or fuchsia, the ties and cummerbunds hand-painted with matching motifs like tropical fruit, naked women, or bass lures" (*V* 218–19). In its earlier incarnations, this fashion statement is adopted by the novels' good guys, passing innocuously enough as just another piece of Pynchonian extravagance. As taken up by Wolfmann, however, it becomes rather more meaningful, suggesting a commentary on the ability of rich, powerful men to brazenly and publicly command a humiliating submission of women, and perhaps also, on the readiness with which some women submit to this for financial profit. One of Wolfmann's lovers is the protagonist Doc's ex-girlfriend Shasta, and Doc worries about "how much she'd come to depend on Wolfmann's guaranteed level of ease and power" (*IV* 5).

Yet it is more difficult, perhaps, to explain away the lack of realism which characterises the sexual responses of many of Pynchon's women; again, this is something which has changed little over Pynchon's career. In *The Crying of Lot 49*, for example, Oedipa, having agreed to a sexual liaison with Metzger but fallen asleep as he was undressing her, awakes "to find herself getting laid" (*L49* 27). Coming in "on a sexual crescendo in progress" (*L49* 27), a rather short period of time elapses before she and Metzger reach simultaneous climax. Similarly, *Against the Day*'s Yashmeen, also being effectively raped – this time by a total stranger in the centre of Venice, is described as submitting to the man "almost by reflex" before, immediately afterwards, asking herself if she had "ever wanted so much to keep looking into a man's eyes" (*ATD* 915–16). But whether or not any proportion of these stereotyped, pornographic, or unrealistic representations of the female – or even the simple abundance of "pleasant-looking women" in the novels – actually represents an expression of misogyny on Pynchon's part is a difficult question to answer. Part of the difficulty stems from feminism's own rejection of the biological determinism of sex and naturalised ideas of gender, achieved on the basis of psychological research. Operating at a further remove from the "real," literary representation (and especially postmodern literary representation) consolidates the constructedness of gender, reflecting, reproducing, or exceeding the normative with varying degrees of self-consciousness. There are thus myriad complications for a male author like Pynchon both in representing the female per se, and particularly, if the aim is to parody misogynistic representations of women, to do this without a very unambiguous feminist rationale.[63]

However, as Stefan Mattessich has pointed out in relation to this very prospect of the parodic use of misogyny in Pynchon's work, "[t]he question of complicity returns at every level, and even parody may be fetishized, may even be the supreme fetish, the fetish of the fetish."[64] There is thus reasonable cause to doubt that the author has entirely transcended his early sexism, which, as noted earlier, he recognised in his short story "Low-lands" and apologised for in his introduction to *Slow Learner*. As I have hinted, this apology was not entirely satisfactory for a number of reasons. Firstly, Pynchon's self-criticism relates only to certain "racist, sexist and proto-Fascist" (*SL* 11) talk, attributed to the perennially offensive recurring character Pig Bodine, failing to acknowledge the generally sexist character of the story (which recounts the protagonist Dennis Flange's abandonment of his shrewish, money-hungry spouse for an ethereal, vertically challenged gipsy girl who idolises him), or indeed the chauvinistic nature of many other representations of women in the short story collection, something even a cursory reading of "The Small Rain" or "Entropy" will confirm. Secondly, although if one examines Bodine's small portion of dialogue, one does find some sexism, there is no evidence of racism or proto-fascism, which engenders the suspicion that the author may have been attempting to divert attention from the true extent of his early sexism by sandwiching that term between two other charges which are hardly borne out.[65] Thirdly, in Pynchon's suggestion that "[m]odern readers will be, at least, put off by" (*SL* 11) such talk, there lurks the implication that contemporary readers in 1960 would not have been – and since the misogyny of "Low-lands" is hard to miss this seems to exclude women (as well as non-misogynistic men) from the category of "readers." The final problematic dimension of this *Slow Learner* apology is its attempt to extract something positive from the representation of Pig Bodine, claiming that Bodine's talk, reflecting Pynchon's "own" voice at the time, is "probably authentic enough" (*SL* 11). Pynchon also excuses Dennis Flange's less than mature attitude to women on the basis that he

Femininity as Fetish: A Flaw in Pynchon's Revolutionary Strategy   155

is typical of the many middle-aged American men who remain like "small boys," unwilling to face the prospect of "developing any real life shared with an adult woman" – the kind of attitude picked up, Pynchon surmises, from "men's magazines, *Playboy* in particular" (*SL* 10). Referring to the short stories alone, the apology suggests that in Pynchon's own view he had progressed away from such sexism as early as *V.*. But when analysed closely, it actually implies that Pynchon's maturation on this issue was far from complete even by 1984.[66]

I thus take issue with Jeffrey Severs's contention that Pynchon's career shows a forward progression in its depictions of women. Severs focuses on *Against the Day*, which he considers a "studied revisitation of the tendencies of [Pynchon's] earliest work" in its portrayal of women, the character of Dally in that novel functioning as "a corrective" to earlier attitudes.[67] Severs considers this demonstrative of a general "maturation" in Pynchon's representations of the female despite the fact, as he admits, *Against the Day*'s "gruesome" sex scenes involving Lake Traverse, along with the "helpless women and caricatured prostitutes" that appear in *Inherent Vice*, "should temper any expectations that Pynchon's construction of female characters has undergone a lasting revolution."[68] Severs finds a "clear indication" of this positive development in a scene which involves the return of "La Jarretière," who had appeared as Mélanie L'Heuremaudit in *V.*. In that novel, she had seemingly met a grisly end while performing in a production of the ballet *The Rape of the Chinese Virgins*. The choreographed dance involved La Jarretière balancing aloft on a pointed pole which would apparently impale her at the crotch. She was supposed to wear a protective device, but for some reason, we are told, she had "left it off" (*V.* 414). Severs recounts how during her reappearance in Pynchon's 2006 novel, "La Jarretière indicts the scene as a product of 'the eternally-adolescent male mind': 'Grand Guignol. They came to see blood. We used the ... raspberry syrup.... A young beauty destroyed before her time, something the eternally-adolescent male mind could tickle itself with.'"[69] As Severs points out, this passage's foregrounding of the "eternally-adolescent male mind" has already received critical attention from Steven Hock, who argues that it refers to "both the Pynchon of *V.*" and the "eternally adolescent" Chums of Chance.[70] Yet I submit that La Jarretière's phrasing, in what is actually less an indictment than an explanation, recalls more powerfully Pynchon's *Slow Learner* apology – his description of his early "puerility" and "adolescent values," and his assertion that "[i]t is no secret nowadays, particularly to women, that many American males, even those of middle-aged appearance, wearing suits and holding down jobs, are in fact, incredible as it sounds, still small boys inside" (*SL* 9–10). I cannot therefore agree with Severs when he says that the scene marks a "distinctive form of maturation."[71] Rather, it emphasises if anything how *little* Pynchon's attitudes have developed since the publication of *Slow Learner*. Pynchon still seeks to excuse male sexism as merely infantile, rather than condemning it as something more malicious.

Whether or not this analysis hits the mark, in the absence of a clear pro-feminist agenda Pynchon's recurrent fetishisation of the female body and narration of women in willing submission to the male will inevitably serve to alienate a proportion of his potential reading public. I argued in Chapter 3 that Pynchon is pursuing a political project in his writing, offering up secret histories and cautionary tales in an anti-didactic manner which requires the reader to engage actively with the text, to consider its multiple meanings, and to pursue their own, individual interpretation, the aim being to foster understanding and awareness of the contemporary sociopolitical situation as well as of the advantages and disadvantages of various approaches to change. By expanding the consciousness of his readership in such a way, I suggested, Pynchon contributes to a counter-cultural politics, encouraging the adoption of anarchist values. If we accept this to be the case, then the kinds of representations of women discussed earlier are certainly counterproductive to his cause, limiting Pynchon's audience to some degree, leading readers to question the motives behind his anti-separatist attitude towards the women's liberation movement and defence of motherhood, and also possibly rendering readers less generally sympathetic to the views his novels express. In this aspect of his fiction Pynchon is seemingly lacking in awareness – that commodity which he has promoted doggedly throughout his career. It thus appears that, in certain aspects of his narrative treatment of women, Pynchon has failed to learn the lessons of the New Left, introducing into his work a rare but significant flaw, a divisive element which works against the egalitarian community he seeks to help build.

Conclusion
A "Little Parenthesis of Light"
Pynchon's Counterculture

One of Pynchon's most vivid and direct descriptions of the 1960s appears in *Vineland*. Here, the narrator offers up a predominantly affirmative vision of a particular atmosphere and attitude which inhered during those years. During a flashback to the wedding of Zoyd and Frenesi, we learn that the assembled well wishers felt no impatience during the reading of the vows because they were inhabiting "the Mellow Sixties":

> a slower-moving time, predigital, not yet so cut into pieces, not even by television. It would be easy to remember the day as a soft-focus shot, the kind to be seen on "sensitivity" greeting cards in another few years. Everything in nature, every living being on the hillside that day, strange as it sounded later whenever Zoyd tried to tell about it, was gentle, at peace – the visible world was a sunlit sheep farm. War in Vietnam, murder as an instrument of American politics, black neighborhoods torched to ashes and death, all must have been off on some other planet.... in later years, try as Zoyd might to remember everything at its most negative, truth was there'd been no brawls or barfing or demolition derbies, everybody had got along magically, it was one of the peak parties of his life, folks loved the music, and it went on all night and then the next, right on through the weekend. Pretty soon bikers and biker chicks, playing at villainy, were showing up in full regalia, then a hay wagon jammed full of back-to-nature acidheads from up the valley out on an old-fashioned hayride, and eventually the sheriff, who ended up doing the Stroll, a dance of his own day, with three miniskirted young beauties.... (*VL* 38)

Saturated with a deep nostalgia for the social harmony and good times of the counterculture at its peak, this passage reconfirms points made throughout this book regarding Pynchon's investment in the sixties' communitarian ideal, his sense of those years as a "little parenthesis of light" (*IV* 254), despite the perhaps overly saccharine pastoral imagery it employs in places. In depicting the unconflicted coming together of wedding guests, Hell's Angels, acidheads, and even the local authorities, it clearly expresses the environmentalist, cross-creedal, pro-diversity attitude that John A.

McClure finds in the work of Pynchon and other post-sixties left-wing writers, and it links such values firmly to a sixties context.[1] Furthermore, the passage asserts that the utopian dream *was* attained, albeit in isolated moments, and embodies, therefore, hope for future re-enactments. But, as always, Pynchon errs on the side of caution, his mention of certain harsh realities occurring contemporaneously with this idyllic wedding party and spurring the activism of the decade – Vietnam, political assassinations, and racial violence – preventing his nostalgia from being mistaken for the kind of naive, free-floating, or escapist idealism he finds, as we have seen, extremely damaging and destructive to the revolutionary cause and responsible, in part, for the demise of the Mellow Sixties.

As I have argued, in Pynchon's novelistic allusions to countercultural intertexts, individuals, and groups, and the various values, theories, and practices they promoted, the uncompromising intellectual rigor (and concomitant earnestness) of his approach, further demonstrated by the passage quoted earlier, marks him out as an important political philosopher as well as a writer of engaging and entertaining fiction. I have sought firstly to shed light on the author's political acuity by clarifying some of the myriad subtleties and ambivalences woven into his representations of the sixties era and its actors, and also to contribute to an awareness of these as justified and necessary characteristics of Pynchon's literary expression of an anti-authoritarian political philosophy. But subtlety and ambivalence do not, as I hope to have demonstrated, equate to obscurity in terms of political sympathies and critiques. Through his novels and non-fiction, Pynchon expresses an anti-capitalist and anarchist sensibility ever more clearly. Moreover, a basic support is also given to certain communist groups and individuals when they speak of human unity and conduct a practical activism based on the positive, humanist rationality Pynchon champions, rather than on illusory future projections or thinly disguised power hunger.[2]

Although Pynchon's leftism is not defined by the 1960s, retaining the timeless quality of a system of values that recurs throughout history during periods of popular revolt against oppression, my interpretations further confirm, I hope, the special relevance of the counterculture as a context for Pynchon's politics. While not to be associated, in particular, with any one movement or philosophy, I would suggest that Pynchon's work, from *V.* to *Inherent Vice*, embodies the essential originating spirit of the counterculture broadly considered. Many of the criticisms of Western society (the "East" being largely exempted) that run through his writing derive from implicit and explicit critiques of alienation and exploitation under capitalist democracy and the rule of the technocracy made by both the Beat Generation and the civil rights movement, critiques that were to form the ideological basis of many countercultural groups. As a result, the author finds something to sympathise with in each of the sixties movements I have considered, while rejecting certain of their theories or tactics which he perceives as compromising core countercultural values or reducing the wider movement's chances of success. And Pynchon does seem to hope for broad-reaching revolutionary change. In the sense that they repeatedly call into question many of the fundamental social, economic, and political structures under which Americans and others in the West now live, and model various anarchist alternatives, Pynchon's novels can certainly be described as politically radical. The presence of Rosa Luxemburg in *Gravity's Rainbow* as an imagined presidential candidate in an escapist fantasy of sudden change points to the improbability of revolution occurring via existing political channels and implies the author's rejection of traditional reformism. Spontaneous revolution, it seems, would be welcomed, but its likelihood is not to be exaggerated – and it is certainly not to be considered inevitable. Yet Pynchon's radicalism, as we have seen, does not extend to questions of gender roles: although his novels support female liberation in many areas of life and recognise gender norms as substantially culturally constructed, they nevertheless suggest a desire for women to conform, at least in some degree, to conventional idealised or pornographic femininity. Pynchon's radicalism also, perhaps, ultimately gives way to a preference for the hetero-normative in the related discourse of sexuality; although there are a number of examples of more sympathetic representations of non-reproductive sexual practices and gay relationships in his recent work, he has received criticism for apparent homophobia in certain of his narratives.[3]

Despite such important exceptions, the values expressed through Pynchon's novels largely converge with those of the counterculture identified in the introduction to this study. The social anarchism that acts as an ideal in his work is based, exactly, on the tenets of egalitarianism, community spirit, participation, and flexibility. It combines a necessary degree of structure with as much anti-structure, or *communitas*, as possible, the aim being to organise society in such a way as to prevent the accumulation of power in any one individual or group. (As evinced by Oberst Enzian's narrative in *Gravity's Rainbow*, consolidated leadership, even within a revolutionary group, may be susceptible or conducive to establishment attitudes like paternalism, self-promotion, superiority, exhibitionism, alienation, and aggression.) In his attachment to such values, Pynchon is much more closely aligned with the earlier, non-violent manifestations of the counterculture than their later, more aggressive counterparts: a non-violent stance demonstrates human dignity and integrity, validating to some degree the motivating faith underlying countercultural movements, the faith that people are capable of forming harmonious communities, and that greed and brutality are not fundamental or incontrovertible human qualities. Further asserting the possibility of functioning, egalitarian communities are the cultures of "unity" existing within the United States and abroad that Pynchon depicts – the native Herero, American outcasts and vagabonds, the Yz-les-Bains anarchists – as well as the various symbols and confirmations of "oneness" that recur throughout his work – the synchronicity of rioting protestors in *Gravity's Rainbow*, the pastoral serenity of *Vineland*'s Mellow Sixties, the "Æther" and the living earth in *Against the Day* and *Mason & Dixon*, to name but a few. But in the light of the failure of the counterculture (women's movement excepted), Pynchon does not overemphasise the practical chances of realising utopia, remaining aware of human weakness and manifold other obstacles – the capitalist system and its creation of manipulative "pornographies," the media and its tendency to misrepresent reality, the prevalence of objective consciousness – to the widespread success of social anarchist groupings. In *this* sense, Sam Thomas's contention that "whilst Pynchon treats the sixties with immense affection he is also one of the era's harshest critics," holds true.[4] Pynchon does criticise sixties politics, but retaining faith in the basic countercultural spirit, and clinging to the core values outlined in the introduction, he does so in the hope that future revolutionaries might learn from the mistakes of their predecessors, and do better next time. He always, as David Cowart puts it, has "an eye to imagining a world in which various oppressive forces can be countered, dismantled, resisted."[5]

Following Pynchon's logic, in choosing the violent route late sixties groups like the Black Panthers, the Weathermen, and many within the student-run New Left showed themselves spellbound by a capitalist "pornography of killing" or perhaps by their own, self-created "pornography of self-sacrifice," both of which ultimately express a desire to usurp or mimic the kind of power enjoyed by "the Man." But Pynchon's preference for non-violence does not, as I have argued, translate to out and out pacifism. In the mid sixties *The Crying of Lot 49* and "A Journey into the Mind of Watts" both assert that their author's reflexes on violence are not as "predictable" (J 82) as those of the government social workers Pynchon finds fault with in the latter text. It seems, in fact, that at the time of publication (when the nascent violence of certain countercultural groups had not yet proven itself intensely counterproductive) Pynchon may have been somewhat attracted to the notion of the violent retaliation of the weak against the strong. If so, however, Pynchon came to realise his mistake; what remains in his mature fiction is only support for the kind of violence represented by Huey P. Newton's concept of revolutionary suicide – the violent act forced by the absence of any alternative in a situation of unbearable oppression, the risk to self motivated by an altruistic love for the members of one's community. As such, revolutionary suicide is also an expression of the kind of blighted yet resilient hope Pynchon's novels embody, as the author acknowledges the vast odds against wide-scale positive change, yet still writes towards that, despite the fact that many will perceive his work as yet another iteration of the general countercultural failure to make realities of ideals. Pynchon's support for revolutionary suicide links, furthermore, to his increasing interest in the family as unit of resistance; family members, when compared to friends or strangers, are typically more given to the kind of intense and selfless love which can motivate the willing sacrifice of the one for the other. This kind of love, which is not manipulative, not used as a hustle or as a means of withdrawal, or combined awkwardly with violence, is at the core of Pynchon's countercultural philosophy.

Altruistic, non-possessive love for others, or what I have elsewhere termed *communitas*, is posited as the ideal basis of social interaction and organisation, but the importance of nurturing the self and environment is also underscored in Pynchon's novels. This manifests itself in their encouragement of openness and enquiry on the part of the reader, following the questioning, exploratory model Pynchon himself adopts. Predicated, at least in part, upon the adventuresome spirit of the Beat Generation who combined the pursuit of a sense of brotherhood with forays into both the geographical and spiritual unknown, Pynchon's work interrogates and destabilises both the officially endorsed historical record and commonly held beliefs about the borders and limitations of the "given world," uncovering secret histories both quirky and depressing and expanding the reader's sense of the possible. Indeed, this spirit of openness in exploration of the (meta)physical beyond runs parallel to a similar availability in social contexts – the two are innately connected. As Pynchon suggests in his introduction to *The Writings of Donald Barthelme*, for Barthelme to move towards "a full Dickensian embrace of human diversity, foolishness and all … to open up instead of shut down," implied "risking the possibility of finding spiritual dimensions sooner or later hiding inside a space he thought he owned and knew."[6] This is all very much in line with the prevalent countercultural valorisation of continuous learning in adults, something expressed most clearly by Timothy Leary amongst those exponents of the counterculture considered in this book. This emphasis on open-mindedness and the thirst for knowledge, surprise, and wonder in Pynchon's work helps to explain, incidentally, the distaste for Marxist dialectical materialism expressed, as I argued in Chapter 4, in *Gravity's Rainbow*. The idea that the future is in any way certain or that history moves forward on the basis of strictly material imperatives runs directly counter to this open approach to reality. Other core countercultural tenets promoted by Pynchon's novels include responsibility and creativity – the complexity, obscurity, and interpretative ambiguity of the works challenging the reader's habitual reliance on a didactic or guiding narrator.

Turning from values to aims and methods, whether politically activist or culturally subversive, a primary objective across countercultural groups was to raise the public's awareness of oppression and its sources. Called "consciousness expansion" by exponents of the psychedelic movement, "raising awareness" by the New Left, and "consciousness raising" by feminists, it was a necessary first step towards effecting real, revolutionary change. Indeed, for many – Leary amongst them – it was the only really essential step. "[C]hange consciousness, change life!": an idea, as Todd Gitlin points out, rooted in the philosophies of Emerson and Thoreau.[7] While Pynchon is certainly aligned with the counterculture at large in seeing consciousness expansion as an important goal, he takes an independent approach to achieving this. Different counterculture groups employed various means of generating public understanding of and sympathy for the revolutionary cause, many of which, as discussed, attract some degree of criticism from Pynchon. Kerouac's *On the Road* promoted escape into the landscape as a simple catalyst for opening the mind to new possibilities of thought, belief, and action, but for Pynchon it seems that the co-optation of the American road to capitalist ends had put paid to this idea, subverting its anarchic promise. Nor was Leary's attempted solution to the problem via a reorientation of the escape route towards internal reality unproblematic. Despite Leary's pronouncements on the difficulty of remaining "dropped out," this form of consciousness expansion is also, the author suggests, both too simple and offers too personal an experience, rendering it conducive to a politically detrimental escapism or hedonism. Moreover, the tool used to effect it, LSD, carries dangers if not used carefully and responsibly. Repeatedly, Pynchon's novels suggest that we cannot circumvent hard work and struggle in effecting significant sociopolitical change.

In seeming to preclude escapism, the direct activism of the New Left might have offered a more viable alternative methodology. Working locally and on the ground, certain New Left organisations would have met with a degree of approval from the author. But again, Pynchon's support is only partial, his fiction pointing to excessive idealism, violence, a lack of awareness of the subtler, more psychological forms of capitalist influence and repression, and also, perhaps, the fragmentation caused by the splitting off of the women's movement, as causes for the overall failure of the New Left. In any case, Pynchon shows little interest in marches, sit-ins, and the like, which despite their ubiquity in the sixties, have negligible presence in his work. Pynchon's own approach to realising positive change, his preferred political methodology, is writing. In both his fiction and journalism Pynchon offers up the written word as trigger for thought, fantasy, and debate towards increased understanding and awareness. This is not, as Seán Molloy claims, an advocation of "a transcendent flight from politics."[8] Thomas's opposing perspective, that "categories such as metaphysics, magic, dream and myth (which are crucial to any reading of Pynchon) … become serious political categories in themselves with material effects inside and outside the dominant political reality" is far more apt.[9] As my analysis of *Against the Day* suggests, Pynchon would consider the heightening of awareness, often achieved via intrusions of the extraliteral, conducive to the adoption of anarchist attitudes and possibly to the eventual overthrow of the capitalist power monopoly. The complexity and irrealism of his novels (and, indeed, of much of his journalism) combines with their emphasis on lesser-known historical episodes, scientific discoveries, or world cultures to counter the socially instilled escapist drives of the reader, while providing, as we have seen, a positive liberation from the routine and the ordinary. In communicating its multifaceted vision, Pynchon's fiction demands effort from its readers and fosters greater awareness and creativity, all of which are essential, the author implies, to effective political action. In this Pynchon definitively gives the lie to the idea that postmodern writing is disinterested in political change, or, as Linda Hutcheon suggested, incapable of proposing practical routes towards this.[10] In fact, his fiction demonstrates how the formal and stylistic innovations of postmodernist literature can be grounded in deeply political considerations and fundamentally motivated by the desire to challenge those assumptions and expectations in readers which reflect the naturalisation of contemporary capitalist culture.

In taking this approach Pynchon by no means distinguishes or distances himself from the counterculture. The political value of art was asserted by many oppositional groups in the sixties; during that decade, at least, the boundaries between the aesthetic, the cultural, and the political were removed or made indistinct. Art supported activism, and activism began to operate in terms of metaphor: flowers were put into the barrels of guns, dollar bills were rained down on the New York stock exchange, a pig received a presidential nomination. Oppositional groups engaged in street theatre and "expressive politics" in order to spread their message; style, colour, and even fun all took on a subversive relevance. Pynchon drew inspiration, no doubt, from such crossovers, as well as from particular works affirming art's practical, motivational potential, including Kerouac's *On the Road* and Simon Rodia's "Watts Towers," discussed in this study. Moreover, as Pynchon's work suggests in both form and content, art can offer a political model. His novels, like the "Watts Towers" or the jazz music he admires, operate on a social anarchist principle. In his discussion of politics and literature quoted in the introduction, Italo Calvino described certain works of literature as influential in their "ability to impose patterns of language, of vision, of imagination, of mental effort, of the correlation of facts, and in short the creation ... of a model of values that is at the same time aesthetic and ethical, essential to any plan of action especially in political life."[11] Each and every Pynchon novel has this ability, which is perhaps epitomised within his *oeuvre* by *Against the Day*.

Returning to the question of the possibility of influencing politics through literature broached in the introduction, it seems that Pynchon is comparatively more hopeful in his later career, having apparently come to believe more strongly in the power of imagining positive alternatives to what is. Thus *The Crying of Lot 49*'s hesitation between nihilism and affirmation – "[b]ehind the hieroglyphic streets there would either be a transcendent meaning, or only the earth" (*L49* 125) – is replaced in the epigraph to *Inherent Vice* by the triumphant "Under the paving-stones, the beach!" Furthermore, enemies become progressively more identifiable in Pynchon's fiction, and the action of the protagonist less and less stultified by misunderstanding. In *V.* Stencil never discovers the truth about V., just as in *Lot 49* Oedipa remains in the dark about the elusive and ambiguously evil Trystero, only just managing to recover from the total disorientation that overwhelms her as her paranoia reaches its climax towards the end of novel. Slothrop in *Gravity's Rainbow* has more luck, discovering the mechanism of his psychological oppression and its perpetrator Lazlo Jamf, and manoeuvring to have his pursuer, the bigoted Major Marvy, castrated. In *Vineland* Prairie joins an alternative community which enjoys a certain independence from state control, and in *Mason & Dixon*

Dixon enacts his dissent against systems of oppression in attacking a slave driver. *Against the Day* features the arch-capitalist Scarsdale Vibe, who acts as the root of all evil throughout and ends up being shot dead by his own assistant, and in *Inherent Vice* Doc performs what can only be described as a heroic escape from his persecutors and succeeds in fatally wounding them. Reflecting this progression towards more decisive, purposive protagonists, the whole tenor of the later novels is less sinister. From *Vineland* onwards they read much more lightly, there are more comic (rather than black comic) moments, the atmosphere is less oppressive – as several commentators have noted, some of Pynchon's more recent work even appears sentimental.

Whether Pynchon's greater optimism is at all warranted by recent political developments remains unclear, but his critics and readers can certainly look forward to the further unravelling of the author's model of values. This book, I hope, stands alongside the published critical work discussed in the introduction in drawing attention to the depth and sincerity of Pynchon's political engagement with his times, in helping us to realise, as Kathryn Hume does, that "Pynchon is not just a quirky bearer of 1960s banners; rather his political vision is complex and is emerging as a serious core value in his work, however much the literary and aesthetic fireworks have obscured that fact."[12] There is still much work to be done in this field, which will, no doubt, offer up many more avenues of investigation and foster stimulating discussion for years to come. The significance of Pynchon's relationship with the sixties counterculture is by no means exhausted by this study or the related criticism that predates it. Furthermore, while the 1960s are the most relevant decade to a discussion of Pynchon's politics, other eras offer comparable contextual insights. Pynchon's novels aim to communicate to us a political vision of reality both inspirational and enraging, enigmatic and demanding, and we must continue to rise to their interpretative challenge.

Notes

Introduction

1 Linda Hutcheon coined the term "historiographic metafiction" in *A Poetics of Postmodernism: History, Theory, Fiction* (London: Routledge, 1988).
2 Thomas Pynchon, *Slow Learner* (1984; repr. London: Vintage, 1995), 18–19. Hereafter cited in text.
3 In *Slaughterhouse-5* writing an "anti-war" book is compared to writing an "anti-glacier" book in its chances of stopping the phenomenon. In *My Death My Life by Pier Paolo Pasolini*, Kathy Acker describes the artist as "powerless" while a repressive society retains "the hype." See Kurt Vonnegut, Jr., *Slaughterhouse-5, or The Children's Crusade* (1969; repr. London: Vintage, 2000), 3, and Kathy Acker, *My Death My Life by Pier Paolo Pasolini*, excerpted in *Essential Acker, the Selected Writings of Kathy Acker*, ed. Amy Scholder and Dennis Cooper (New York: Grove Press, 2002), 201.
4 Thomas Pynchon, *Gravity's Rainbow* (1973; repr. London: Vintage, 1995), 155. Hereafter cited in text.
5 Shorter pieces addressing Pynchon's politics have been appearing in journals for many years. Recent examples include Molly Hite's "'Fun Actually Was Becoming Quite Subversive': Herbert Marcuse, the Yippies, and the Value System of *Gravity's Rainbow*," *Contemporary Literature* 51, no. 4 (2010): 677–702, and Seán Molloy's "Escaping the Politics of the Irredeemable Earth – Anarchy and Transcendence in the Novels of Thomas Pynchon," *Theory & Event* 13, no. 3 (2010): n. p., http://muse.jhu.edu.ezproxy.sussex.ac.uk/journals/theory_and_event/v013/13.3.molloy.html.
6 Kathryn Hume, "Thomas Pynchon: Reading from the Margins," *Studies in the Novel* 37, no. 1 (Spring 2005): par. 2, http://gateway.proquest.com/openurl?ctx_ver=Z39.88-2003&xri:pqil:res_ver=0.2&res_id=xri:lion&rft_id=xri:lion:ft:abell:R03544941:0.
7 Sam Thomas, *Pynchon and the Political* (New York: Routledge, 2007), 128.
8 David Cowart, *Thomas Pynchon and the Dark Passages of History* (Athens and London: University of Georgia Press, 2011), 85.
9 Victor Strandberg, "Dimming the Enlightenment: Thomas Pynchon's *Mason & Dixon*," in *Pynchon and "Mason & Dixon,"* ed. Brooke Hovarth and Irving Malin (Newark: University of Delaware Press, 2000), 103.

10 Andrew Gordon, "Smoking Dope with Thomas Pynchon: A Sixties Memoir," in *The Vineland Papers: Critical Takes on Pynchon's Novel*, ed. Geoffrey Green, Donald J. Greiner, and Larry McCaffery (Normal, IL: Dalkey Archive Press, 1994), 168.

11 Todd Gitlin, *The Sixties: Years of Hope, Days of Rage* (New York: Bantam Books, 1987), 243.

12 Leary said this in a television interview available online: "Meeting Thomas Pynchon," YouTube video clip, http://www.youtube.com/watch?v=tSJ1Pzzhwmw. The confluence between the outlooks of Leary and Pynchon this suggests is explored in Chapter 3 of this study.

13 Cowart's chapter is a reworking and elaboration of an earlier article entitled "Pynchon and the Sixties" and published in *Critique* 41, no. 1 (1999): 3–13. See Jeffrey S. Baker, "A Democratic Pynchon: Counterculture, Counterforce and Participatory Democracy," *Pynchon Notes* 32–33 (1993): 99–131, and Frederick Ashe, "Anachronism Intended: *Gravity's Rainbow* in the Sociopolitical Sixties," *Pynchon Notes* 28–29 (1991): 59–75.

14 Thomas H. Schaub, *Pynchon: The Voice of Ambiguity* (Urbana: University of Illinois Press, 1981), 150–1, 152.

15 Thomas, *Pynchon and the Political*, 11.

16 Alan Wilde, "Love and Death in and around Vineland, U. S. A.," *boundary 2* 18, no. 2 (1991): 169–70.

17 Linda Hutcheon, *The Politics of Postmodernism*, 2nd ed. (Oxon: Routledge, 2002), 3.

18 I would note, however, that although I consider Pynchon deeply serious politically, I do not suggest that his work is entirely motivated by political goals. Often his desire is simply to entertain or interest us.

19 Molloy, "Escaping the Politics," par. 3.

20 Charles Hollander, "Pynchon's Politics: The Presence of an Absence," *Pynchon Notes* 26–27 (1990): par. 2, http://www.vheissu.net/art/art_eng_SL_hollander.htm.

21 Ibid., par. 3.

22 Amongst those critics who agree with me on this point is David Cowart, who claims in the "Pynchon and the Sixties" chapter of his recent monograph that "Pynchon makes his political sympathies plain enough," and that Pynchon is "an author who leaves his readers in no doubt regarding his attitude towards racism, oppressive economic practices, genocidal violence, skullduggery in high places, and police-state repression." *Thomas Pynchon and the Dark Passages of History*, 121, 84.

23 Italo Calvino, "Right and Wrong Political Uses of Literature," in *Literature in the Modern World: Critical Essays and Documents*, ed. Dennis Walder (Oxford: Oxford University Press, 1990), 101.

24 Schaub, *Pynchon: The Voice of Ambiguity*, 152.

25 See Victor Turner, *The Ritual Process: Structure and Anti-Structure* (New York: Aldine, 1969), 127.

26 Students for a Democratic Society, *The Port Huron Statement* (Chicago: Charles H. Kerr, 1990), 8, 7. First published 1962.

27 See Karl Marx, "The British Rule in India," *New-York Daily Tribune*, 25 June 1853, 5.
28 Theodore Roszak, *The Making of a Counterculture: Reflections on the Technocratic Society and Its Youthful Opposition* (Doubleday: New York, 1969), 42.
29 Alexander Bloom, "Why Read about the 1960s at the Turn of the Twenty-first Century?," introduction to *Long Time Gone: Sixties America Then and Now*, ed. Alexander Bloom (Oxford: Oxford University Press, 2001), 8.
30 Roszak, *The Making of a Counterculture*, 64.
31 Molloy, "Escaping the Politics," par. 3.
32 In creating this list I draw primarily on the aforementioned works by Roszak, Bloom, Gitlin, as well as on Charles A Reich's *The Greening of America* (London: Penguin, 1971), Jerome Klinkowitz's *The American 1960s: Imaginative Acts in a Decade of Change* (Ames: Iowa State University Press, 1980), Assar Lindbeck's *The Political Economy of the New Left: An Outsider's View*, 2nd ed. (New York: Harper & Row, 1977), and David Farber, ed., *The Sixties: From Memory to History* (Chapel Hill and London: University of North Carolina Press, 1994).

1 On the Road to Anti-Structure

1 Civil rights activists were, of course, also extremely influential on the sixties counterculture, as discussed at greater length in the fourth chapter of this book.
2 As recounted by Kerouac in a 1959 interview by Al Aronowitz, "St. Jack (Annotated by Jack Kerouac)," in *Conversations with Jack Kerouac*, ed. Kevin J. Hayes (Jackson: University Press of Mississippi, 2005), 31.
3 Dana Heller, "Holy Fools, Secular Saints, and Illiterate Saviors in American Literature and Popular Culture," *CLCWeb: Comparative Literature and Culture* 5, no. 3 (2003): 11, http://docs.lib.purdue.edu/clcweb/vol5/iss3/4/.
4 Jack Kerouac, *On the Road* (London: Penguin, 2003), 38. First published 1957. Hereafter cited in text.
5 See Pierre-Yves Petillon, "A Re-cognition of Her Errand into the Wilderness," in *New Essays on "The Crying of Lot 49,"* ed. Patrick O'Donnell (Cambridge: Cambridge University Press, 1991), 127–70.
6 Ibid., 130.
7 David Cowart, *Thomas Pynchon: The Art of Allusion* (Carbondale: Southern Illinois University Press, 1980), 29.
8 William Burroughs, interview by Philippe Mikriammos, "The Last European Interview," in *Conversations with William S. Burroughs*, ed. Allen Hibbard (Jackson: University Press of Mississippi, 1999), 82.
9 Ibid.
10 Richard Pearce, *The Novel in Motion: An Approach to Modern Fiction* (Columbus: Ohio State University Press, 1983), xii.
11 Originally inspired by the intensely energetic rhythm of the sparsely punctuated prose of a letter written by Neal Cassady (which, in Kerouac's view at the time, was "painfully necessary" in its quality of intrinsic openness),

"spontaneous prose" was a style which matched form to content, recreating the experience of velocity and immediacy and enabling a greater connection between author and reader. See Jack Kerouac, "Essentials of Spontaneous Prose," *Evergreen Review* 2 (1958): 72–3. Quotation taken from a letter from Kerouac to Neal Cassady, excerpted in Ann Charters's introduction to Kerouac, *On the Road*, xviii.

12 Allen Ginsberg, "Kaddish," in *Beat Collection*, ed. Barry Miles (London: Virgin Books, 2005), 112.
13 For an in-depth discussion of mobility's fundamental role in the American imago see John A. Kouwenhoven, *The Beer Can by the Highway: Essays on What's American about America* (Garden City, NY: Doubleday, 1961).
14 As Ronald Primeau argues in *Romance of the Road: The Literature of the American Highway* (Bowling Green, OH: Bowling Green State University Popular Press, 1966), ix, 1.
15 Norman Mailer, "The White Negro: Superficial Reflections on the Hipster," *Dissent* 4, no. 3 (1957): sec. 1, par. 3; sec. 4, par. 3, http://www.dissentmagazine.org/online.php?id=26.
16 William Burroughs quoted in Charters's introduction to Kerouac, *On the Road*, xxvii.
17 Thomas Pynchon, *The Crying of Lot 49* (1966; repr. London: Vintage, 2000), 118. Hereafter cited in text.
18 Gilles Deleuze and Félix Guattari, *A Thousand Plateaus*, trans. Brian Massumi (New York: Continuum, 2004), 13.
19 Despite his attraction to Beat poetry, as he makes clear in the *Slow Learner* introduction, Pynchon also admired modernist literature, which was after all not diametrically opposed to that of the Beats, and in his own postmodern prose the influence of both literary schools is evident (*SL 9*).
20 Howard Cunnell, "Fast This Time: Jack Kerouac and the Writing of *On the Road*," introduction to *On the Road: The Original Scroll*, by Jack Kerouac (London: Penguin, 2007), 4.
21 Thomas Pynchon, *V.* (1963; repr. London: Vintage, 2000), 55. Hereafter cited in text.
22 Allen Ginsberg, "Howl," in *Howl and Other Poems* (San Francisco: City Lights, 1956), 9–28, 10.
23 Joseph W. Slade, *Thomas Pynchon* (New York: P. Lang, 1990), 73.
24 Wittgenstein made this assertion in his *Tractatus Logico-Philosophicus*, first published in 1921.
25 The word "ambiguous" has etymological roots in "*ambigere* go round, wander about, argue, f. *amb-* both ways + *agere* drive." C. T. Onions, ed., *The Oxford Dictionary of English Etymology* (London: Oxford University Press, 1966), 30.
26 Relevant to this is Pierre-Yves Petillon's suggestion that the forty-nine-day duration of the novel's action can refer to both the interim period preceding Pentecost, "when the Holy Ghost, speaking in a babble of voices, will typologically foreshadow the Day of Doom and ultimate revelation," and to the time it takes for "the newly deceased [to] slowly work their way toward final death and rest" according to the Tibetan *Book of the Dead*. "A Re-cognition," 137.

27 Kouwenhoven, *The Beer Can by the Highway*, 19, 16.
28 The unrolling or unreeling road is a recurrent image in *On the Road*.
29 Lawrence Ferlinghetti, "In Goya's Greatest Scenes We Seem to See," in *A Coney Island of the Mind* (New York: New Directions, 1958), 9.
30 Thomas Pynchon, *Mason & Dixon* (London: Vintage, 1998), 448. Hereafter cited in text.
31 Edward Mendelson, "The Sacred, the Profane, and *The Crying of Lot 49*," in *Thomas Pynchon: A Collection of Critical Essays*, ed. Edward Mendelson (Englewood Cliffs, NJ: Prentice-Hall, 1978), 117.
32 Stephen Prothero describes them thus in "On the Holy Road: The Beat Movement as Spiritual Protest," *The Harvard Theological Review* 84, no. 2 (1991): 208.
33 Timothy Gray, *Gary Snyder and the Pacific Rim: Creating Countercultural Community* (Iowa City: University of Iowa Press, 2006), 38.
34 For a good biography of Kerouac see Ann Charters, *Kerouac: A Biography* (New York: St. Martin's Press, 1994).
35 John Clellon Holmes quoted in Charters, introduction to Kerouac, *On the Road*, xxix.
36 Ann Charters notes the public focus on the character of Dean Moriarty in her introduction to Kerouac, *On the Road*, ix.
37 In later novels Pynchon seems to take a slightly more generous view of Buddhism. In *Against the Day*, for instance, Buddhist practice offers Kit access to a dubiously useful but nonetheless magical transcendent experience, described with imaginative vibrancy. See Chapter 3 of this study.
38 Onions, ed., *The Oxford Dictionary of English Etymology*, 38.
39 Heller, "Holy Fools, Secular Saints," 10.
40 See Amy J. Elias, "Plots, Pilgrimage, and the Politics of Genre in *Against the Day*," in *Pynchon's "Against the Day": A Corrupted Pilgrim's Guide*, ed. Jeffrey Severs and Christopher Leise (Newark: University of Delaware Press, 2011), 29–46.
41 See Prothero, "On the Holy Road," 205–22, and Steve Wilson, "The Author as Spiritual Pilgrim: The Search for Authenticity in Jack Kerouac's *On the Road* and *The Subterraneans*," in *The Beat Generation: Critical Essays*, ed. Kostas Myrsiades (New York: Peter Lang, 2002), 77–91.
42 Prothero, "On the Holy Road," 211.
43 Ben Giamo, *Kerouac, the Word and the Way: Prose Artist as Spiritual Quester* (Carbondale: University of Southern Illinois Press, 2000), 3.
44 Victor Turner, "The Center out There: Pilgrim's Goal," *History of Religions* 12, no. 3 (1973): 214.
45 Well respected in his field, the work of Turner is also drawn upon by Amy J. Elias and Stephen Prothero in their respective analyses of the role of the pilgrimage in Pynchon's *Against the Day* and Beat literature.
46 Arnold van Gennep, *The Rites of Passage*, quoted in Turner, *The Ritual Process*, 94.
47 Ibid., 95.
48 Ibid., 127.

49 Ibid., 95.
50 Ibid.
51 Ibid.
52 Ibid., 112.
53 Ibid., 112–13.
54 *The Ritual Process* confirms the experience of "anti-structure" as providing a positive balance in our structured, hierarchical human societies. In many of the social groups Turner observed, there occurred rites of "status reversal," which were often carried out at particular times of year, coinciding with festivals, for example. Their function was to redress the established balance between weak and powerful, allowing everyone to understand the value of their role or the nature of their privilege. In such rites, the shared experience of liminality "implies that the high could not be high unless the low existed, and he who is high must experience what it is like to be low." It is "a matter of giving recognition to an essential and generic human bond, without which there could be *no* society" (97). Turner does not suggest that humans can function without structure, but that effective social relations require an element of anti-structure; as he explains, "[c]ommunitas, with its unstructured character, representing the 'quick' of human interrelatedness, what Buber has called *das Zwischenmenschliche*, might well be represented by the 'emptiness at the center,' which is nevertheless indispensable to the functioning of the structure of the wheel" (127).
55 Michael Sean Bolton provides a fascinating analysis of alienation as a tool of revolt in Burroughs's work in "From Self-Alienation to Posthumanism: The Transmigration of the Burroughsian Subject," in *The Philosophy of the Beats*, ed. Sharin N. Elkholy (Lexington: University of Kentucky Press, 2012), 65–78, 66.
56 Ginsberg, "A Supermarket in California," in Miles, ed., *Beat Collection*, 98.
57 Stephen Prothero argues that for Kerouac and Ginsberg, Neal Cassady personified "the sacred connections of *communitas*." "On the Holy Road," 214.
58 Pierre-Yves Petillon also considers Oedipa's experience to be one of liminality, likening it, further, to a rite of passage as described by Van Gennep. He does not, however, connect such liminality with either communitas or the Beat sensibility. See "A Re-cognition," 137.
59 Prothero, "On the Holy Road," 212.
60 Petillon, "A Re-cognition," 131.
61 See, for instance, Jon Panish's discussion of such stereotyping in one of Kerouac's later novels in "Kerouac's *The Subterraneans*: A Study of 'Romantic Primitivism'" *MELUS* 19, no. 3 (Autumn 1994): 107–23.
62 The role of jazz within Kerouac's novel has been the subject of a substantial amount of critical commentary. See, for instance, Douglas Malcolm, "'Jazz America': Jazz and African American Culture in Jack Kerouac's *On the Road*," *Contemporary Literature* 40, no. 1 (1999): 85–110.
63 Erik R. Mortenson, "Beating Time: Configurations of Temporality in Jack Kerouac's *On the Road*," in Myrsiades, ed., *The Beat Generation*, 72.

64 For Turner, "*existential* or *spontaneous* communitas," which corresponds to that intuitive feeling of oneness with humanity and unchannelled anarchy we have been describing, is one of three possible forms communitas can take. The second form is "normative communitas," which is a toned-down version of the first form. It is still a feeling of brotherhood but it has to some extent been normalised; structures have been formed which reduce its effect – as when a pilgrimage route becomes established and businesses spring up along the route to cater to the passing traveller, making the pilgrimage more an experience of ordered anti-structure. The third form is "ideological communitas," which involves utopian imaginings of more organised societies which would allow for maximum existential communitas. As Turner explains, existential communitas tends to decline into its normative form, and is thus a rare and transient experience. *The Ritual Process*, 132.

65 Ginsberg, "Howl," 21.

66 Kerouac to Lawrence Ferlinghetti, 25 May 1961, in *Jack Kerouac: Selected Letters 1957–1969*, ed. Ann Charters (New York: Viking Penguin, 1999), 291.

67 Kerouac to Fernanda Pivano, early 1964, in Charters, ed., *Selected Letters 1957–1969*, 377.

68 Further evidence of this is available in Charters, introduction to Kerouac, *On the Road*, ix.

69 Jack Kerouac in conversation with an anonymous interviewer, "On the Road Back: How the Beat Generation Got That Way, According to Its Seer," *San Francisco Examiner*, 5 October 1958, *Highlight* sec., 18.

70 SDS, *The Port Huron Statement*, 8, 7.

71 Ibid., 9.

72 Ibid., 11.

2 Love, Violence, and Yippie Subversion in *Gravity's Rainbow*

1 SNCC, "SNCC Position Paper: Vietnam," in *The Sixties Papers: Documents of a Rebellious Decade*, ed. J. C. Albert and S. E. Albert (New York: Praeger, 1984), 117–18. Reprinted from *The Movement*, January 1966.

2 SDS, *The Port Huron Statement*, 7.

3 See Introduction, pp. 12–13.

4 For a detailed modern history of the New Left see John McMillian and Paul Buhle, eds., *The New Left Revisited* (Philadelphia: Temple University Press, 2003).

5 Pynchon's comment is reprinted in Clifford Mead, *Thomas Pynchon: A Bibliography of Primary and Secondary Materials* (Elmwood Park, IL: Dalkey Archive, 1989), 44. Frederick Ashe also draws attention to this endorsement, which he describes as "Pynchon's most explicit identification with New Left thought," in "Anachronism Intended," 63.

6 See David Witzling, *Everybody's America: Thomas Pynchon, Race, and the Cultures of Postmodernism* (New York: Routledge, 2008); Baker, "A Democratic Pynchon," 99–131; Sean McCann and Michael Szalay, "Do You Believe in

Notes to pages 41–50

Magic? Literary Thinking after the New Left," *The Yale Journal of Criticism* 18, no. 2 (2005): 435–68; and Ashe, "Anachronism Intended," 59–75.

7   Thomas Pynchon, introduction to *Been Down So Long It Looks Like Up To Me* (1983), by Richard Fariña (1966; repr. London: Penguin, 1996), vi–vii.

8   Thomas Pynchon, "A Journey into the Mind of Watts," *The New York Times Magazine*, 12 June 1966, 78. Hereafter cited in text.

9   As Howard Zinn recounts in *SNCC: The New Abolitionists* (Cambridge, MA: South End Press, 2002), 12.

10 The phrase comes from a 1964 pamphlet "An Interracial Movement of the Poor?," co-authored by Tom Hayden and Carl Wittman and distributed by SDS.

11 See Richard Rothstein, "A Short History of ERAP," University of California Calisphere, http://content.cdlib.org/view?docId=kt4k4003k7.

12 For a detailed account of SDS history see Gitlin, *The Sixties*.

13 Thomas Pynchon, "The Heart's Eternal Vow," *The New York Times*, 10 April 1988, http://www.nytimes.com/1988/04/10/books/the-heart-s-eternal-vow.html?scp=1&sq=heart%27s+eternal+vow+pynchon+marquez&st=nyt#.

14 SDS, *The Port Huron Statement*, 12; SNCC, "SNCC: Founding Statement," in Albert and Albert, eds., *The Sixties Papers*, 113.

15 Stephen Gaskin quoted in James J. Farrell, *The Spirit of the Sixties: The Making of Postwar Radicalism* (New York: Routledge, 1997), 216.

16 Leo Bersani, "Pynchon, Paranoia, and Literature," *Representations* 25 (1989): 103.

17 Ibid., 109.

18 Ibid., 104.

19 Nadine Attewell, "'Bouncy Little Tunes': Nostalgia, Sentimentality, and Narrative in *Gravity's Rainbow*," *Contemporary Literature* 45, no. 1 (2004): 33.

20 Ibid., 33–4.

21 Thomas Pynchon, *Inherent Vice* (London: Jonathan Cape, 2009), 5. Hereafter cited in text.

22 Quoted in Simon Wells, *Charles Manson: Coming Down Fast* (London: Hodder and Stoughton, 2009), 122.

23 Ibid.

24 Ibid., 123.

25 Bersani, "Pynchon, Paranoia, and Literature," 104.

26 A related close reading of this episode appears in Stefan Mattessich's *Lines of Flight: Discursive Time and Countercultural Desire in the Work of Thomas Pynchon* (Durham, NC and London: Duke University Press, 2002), 95–113.

27 Wes Chapman, "Male Pro-Feminism and the Masculinist Gigantism of *Gravity's Rainbow*," *Postmodern Culture* 6, no. 3 (1996): par. 11.

28 Pynchon's formulation of this theory of pornographies may well have been influenced by Herbert Marcuse and Norman O. Brown's related discussions of sexual repression in modern society mentioned earlier.

29 Chapman, "Male Pro-Feminism," par. 10.

30 Ibid.

31 For a discussion of Pynchon's frustration of detective genre expectations in *The Crying of Lot 49* see, for instance, Theodore D. Kharpertian, "*The Crying of Lot 49*: History as Mail Conspiracy," in *A Hand to Turn the Time: The Menippean Satires of Thomas Pynchon* (Cranbury, NJ: Associated University Presses, 1990), 85–107.

32 The motto "an army of lovers cannot lose" was used on placards by the Gay Liberation Movement, and appears in related official manifestoes. In the "Statement of the Male Homosexual Workshop" to the Revolutionary People's Constitution Convention (5–7 September 1970), for example, it appears before the list of demands. This statement is reprinted in Mark Blasias and Shane Phelan, eds., *We Are Everywhere: A Historical Sourcebook in Gay and Lesbian Politics* (New York: Routledge, 1997), 402–3. As Stephen Weisenburger notes, the motto seems to derive from Plato's *Symposium*, "in which Phaedrus argues that an army of (homosexual) lovers *cannot* be beaten. As he puts it: 'If only there were a way to start a city or an army made up of lovers and the boys they love! Theirs would be the best possible system of society, for they would hold back from all that is shameful, and seek honor in each other's eyes. Even a few of them, in battle side by side, would conquer the world, I'd say.'" Stephen Weisenburger, *A "Gravity's Rainbow" Companion: Sources and Contexts for Pynchon's Novel*, 2nd ed. (Athens: University of Georgia Press, 2006), 108.

33 Bernard Duyfhuizen, "'God Knows, Few of Us Are Strangers to Moral Ambiguity': Thomas Pynchon's *Inherent Vice* (review)," *Postmodern Culture* 19, no. 2 (2009): par. 1. Frederick Ashe interprets the slogan in analogous fashion as mimicking the Weathermen's "ostentatious contempt for the hippie resolve to 'make love not war,'" in "Anachronism Intended," 66.

34 Mattessich, *Lines of Flight*, 113.

35 Critics who have taken this position include George Levine in his essay "Risking the Moment: Anarchy and Possibility in Pynchon's Fiction," in *Mindful Pleasures: Essays on Thomas Pynchon*, ed. George Levine and David Leverenz (Boston: Little Brown, 1976), 113–34, and Peter L. Cooper in *Signs and Symptoms: Thomas Pynchon and the Contemporary World* (Berkeley: University of California Press, 1983).

36 Thomas Pynchon, *Against the Day* (2006; repr. London: Vintage, 2007), 417. Hereafter cited in text.

37 Ashe, "Anachronism Intended," 66.

38 Steven Weisenburger considers the German president a reference to Paul von Hindenburg, president of Germany 1925–34, basing this on the attribution to him of a "clogged and nasal voice" (*GR* 158) for which von Hindenburg was well known. However, Germany was not at war during these years, and although it increased its military spending, von Hindenburg would have had no reason to ask for a "war appropriation." Richard Nixon also had an unusual, clogged voice (which Pynchon's onomatopoeic name for him in this novel, Richard M. Zhlubb, suggests the author had an appreciation for) and while von Hindenburg may well be the historical reference, there are

considerable grounds for considering Nixon the contemporary analogue. See Weisenburger, *A "Gravity's Rainbow" Companion*, 109.
39 Gitlin, *The Sixties*, 124.
40 Rosa Luxemburg and Nikolai I. Bukharin, *The Accumulation of Capital – An Anti-Critique: Imperialism and the Accumulation of Capital*, ed. Kenneth J. Tarbuck, trans. Rudolf Wichmann (New York: Monthly Review Press, 1972), 62.
41 As A. J. Ryder notes in *The German Revolution of 1918: A Study of German Socialism in War and Revolt* (Cambridge: Cambridge University Press, 1967), 27. See Luxemburg, *The Accumulation of Capital*.
42 Tony Cliff, introduction to *Rosa Luxemburg*, by Paul Frölich, trans. J. Hoornweg (Chicago, IL: Haymarket Books, 2010), x.
43 See Rosa Luxemburg, "The Militia and Militarism" (1899), in *Rosa Luxemburg: Selected Political Writings*, ed. Robert Looker (London: Jonathon Cape, 1972), 76–92.
44 Mark Rudd, "The Death of SDS," par. 17, http://www.markrudd.com/?sds-and-weather/the-death-of-sds.html.
45 Paul Frölich quotes Luxemburg's *Gesammelte Werke IV*, in which she asserts that "[v]iolence is and remains the *ultima ratio* (last resort) even for the working class." See Frölich, *Rosa Luxemburg*, 69. As Kathryn Hume argues, Pynchon expresses a very similar view of political violence in *Against the Day*, a standpoint which I suggest in Chapter 4 is actually well established earlier in his career. See Kathryn Hume, "The Religious and Political Vision of *Against the Day*," in Severs and Leise, eds., *Pynchon's "Against the Day*," 168.
46 Luxemburg, letter to Karl Kautsky, 1 September 1904, quoted in Frölich, *Rosa Luxemburg*, 70.
47 Gitlin, *The Sixties*, 134–5.
48 Molly Hite, "'Fun Was Actually Becoming Quite Subversive': Herbert Marcuse, the Yippies, and the Value System of *Gravity's Rainbow*," *Contemporary Literature* 51, no. 4 (2010): 677.
49 Bersani, "Pynchon, Paranoia, and Literature," 103–4.
50 Ibid.
51 Weisenburger, *A "Gravity's Rainbow" Companion*, 6.
52 Jerry Rubin, "Yippie Manifesto" (1969), free pamphlet published by The Not Guilty Bookshop, 3.
53 Jerry Rubin, "Yippie Manifesto" (1968), in *Takin' It to the Streets: A Sixties Reader*, ed. Alexander Bloom and Wini Breines (Oxford: Oxford University Press, 1995), 324. (This "Yippie Manifesto," published a year earlier, differs from that listed in the previous note.)
54 See especially Baker, "A Democratic Pynchon."
55 See the following chapter for a fuller discussion of the role of Situationist theory in Pynchon's work.
56 Thomas Moore argues that this metaphor works to undermine the notion of the "Romantic self," in *The Style of Connectedness: "Gravity's Rainbow" and Thomas Pynchon* (Columbia: University of Missouri Press, 1987), 199.

57 The term "Thermidor" here relates to the "Thermidorian Reaction" of the French Revolution and connotes an ebbing away of revolutionary zeal.
58 Tom Wolfe, "Radical Chic: That Party at Lenny's," *New York Magazine*, 8 June 1970, http://nymag.com/news/features/46170/.
59 Rubin, "Yippie Manifesto" (1969), 12. In the same pamphlet Rubin also relates his reaction to a girl picketing a George Wallace rally. Telling her that she was "legitimizing" Wallace by picketing, Rubin advises her instead to "support him, kiss him. When he says the next hippie in front of his car will be the last hippie, cheer! Loudly!" (10).
60 The idea that unplanned actions may be more effective than organised demonstrations is further supported by what might be termed the primary narrative in *Gravity's Rainbow* because Slothrop repeatedly relies on spontaneous ingenuity as well as on coincidence in evading his pursuer Major Marvy and finally putting him out of action. This is also true of Pynchon's latest "hero," the hippie private detective Doc Sportello, in his encounters with the Golden Fang in *Inherent Vice*.

3 The Psychedelic Movement, Fantasy, and Anarchism in *The Crying of Lot 49* and *Against the Day*

1 As Todd Gitlin contends, "[f]or Leary and Alpert, all political systems were equal oppressors and power-trippers." *The Sixties*, 208.
2 Timothy Leary, *Flashbacks: An Autobiography* (Los Angeles: J. P. Tarcher, 1983), 67.
3 Timothy Leary, *The Politics of Ecstasy* (1968; repr. Berkeley, CA: Ronin, 1990), 1. Hereafter cited in text.
4 See Chapter 1 for a discussion of Pynchon's perspective on the viability of accessing freedom through spatial motion.
5 For an engaging and objective biography of Timothy Leary see John Higgs, *I Have America Surrounded: The Life of Timothy Leary* (London: Friday Books, 2006).
6 I refer here especially to R. D. Laing's *The Politics of Experience and the Bird of Paradise* (1967) and Norman O. Brown's *Life against Death: The Psychoanalytical Meaning of History* (1959) and *Love's Body* (1966).
7 Aldous Huxley, *The Doors of Perception: Heaven and Hell* (London: Thinking Ink, 2011), 8. First published 1956.
8 Ibid., 35.
9 Ibid., 35–6.
10 Leary coined this popular counterculture motto in September 1966 at a press conference he gave in New York City.
11 Gitlin, *The Sixties*, 208.
12 Higgs, *I Have America Surrounded*, 76.
13 As Tom Wolfe describes, Kesey and the Pranksters got a slightly frosty reception from Leary's followers when they stopped off at Millbrook during their journey around America in their psychedelic school bus. According to Wolfe, while the

Pranksters were "expecting the most glorious reception ever," the atmosphere when they arrived was friendly but cool, and Leary himself declined to emerge from the three-day acid trip he was engaged in. It was as if members of Leary's League for Spiritual Discovery were thinking, "We have something rather deep and meditative going on here, and you California crazies are a sour note." *The Electric Kool-Aid Acid Test* (New York: Bantam, 1969), 93–4.

14 Quotations are taken from the version of this lecture published as "The Seven Tongues of God" in *The Politics of Ecstasy*, 55–6.
15 Richard Alpert was sacked from Harvard a month later. Higgs, *I Have America Surrounded*, 56.
16 See, for instance, Cooper, *Signs and Symptoms*, 78.
17 See also Gordon, "Smoking Dope with Thomas Pynchon."
18 Cyrus R. K. Patell, *Negative Liberties: Morrison, Pynchon, and the Problem of Liberal Ideology* (Durham, NC and London: Duke University Press, 2001), 146.
19 Petillon, "A Re-Cognition," 127. As he further explains, the Leary influence did not stop with one character: 1966 "was the year when Dr. Leary, spurred on by Marshall McLuhan, coined his slogan 'Turn On, Tune In, Drop Out' – and at the time this seemed a fairly adequate summary of the story told in *The Crying of Lot 49*" (127).
20 This particular headline appeared on the cover of *Life* magazine, 25 March 1966.
21 Martin Mayer, "Getting Alienated with the Right Crowd at Harvard," quoted in Leary, *The Politics of Ecstasy*, 72–3.
22 Stephen Bello, "Timothy Leary," *The Harvard Crimson*, 13 October 1965, http://www.thecrimson.com/article/1965/10/13/timothy-leary-ptalking-to-timothy-leary/.
23 Higgs, *I Have America Surrounded*, 88.
24 His specific argument is that "[t]he behaviorism and experimentalism of twentieth-century western psychology is so narrow as to be mostly trivial. Consciousness is eliminated from the field of inquiry. Social application and social meaning are largely neglected. … Eastern psychology, by contrast, offers us a long history of detailed observation and systematization of the range of human consciousness along with an enormous literature of practical methods for controlling and changing consciousness." Timothy Leary, Ralph Metzner, and Richard Alpert in *The Psychedelic Experience: A Manual Based on The Tibetan Book of the Dead* (London: Penguin, 2008), 9. First published 1964.
25 Timothy Leary, "Timothy Leary Revisited," interview by Paul Krassner, in *Paul Krassner's Impolite Interviews* (New York: Seven Stories Press, 1999), 304.
26 It might be argued that Pynchon is in fact criticising certain aspects of Leary's career via the tale of Hilarius's involvement in severely unethical experiments at Buchenwald. Leary has been accused of involvement in the MK-ULTRA programme of CIA-led mind control experiments utilising LSD. However, I think that any similarity here must be purely coincidental; it is highly unlikely given the dates involved that Pynchon could have known anything about

such experiments, the details of which were not made public until 1977, or have suspected Leary's involvement. At the time of *The Crying of Lot 49*'s publication, Leary was very popular amongst the counterculture, and Pynchon would more probably have absorbed a positive view of Leary from his Beat supporters, among them in particular Allen Ginsberg, himself a major figure in the psychedelic movement.

27 As described in Leary, Metzner, and Alpert, *The Psychedelic Experience*, 12. Petillon does not relate *The Tibetan Book of the Dead* to *The Psychedelic Experience*. Petillon, "A Re-cognition," 137.

28 Pynchon also refers to the *Book of the Dead* in *Vineland* (specifying that it is the Tibetan *Book* or the *Bardo Thödol* he is referring to, not the Egyptian equivalent) in connection with its role as guidebook for "the soul newly in transition." Thomas Pynchon, *Vineland* (London: Secker & Warburg, 1990), 218. Hereafter cited in text.

29 Chris Hall, "'Behind the Hieroglyphic Streets': Pynchon's Oedipa Maas and the Dialectics of Reading," *Critique* 33, no. 1 (1991): 70.

30 See Leary, Metzner, and Alpert, *The Psychedelic Experience*, 52.

31 Ibid., 60–1.

32 Ibid., 103.

33 Gitlin, *The Sixties*, 253.

34 Frank Kermode, "Decoding the Trystero," in Mendelson, ed., *Pynchon: A Collection of Critical Essays*, 163. Oedipa as reader or literary critic is also discussed in Hall, "Behind the Hieroglyphic Streets," 63–77, Alfred MacAdam, "Pynchon as Satirist: To Write, To Mean," *Yale Review* 67, no. 4 (1978): 555–66, and C. E. Nicholson and R. W. Stevenson, "'Words You Never Wanted to Hear': Fiction, History and Narratology in *The Crying of Lot 49*," *Pynchon Notes* 16 (1985): 83–7.

35 Melissa Lam, *Disenfranchised from America: Reinventing Language and Love in Nabokov and Pynchon* (Lanham, MD: University Press of America, 2009), 42.

36 Roszak, *The Making of a Counterculture*, 217.

37 Of course, Roszak's ideas here are deeply rooted in the political theory of Marx and the Frankfurt School.

38 Farrell, *The Spirit of the Sixties*, 208.

39 Baker, "A Democratic Pynchon," 119.

40 See my comments on postmodernism, political agency, and Linda Hutcheon's arguments in *The Politics of Postmodernism* in the introduction to this study.

41 Thomas, *Pynchon and the Political*, 33.

42 Graham Benton, "Daydreams and Dynamite: Anarchist Strategies of Resistance and Paths for Transformation in *Against the Day*," in Severs and Leise, eds., *Pynchon's "Against the Day*," 198.

43 Patricia A. Bergh, "(De)constructing the Image: Thomas Pynchon's Postmodern Woman," *Journal of Popular Culture* 30, no. 4 (Spring 1997): 5.

44 Ibid.

45 See Robert E. Kohn, "Seven Buddhist Themes in Pynchon's *The Crying of Lot 49*," *Religion and Literature* 35, no. 1 (Spring 2003): 73–96, and Kathryn Hume,

"Books of the Dead: Postmortem Politics in Novels by Mailer, Burroughs, Acker, and Pynchon," *Modern Philology* 97, no. 3 (2000): 417–44.
46 Justin St. Clair describes the Itinerary thus in "Binocular Disparity and Pynchon's Panoramic Paradigm" in Severs and Leise, eds., *Pynchon's "Against the Day,"* 87.
47 Douglas Fowler, *A Reader's Guide to "Gravity's Rainbow"* (Ann Arbor, MI: Ardis Press, 1980), 55. Fowler uses this phrase to describe *Gravity's Rainbow*.
48 Thomas, *Pynchon and the Political*, 56.
49 See the second chapter of this book.
50 Guy Debord, *Society of the Spectacle* (Detroit: Black & Red, 1983), par. 1.
51 Ibid., par. 6, par. 143.
52 Ibid., par. 15.
53 For an in-depth discussion of Pynchon's relationship with "white liberal guilt," albeit earlier in his career, see David Witzling, "The Sensibility of Postmodern Whiteness in *V*, or Thomas Pynchon's Identity Problem," *Contemporary Literature* 47, no. 3 (2006): 381–415.
54 This in turn recalls again Oedipa's experience with the epileptic sailor in *The Crying of Lot 49*, who, "[c]ammed each night out of that safe furrow the bulk of this city's waking each sunrise again set virtuously to plowing," causes Oedipa to wonder "what rich soils had he turned, what concentric planets uncovered?" (*L49* 87). But there are two differences: whereas Oedipa's experience is vicarious, Lew's is direct; while the sailor's experience seems to be, as discussed, relatively destructive and isolating, Lew's is productive and leads to political engagement.
55 A quote from *The Psychedelic Experience* from the section "Instructions for the Wrathful Visions": "O nobly born, listen carefully: / You were unable to maintain the perfect Clear Light of the First Bardo. / Or the serene peaceful visions of the Second. / You are now entering Second Bardo nightmares. / Recognize them. / They are your own thought-forms made visible and audible. / They are products of your own mind with its back to the wall. / They indicate that you are close to liberation. / Do not fear them. / No harm can come to you from these hallucinations. / They are your own thoughts in frightening aspect. / They are old friends. / Welcome them. Merge with them. Join them. / Lose yourself in them. / They are yours. / *Whatever* you see, no matter how strange and terrifying, / Remember above all that it comes from within you. / Hold onto that knowledge. / As soon as you recognize that, you will obtain liberation" (110).
56 Reinforcing the analogy between light and destructive power that runs throughout *Against the Day*, the "Interdikt" has a certain genealogy in Pynchon's fiction, a proposal for the light weapon L-5227, "a new airborne ray which could turn whole populations, inside a ten-kilometer radius, stone blind" (*GR* 163), being rejected by *Gravity's Rainbow*'s plutocrats for the repercussions it would have on the dye market.
57 Pierre-Joseph Proudhon, *What is Property? An Inquiry into the Principle and Right of Government*, eds. Donald R. Kelley and Bonnie G. Smith (Cambridge: Cambridge University Press, 1994), 209. First published 1840.

58 Daniel Guérin, *Anarchism: From Theory to Practice*, trans. Mary Klopper (New York: Monthly Review Press, 1970), 16–17. For Proudhon and Bakunin this state was communist, whereas for Pynchon it was capitalist, reflecting the sociopolitical situation in their respective home countries.
59 Mikhail Bakunin, "Deuxième discours au deuxième Congres de la Pais et de la Liberté," 23 September 1868, quoted in Guérin, *Anarchism*, 22.
60 Ruth Kinna, *Anarchism: A Beginner's Guide* (Oxford: Oneworld, 2005), 3.
61 Benton, "Daydreams and Dynamite," 191. Benton's doctoral thesis on the topic has also recently been published in book form. See Graham Benton, *Unruly Narratives: The Anarchist Dimension in the Novels of Thomas Pynchon* (Saarbrücken, Germany: LAP Lambert, 2012).
62 Kinna, *Anarchism*, 3–4.
63 Peter Kropotkin, *Anarchism: A Collection of Revolutionary Writings* (New York: Dover, 2002), 293.
64 Paul Avrich, *Anarchist Portraits* (Princeton, NJ: Princeton University Press, 1988), 243.
65 Seán Molloy also describes these differing views on anarchist violence in *Against the Day* in his article "Escaping the Politics of the Irredeemable Earth."
66 See the first and second chapters of this study for related discussions of other instances of such anarchic synchronicity.
67 Farrell, *The Spirit of the Sixties*, 229.
68 Michael Lerner, "Anarchism and the American Counter-Culture," *Government and Opposition* 5, no. 4 (October 1970): 431.
69 Wolfe, *The Electric Kool-Aid Acid Test*, 125.
70 Leary, Metzner, and Alpert, *The Psychedelic Experience*, 43.
71 Molloy opines that "[d]espite his obviously sympathetic representation of Anarchist communities in *Against the Day*, e.g., the Yz-les-Bains collective, Pynchon's ultimate statement on the politics of resistance is one of rejection due to the futility of idealist schemes in relation to human realities," in "Escaping the Politics of the Irredeemable Earth," par. 29.
72 Benton, "Daydreams and Dynamite," 191.

4 The Black Panther Party, Revolutionary Suicide, and *Gravity's Rainbow*

1 SDS, *The Port Huron Statement*, 7.
2 Charles A. Reich, *The Greening of America* (London: Penguin, 1971), 164, 197.
3 Such clues include the insistent association of the Trystero with the colour black, their status as a threatening, subversive presence in white America, and their designation as "disinherited," a term often used (by such prominent commentators as W. E. B. Du Bois and Malcolm X) to describe the situation of African Americans in the United States.
4 Gerald Horne speculates that Pynchon might have written "A Journey" in direct response to some of the more bizarre explanations for Watts, in *Fire This Time: The Watts Uprising and the 1960s* (Charlottesville and London: University Press of Virginia, 1995), 39.

5 See letter from Pynchon to Thomas F. Hirsch, 8 January 1969, in David Seed, *The Fictional Labyrinths of Thomas Pynchon* (Basingstoke: MacMillan, 1988), 241. In such a view racial politics is secondary to a politics of consciousness, the ultimate aim being to homogenise the world in America's image, enabling the unopposed rise of free market capitalism.

6 See p. 78.

7 The Black Panther Party, "The Black Panther Party: Platform and Program," in *The Sixties Papers: Documents of a Rebellious Decade*, eds. J. C. Albert and S. E. Albert (New York: Praeger, 1984), 159–64. Reprinted from *The Black Panther*, 5 July 1969.

8 Huey P. Newton, *Revolutionary Suicide* (New York: Harcourt Brace Jovanovich, 1973), 70. Hereafter cited in text.

9 Charles E. Jones and Judson L. Jeffries, "'Don't Believe the Hype': Debunking the Panther Mythology," in *The Black Panther Party [Reconsidered]*, ed. Charles E. Jones (Baltimore, MD: Black Classic Press: 1998), 27.

10 Henry Hampton and Steve Fayer describe the Panthers' uniform in *Voices of Freedom: An Oral History of the Civil Rights Movement from the 1950s through the 1980s* (New York: Bantam, 1990), 351.

11 Gitlin, *The Sixties*, 348, 350.

12 Quite why this conversation is staged between these two characters rather than between members of Schwarzkommando is a matter for speculation. One interpretation might be that his choice of dialogists allows Pynchon to more readily connect Panther ideology back to those classical political standpoints – the Marxist and the Capitalist.

13 Dialectical materialism is one of the central tenets of Marxist thought. Essentially it is a materialist reconception of Hegel's idealist dialectics. Dialectical materialism considers the movement of history to occur as a result of material factors, developing in stages as successive revolutions impel society towards communism. For a detailed description of dialectical materialism and its genesis see (e.g.) Paul Thomas, *Marxism and Scientific Socialism: From Engels to Althusser* (New York: Routledge, 2008), 86–105.

14 Newton is described thus in The Huey P. Newton Foundation, *The Black Panther Party: Service to the People Programs*, ed. David Hilliard (Albuquerque: University of New Mexico Press, 2008), 129.

15 As Newton himself notes in *Revolutionary Suicide*, 5.

16 This was published in 1973, the same year as *Gravity's Rainbow*. The concept of "revolutionary suicide" had already been publicised, however, via an edited collection of Newton's writings, *To Die for the People*, published in 1972, and via Newton's prison interviews which were released on Paredon Records in January 1970.

17 Karl Marx, *Critique of Hegel's "Philosophy of Right,"* ed. Joseph O'Malley, trans. Annette Jolin and Joseph O'Malley (Cambridge: University of Cambridge Press, 1977), 131. First published 1843.

18 Michael L. Clemons and Charles E. Jones describe the speech thus in "Global Solidarity: The Black Panther Party in the International Arena," in *Liberation*,

Imagination, and the Black Panther Party: A New Look at the Panthers and Their Legacy, eds. Kathleen Cleaver and George Katsiaficas (New York: Routledge, 2001), 27.
19 Huey P. Newton, "Speech Delivered at Boston College," 18 November 1970, in *The Huey P. Newton Reader*, eds. David Hilliard and Donald Weise (New York: Seven Stories Press, 2002), 163.
20 Ibid., 166.
21 Ibid., 165.
22 Karl Marx, "The British Rule in India," *New-York Daily Tribune*, 25 June 1853, 5.
23 See Chapter 2.
24 David Witzling arrives at a very similar point by reading Pynchon's critique of colonial brutality alongside his mention of the Counterforce's cooption into dominant power structures – as symbolised by the *Wall Street Journal*. See Witzling, *Everybody's America*, 156–7.
25 Lawrence C. Wolfey, "Repression's Rainbow: The Presence of Norman O. Brown in Pynchon's Big Novel," *PMLA* 92, no. 5 (October 1977): 878.
26 A group called the "Otzovists" appears in *Against the Day*. The historical Otzovists were a Marxist faction with anarchist and humanist leanings which split from Lenin's Bolsheviks (Lenin first elaborated the theory of dialectical materialism). In *Against the Day* they are believers in the fourth dimension and as such they are anti-materialist.
27 Hume, "The Religious and Political Vision," 168.
28 Ibid., 185.
29 Herbert Marcuse, *Counterrevolution and Revolt* (Boston: Beacon Press, 1972), 53. Marcuse's use of the term "revolutionary suicide" here is not original, but refers to Newton's theory. The larger context of the quoted passage is a discussion of the contemporary oppositional practices of the New Left.
30 Ashe, "Anachronism Intended," 67.
31 Judson L. Jeffries, *Huey P. Newton: The Radical Theorist* (Jackson: University Press of Mississippi, 2002), 43.
32 This phrase has been discussed critically with reference to the life of Christ. See, for example, Kathryn Hume, "Views from Above, Views from Below: The Perspectival Subtext in *Gravity's Rainbow*," *American Literature* 60, no. 4 (December 1988): 625–42. While I agree with such interpretations in that Christ is clearly an important referent here, I suggest that the contemporary sociopolitical frame is equally, if not more, important to a rounded understanding of the Schwarzkommando narrative.
33 Jenifer Warren, "Former Black Panther Eldridge Cleaver Dies at 62," *The Los Angeles Times*, 2 May 1998, http://articles.latimes.com/1998/may/02/news/mn-45607.
34 Pynchon's concept of charisma is closely tied to his reading of Max Weber. William M. Plater has written on this subject in *The Grim Phoenix: Reconstructing Thomas Pynchon* (Bloomington: Indiana University Press, 1978).

35 Gitlin, *The Sixties*, 342.
36 Ibid., 351.
37 Witzling, *Everybody's America*, 168.
38 Ibid., 168.
39 Debord, *The Society of the Spectacle*, par. 57.
40 Jones and Jeffries, "Don't Believe the Hype," 41–3.
41 "The Black Panther Coloring Book" can be found online at http://www.nd.edu/~dmyers/courses/old/102au98/blpan.html.
42 Much of this controversy was triggered by an article published by Arthur R. Jenson in which he claimed that "on the average, Negroes test about 1 standard deviation (15 IQ points) below the average of the white population in IQ." "How Much Can We Boost IQ and Scholastic Achievement?," *Harvard Educational Review* 39, no. 1 (Winter 1969): 81.
43 Huey P. Newton, "A Spokesman for the People: In Conversation with William F. Buckley" (1973), in Hilliard and Weise, eds., *The Huey P. Newton Reader*, 282.

5 Feminism Moderate and Radical in *The Crying of Lot 49* and *Vineland*

1 The National Organization for Women (NOW), "Statement of Purpose" (1966), in *"It Changed My Life": Writings on the Women's Movement*, by Betty Friedan (Cambridge, MA: Harvard University Press, 1998), 112.
2 Valerie Solanas, *SCUM Manifesto* (Edinburgh: AK Press, 1996), 1. First published 1967.
3 Gitlin, *The Sixties*, xvii.
4 Christopher Gair, *The American Counterculture* (Edinburgh: Edinburgh University Press, 2007), 9.
5 Debra Michals, "From 'Consciousness Expansion' to 'Consciousness Raising': Feminism and the Countercultural Politics of the Self," in *Imagine Nation: The American Counterculture of the 1960s and '70s*, eds. Peter Braunstein and Michael William Doyle (New York: Routledge, 2002), 41–68, 45.
6 For Friedan educational functionalism taught women that their only role in society was that of the housewife, its aim being to maintain the social structure as it was. See Betty Friedan, *The Feminine Mystique* (1963; repr. Harmondsworth: Penguin, 1983), Chapter 7: "The Functional Freeze."
7 Daniel Horowitz, *Betty Friedan and the Making of "The Feminine Mystique": The American Left, the Cold War, and Modern Feminism* (Amherst: University of Massachusetts Press, 2000), 226.
8 Oedipa's resemblance to a Friedanian housewife has been noted by Cathy N. Davidson in her article "Oedipa as Androgyne in Thomas Pynchon's *The Crying of Lot 49*," *Contemporary Literature* 18, no. 1 (Winter 1977): 38–50. Other critics, including Charles Hollander and Thomas Schaub, have noted the relevance of Friedan's work as a (countercultural) context for the novel. See Thomas H. Schaub, "Influence and Incest: Relations between *The Crying*

of Lot 49 and *The Great Gatsby*," in *Thomas Pynchon: Reading from the Margins*, ed. Niran Abbas (Madison, NJ: Fairleigh Dickenson University Press, 2003), 152, and Charles Hollander, "Pynchon, JFK and the CIA: Magic Eye Views of *The Crying of Lot 49*," *Pynchon Notes* 40–41 (1997): 61.

9 In a related reading, Tracey Sherard discusses the abundance of "linguistic tags" designating the female in the opening to the novel. "The Birth of the Female Subject in *The Crying of Lot 49*," *Pynchon Notes* 32–33 (1993): 61.

10 The reproductive cycle as leitmotif in *The Crying of Lot 49* is discussed by Dana Medoro in her study of menstruation in modern novels *The Bleeding of America: Menstruation as Symbolic Economy in Pynchon, Faulkner, and Morrison* (Westport, CT: Greenwood Press, 2002), 35.

11 Davidson, "Oedipa as Androgyne," 40–1; Sherard, "The Birth of the Female Subject," 60–74.

12 Oedipa does suffer somewhat from vulnerability, but this is not an exclusively feminine quality in the novel.

13 Alice A. Jardine, *Gynesis: Configurations of Woman and Modernity* (Ithaca, NY and London: Cornell University Press, 1985), 252. Stefan Mattessich may be another exception here. Discussing Pynchon's apparently parodic use of misogyny in his first novel, Mattessich remains undecided as to whether this expresses a level of misogyny on the author's part. See Stefan Mattessich, "Imperium, Misogyny, and Postmodern Parody in Thomas Pynchon's *V.*," *ELH* 65, no. 2 (Summer 1998): 503–21.

14 Molly Hite, "Feminist Theory and the Politics of *Vineland*," in Green, Greiner, and McCaffery, eds., *The Vineland Papers*, 136. Indeed Hite locates sexism in each of Pynchon's first three novels, with reference to "*V.*'s perversity, Oedipa's vulnerability, and *Gravity's Rainbow*'s use of women as sexual icons on the periphery of the rocket's monolithic phallic signification," as described by her reviewer Donald Brown in "A Pynchon for the Nineties," *Poetics Today* 18, no. 1 (Spring 1997): 103. In this Hite's analysis runs directly counter to that of Marjorie Kaufman who, albeit in rather underwhelming fashion, asserts that Pynchon "give[s] a fair shake to his women characters" in each of his first three novels. Marjorie Kaufman, "Brünnehilde and the Chemists: Women in *Gravity's Rainbow*," in Levine and Leverenz, eds., *Mindful Pleasures: Essays on Thomas Pynchon*, 199.

15 David Cowart describes the parallels between the biographies of Pynchon and Oedipa in "Pynchon and the Sixties," 9.

16 Friedan, *The Feminine Mystique*, 164.

17 Ibid., 16.

18 Ibid., 211.

19 This tendency of Oedipa's to seek male help remains strong throughout the novel, evincing the depth of her conditioning to passive femininity, as Cathy N. Davidson has noted in "Oedipa as Androgyne," 43.

20 Friedan, *The Feminine Mystique*, 179–80.

21 Ibid., 113.

22 Friedan devotes chapter 11 of *The Feminine Mystique*, "The Sex-Seekers," to this topic.

23 Tracey Sherard links the Trystero to women more generally, noting how Emory Bortz's description of their tendency to "silence, impersonation, opposition masquerading as allegiance" (*L49* 120) recalls "the position women have been forced into in our culture." "The Birth of the Female Subject," 72. As discussed in Chapter 4, the Trystero also encapsulates allusions to Black Power.
24 Davidson, "Oedipa as Androgyne," 38–50.
25 Ibid., 45.
26 Friedan, *The Feminine Mystique*, 181.
27 Horowitz, *Betty Friedan*, 253.
28 Rachel Bowlby, "'The Problem with No Name': Rereading Friedan's *The Feminine Mystique*," *Feminist Review* 27 (Autumn 1987): 71.
29 Friedan, *The Feminine Mystique*, 181.
30 Gitlin, *The Sixties*, 365.
31 Ibid., 367.
32 Ibid., 371.
33 Robin Morgan, "Goodbye to All That" (1970), reprinted in Albert and Albert, eds., *The Sixties Papers*, 513, 515.
34 Alice Echols considers both Todd Gitlin and Tom Hayden, in their respective accounts of the decade *The Sixties: Years of Hope, Days of Rage* and *Reunion: A Memoir*, to take an ultimately negative view of the women's movement as contributing to the decline of the (more important) New Left. This attitude, she further argues, "plays a role … in the diminished narrative status accorded to the women's liberation movement in sixties books." See "'We Gotta Get Out of This Place': Notes toward a Remapping of the Sixties," in *Cultural Politics and Social Movements*, eds. Marcy Darnovsky, Barbara Epstein, and Richard Flacks (Philadelphia: Temple University Press, 1995), 110–32, 114.
35 See Chapter 4.
36 Maren Lockwood Carden provides further details pertaining to this schism in *The New Feminist Movement* (New York: Russell Sage, 1974).
37 Morgan, "Goodbye to All That," 514.
38 Genie Plamondon, "Hello to All That" (1970), reprinted in Albert and Albert, eds., *The Sixties Papers*, 522.
39 Germaine Greer, *The Female Eunuch* (London: Harper Perennial, 2006), 74. First published 1970.
40 Shulamith Firestone, *The Dialectic of Sex: The Case for Feminist Revolution* (London: Women's Press, 1980), 19.
41 As Frederick Ashe points out, Pynchon's depiction of Leni's group of pre–Second World War communist revolutionaries "as mildly alienated by the '*male supremacy*' of their cohorts … allud[es] to the origins of Women's Liberation among disgruntled participants in the youth movement." Ashe, "Anachronism Intended," 66.
42 Vond asserts this, we learn, because of his own fear of mortality. Thus, again, Pynchon gives a problem that would seem to be female specific a universal dimension.

43 Ti-Grace Atkinson, *Amazon Odyssey* (New York: Links Books, 1974), vii.
44 Firestone, *The Dialectic of Sex*, 19.
45 Bernice E. Lott, "Who Wants the Children?: Some Relationships among Attitudes toward Children, Parents, and the Liberation of Women," *American Psychologist* 28 (July 1973): 573.
46 Frenesi apparently refers to the Spanish *frenesí*, which has these meanings.
47 See Attewell, "Bouncy Little Tunes."
48 Graham Benton offers a differing interpretation of Webb's parental choices in his essay "Daydreams and Dynamite," 205–6.
49 In his introduction to *Slow Learner* Pynchon hints that he now has parenting experience (*SL* 10).
50 Jocelyn Elise Crowley, *Defiant Dads: Fathers' Rights Activists in America* (Ithaca, NY: Cornell University Press, 2008), 37.
51 Plaskow continues to recount the more submissive Eve's creation from Adam's rib following Lilith's departure; how Lilith attempted to rejoin the human community in the garden, engaged in battle with Adam, and was defeated; how Eve, filled with curiosity following her witnessing of this battle, began to visit Lilith outside the garden walls, developing a bond of sisterhood with her, and making both Adam and God ill at ease. See Judith Plaskow, "The Coming of Lilith: Toward a Feminist Theology," in *The Coming of Lilith: Essays on Feminism, Judaism, and Sexual Ethics, 1972–2003*, eds. Judith Plaskow and Donna Berman (Boston: Beacon Press, 2005), 23–34, 31–2.
52 The novel's essential concern over the equality of the sexes is further affirmed by the narrator's mention of the pay divide, of American women's "59¢ on the male dollar" (*VL* 345).
53 Hite, "Feminist Theory," 136.
54 For an analysis of the relevance of these references see ibid., 136–9.
55 Something which, as Hite points out, Rochelle herself appears to be aware of, her thesis being put forward "tactically and perhaps only provisionally." Ibid., 146.
56 Carrie Pitzulo, "The Battle in Every Man's Bed: *Playboy* and the Fiery Feminists," *Journal of the History of Sexuality* 17, no. 2 (May 2008): 270.
57 Greer, *The Female Eunuch*, 343–4. See also Judith Brown and Beverly Jones, *Toward a Female Liberation Movement* (Boston: New England Free Press, 1968).
58 Kate Millett draws on Robert J. Stoller's research in one of the earliest feminist assertions of "the overwhelmingly *cultural* character of gender" in *Sexual Politics* (1970; repr. Urbana: University of Illinois Press, 2000), 29.
59 John D. Caputo, ed., *Deconstruction in a Nutshell: A Conversation with Jacques Derrida* (New York: Fordham University Press, 1997), 104.
60 Robin Morgan, *Going Too Far: The Personal Chronicle of a Feminist* (New York: Random House, 1977), 169.
61 Andrea Dworkin and Catharine A. MacKinnon, *Pornography and Civil Rights: A New Day for Women's Equality* (Minneapolis: Organizing Against Pornography: 1988), 134.

62 Barbara Dority, "Feminist Moralism, Pornography and Censorship," (lecture given at several universities and colleges), http://privat.ub.uib.no/bubsy/dority.htm.
63 Pynchon's preference for ambiguity on such matters, his tendency to leave it up to the reader to decide, is well known. As Kathryn Hume asserts, through Pynchon's prose "[w]e learn to accept uncertainty, make personal arrangements of local order, and go with the flow." Kathryn Hume, *Pynchon's Mythography: An Approach to Gravity's Rainbow* (Carbondale: Southern Illinois University Press, 1987), 201.
64 Mattessich, "Imperium, Misogyny," 514.
65 Curiously, looking over the story as a whole, there are only a couple of dubiously racist or proto-fascist elements – Bollingbroke's position as garbage man and his description as stereotypically wearing a pork-pie hat; Nerissa's worship of Dennis, a tall, blond "Anglo" – which pale in comparison with the depth of the story's misogyny. With regard to this, it is untenable to suggest that the Pynchon of 1984 has somehow forgotten what he wrote, even though "Low-lands" was written nearly thirty years previously, because he mentions rereading the stories – to his considerable embarrassment – at the start of the introduction.
66 It may be objected, at this point, that there is a substantial question mark over the authenticity of Pynchon's commentary in the *Slow Learner* introduction. Mark Hawthorne, for example, contends that Pynchon "may well write disingenuously" in constructing the modest self-portrait he offers us. Pynchon being a serial prankster, it is entirely feasible that this is the case in at least some parts of the introduction. In terms of my present argument, however, this would mean that Pynchon was either aiming to make himself appear more racist and proto-fascist than he was, on the basis of a superficial reading, or more sexist than he in fact was (in his evasions and explications), for those who would analyse closely. Quite why he would want to do this is rather difficult to comprehend. See Mark D. Hawthorne, "Pynchon's Early Labyrinths," *College Literature* 25, no. 2 (Spring 1998): 79.
67 Jeffrey Severs, "'The abstractions she was instructed to embody': Women, Capitalism and Artistic Representation in *Against the Day*," in Severs and Leise, eds., *Pynchon's "Against the Day*," 217, 234.
68 Ibid., 235, 217.
69 Ibid., 234–5.
70 Ibid., 235. Here Severs refers to a paper given by Stephen Hock at the Northeast Modern Language Association Convention in Buffalo, New York, in April 2008. The paper was entitled "*Against the Day* and 'The Eternally-Adolescent Male Mind' of Thomas Pynchon."
71 Ibid.

Conclusion

1 John A. McClure, "Do They Believe in Magic? Politics and Postmodern Literature," *boundary 2* 36, no. 2 (2009): 133–4.

2 Pynchon's respect for anarchism suggests, of course, that he would not sympathise with communism's faith in centralised organisation and bureaucracy, however.
3 This criticism tends to relate particularly to Pynchon's treatment of homosexuality as a perversion in *Gravity's Rainbow*. See, for instance, Julie Christine Sears, "Black and White Rainbows and Blurry Lines: Sexual Deviance/Diversity in *Gravity's Rainbow* and *Mason & Dixon*," in Abbas, ed., *Reading from the Margins*, 108–21, and Wolfey, "Repression's Rainbow," 873–89.
4 Thomas, *Pynchon and the Political*, 144.
5 Cowart, *Thomas Pynchon and the Dark Passages of History*, 161.
6 Thomas Pynchon, Introduction to *The Teachings of Don B.: Satires, Parodies, Fables, Illustrated Stories, and Plays of Donald Barthelme* (1992), ed. Kim Herzinger (Berkeley: Counterpoint, 2008), xx.
7 Gitlin, *The Sixties*, 213.
8 Molloy, "Escaping the Politics," par. 48.
9 Thomas, *Pynchon and the Political*, 9.
10 Hutcheon, *The Politics of Postmodernism*, 3.
11 Italo Calvino, "Right and Wrong Political Uses of Literature," 101.
12 Hume, "Thomas Pynchon: Reading from the Margins," par. 2.

Bibliography

Abbas, Niran, ed. *Thomas Pynchon: Reading from the Margins*. Madison, NJ: Fairleigh Dickinson University Press, 2003.

Acker, Kathy. *My Death My Life by Pier Paolo Pasolini*. 1984. Excerpted in *Essential Acker, the Selected Writings of Kathy Acker*, edited by Amy Scholder and Dennis Cooper, 185–201. New York: Grove Press, 2002.

Albert, J. C., and S. E. Albert, eds. *The Sixties Papers: Documents of a Rebellious Decade*. New York: Praeger, 1984.

Ashe, Frederick. "Anachronism Intended: *Gravity's Rainbow* in the Sociopolitical Sixties." *Pynchon Notes* 28–29 (1991): 59–75.

Atkinson, Ti-Grace. *Amazon Odyssey*. New York: Links Books, 1974.

Attewell, Nadine. "'Bouncy Little Tunes': Nostalgia, Sentimentality, and Narrative in *Gravity's Rainbow*." *Contemporary Literature* 45, no. 1 (2004): 22–48.

Avrich, Paul. *Anarchist Portraits*. Princeton, NJ: Princeton University Press, 1988.

Baker, Jeffrey S. "A Democratic Pynchon: Counterculture, Counterforce and Participatory Democracy." *Pynchon Notes* 32–33 (1993): 99–131.

Bakunin, Mikhail. "Deuxième discours au deuxième Congres de la Pais et de la Liberté." 23 September 1868.

Bello, Stephen. "Timothy Leary." *The Harvard Crimson*, 13 October 1965. http://www.thecrimson.com/article/1965/10/13/timothy-leary-ptalking-to-timothy-leary/.

Benton, Graham. "Daydreams and Dynamite: Anarchist Strategies of Resistance and Paths for Transformation in *Against the Day*." In Severs and Leise, eds., *Pynchon's "Against the Day,"* 191–213.

Bergh, Patricia A. "(De)constructing the Image: Thomas Pynchon's Postmodern Woman." *Journal of Popular Culture* 30, no. 4 (Spring 1997): 1–12.

Bersani, Leo. "Pynchon, Paranoia, and Literature." *Representations* 25 (1989): 99–118.

Black Panther Coloring Book, The. Unknown author. http://www.nd.edu/~dmyers/courses/old/1 02au98/blpan.html.

Black Panther Party, The. "The Black Panther Party: Platform and Program." In Albert and Albert, eds., *The Sixties Papers*, 159–64. Reprinted from *The Black Panther*, 5 July 1969.

Bloom, Alexander. *Long Time Gone: Sixties America Then and Now*. Oxford: Oxford University Press, 2001.

"Why Read about the 1960s at the Turn of the Twenty-first Century?" Introduction to Bloom, ed., *Long Time Gone*, 3–9.

Bolton, Michael Sean. "From Self-Alienation to Posthumanism: The Transmigration of the Burroughsian Subject." In *The Philosophy of the Beats*, edited by Sharin N. Elkholy, 65–78. Lexington: University of Kentucky Press, 2012.

Bowlby, Rachel. "'The Problem with No Name': Rereading Friedan's *The Feminine Mystique*." *Feminist Review* 27 (Autumn 1987): 61–75.

Brown, Donald. "A Pynchon for the Nineties." *Poetics Today* 18, no. 1 (Spring 1997): 95–112.

Brown, Judith, and Beverly Jones. *Toward a Female Liberation Movement*. Boston: New England Free Press, 1968.

Burroughs, William. "The Last European Interview." Interview by Philippe Mikriammos. In *Conversations with William S. Burroughs*, edited by Allen Hibbard, 80–9. Jackson: University Press of Mississippi, 1999.

Calvino, Italo. "Right and Wrong Political Uses of Literature." In *Literature in the Modern World: Critical Essays and Documents*, edited by Dennis Walder, 99–102. Oxford: Oxford University Press, 1990.

Caputo, John D., ed. *Deconstruction in a Nutshell: A Conversation with Jacques Derrida*. New York: Fordham University Press, 1997.

Carden, Maren Lockwood. *The New Feminist Movement*. New York: Russell Sage, 1974.

Chapman, Wes. "Male Pro-Feminism and the Masculinist Gigantism of *Gravity's Rainbow*." *Postmodern Culture* 6, no. 3 (1996): n. p.

Charters, Ann. Introduction (1991) to Kerouac, *On the Road*, vii–xxix.

———. *Kerouac: A Biography*. New York: St. Martin's Press, 1994.

Charters, Ann, ed. *Jack Kerouac: Selected Letters 1957–1969*. New York: Viking Penguin, 1999.

Clemons, Michael L., and Charles E. Jones. "Global Solidarity: The Black Panther Party in the International Arena." In *Liberation, Imagination, and the Black Panther Party: A New Look at the Panthers and their Legacy*, edited by Kathleen Cleaver and George Katsiaficas, 20–39. New York: Routledge, 2001.

Cliff, Tony. Introduction to Frölich, *Rosa Luxemburg*, ix–xi.

Cooper, Peter L. *Signs and Symptoms: Thomas Pynchon and the Contemporary World*. Berkeley: University of California Press, 1983.

Cowart, David. *Thomas Pynchon: The Art of Allusion*. Carbondale: Southern Illinois University Press, 1980.

———. "Pynchon and the Sixties." *Critique* 41, no. 1 (1999): 3–13.

———. *Thomas Pynchon and the Dark Passages of History*. Athens and London: University of Georgia Press, 2011.

Crowley, Jocelyn Elise. *Defiant Dads: Fathers' Rights Activists in America*. Ithaca, NY: Cornell University Press, 2008.

Cunnell, Howard. "Fast This Time: Jack Kerouac and the Writing of *On the Road*." Introduction to *On the Road: The Original Scroll*, by Jack Kerouac, 1–52. London: Penguin, 2007.

Davidson, Cathy N. "Oedipa as Androgyne in Thomas Pynchon's *The Crying of Lot 49.*" *Contemporary Literature* 18, no. 1 (Winter 1977): 38–50.
Debord, Guy. *The Society of the Spectacle.* Detroit: Black & Red, 1983.
Deleuze, Gilles, and Félix Guattari. *A Thousand Plateaus.* Translated by Brian Massumi. New York: Continuum, 2004.
Dority, Barbara. "Feminist Moralism, Pornography and Censorship." Lecture given at several universities and colleges. http://privat.ub.uib.no/bubsy/dority.htm.
Duyfhuizen, Bernard. "'God Knows, Few of Us Are Strangers to Moral Ambiguity': Thomas Pynchon's *Inherent Vice* (review)." *Postmodern Culture* 19, no. 2 (2009): n. p.
Dworkin, Andrea, and Catharine A. MacKinnon. *Pornography and Civil Rights: A New Day for Women's Equality.* Minneapolis, MN: Organizing Against Pornography, 1988.
Echols, Alice. "'We Gotta Get Out of This Place': Notes toward a Remapping of the Sixties." In *Cultural Politics and Social Movements*, edited by Marcy Darnovsky, Barbara Epstein, and Richard Flacks, 110–32. Philadelphia: Temple University Press, 1995.
Elias, Amy J. "Plots, Pilgrimage, and the Politics of Genre in *Against the Day.*" In Severs and Leise, eds., Pynchon's *"Against the Day,"* 29–46.
Farber, David, ed. *The Sixties: From Memory to History.* Chapel Hill and London: University of North Carolina Press, 1994.
Farrell, James J. *The Spirit of the Sixties: The Making of Postwar Radicalism.* New York: Routledge, 1997.
Ferlinghetti, Lawrence. "In Goya's Greatest Scenes We Seem to See." In *A Coney Island of the Mind*, 9–10. New York: New Directions, 1958.
Firestone, Shulamith. *The Dialectic of Sex: The Case for Feminist Revolution.* London: Women's Press, 1980.
Fowler, Douglas. *A Reader's Guide to "Gravity's Rainbow".* Ann Arbor, MI: Ardis Press, 1980.
Friedan, Betty. *The Feminine Mystique.* 1963. Reprint, Harmondsworth: Penguin, 1983.
Frölich, Paul. *Rosa Luxemburg.* Translated by J. Hoornweg. Chicago, IL: Haymarket Books, 2010.
Gair, Christopher. *The American Counterculture.* Edinburgh: Edinburgh University Press, 2007.
Giamo, Ben. *Kerouac, the Word and the Way: Prose Artist as Spiritual Quester.* Carbondale: University of Southern Illinois Press, 2000.
Ginsberg, Allen. "Howl." In *Howl and Other Poems*, 9–28. San Francisco: City Lights, 1956.
——. "Kaddish." In *Beat Collection*, edited by Barry Miles, 107–29. London: Virgin Books, 2005. First published 1961.
Gitlin, Todd. *The Sixties: Years of Hope, Days of Rage.* New York: Bantam Books, 1987.
Gordon, Andrew. "Smoking Dope with Thomas Pynchon: A Sixties Memoir." In Green, Greiner, and McCaffery, eds., *The Vineland Papers*, 167–78.

Gray, Timothy. *Gary Snyder and the Pacific Rim: Creating Countercultural Community*. Iowa City: University of Iowa Press, 2006.

Green, Geoffrey, Donald J. Greiner, and Larry McCaffery, eds. *The Vineland Papers: Critical Takes on Pynchon's Novel*. Normal, IL: Dalkey Archive Press, 1994.

Greer, Germaine. *The Female Eunuch*. London: Harper Perennial, 2006. First published 1970.

Guérin, Daniel. *Anarchism: From Theory to Practice*. Translated by Mary Klopper. New York: Monthly Review Press, 1970.

Hall, Chris. "'Behind the Hieroglyphic Streets': Pynchon's Oedipa Maas and the Dialectics of Reading." *Critique* 33, no. 1 (1991): 63–77.

Hampton, Henry, and Steve Fayer. *Voices of Freedom: An Oral History of the Civil Rights Movement from the 1950s through the 1980s*. New York: Bantam, 1990.

Hawthorne, Mark D. "Pynchon's Early Labyrinths." *College Literature* 25, no. 2 (Spring 1998): 78–93.

Hayden, Tom, and Carl Wittman. "An Interracial Movement of the Poor?" 1964. Pamphlet distributed by SDS.

Heller, Dana. "Holy Fools, Secular Saints, and Illiterate Saviors in American Literature and Popular Culture." *CLCWeb: Comparative Literature and Culture* 5, no. 3 (2003): 1–15. http://docs.lib.purdue.edu/clcweb/vol5/iss3/4/.

Higgs, John. *I Have America Surrounded: The Life of Timothy Leary*. London: Friday Books, 2006.

Hilliard, David, and Donald Weise, eds. *The Huey P. Newton Reader*. New York: Seven Stories Press, 2002.

Hite, Molly. "Feminist Theory and the Politics of *Vineland*." In Green, Greiner, and McCaffery, eds., *The Vineland Papers: Critical Takes on Pynchon's Novel*, 135–53.

——— "'Fun Actually Was Becoming Quite Subversive': Herbert Marcuse, the Yippies, and the Value System of *Gravity's Rainbow*." *Contemporary Literature* 51, no. 4 (2010): 677–702.

Hock, Stephen. "*Against the Day* and 'The Eternally-Adolescent Male Mind' of Thomas Pynchon." Presentation at the *Against the Day* panel. Northeast Modern Language Association Convention, Buffalo, NY. April 2008.

Hollander, Charles. "Pynchon's Politics: The Presence of an Absence." *Pynchon Notes* 26–27 (1990): 5–59. http://www.vheissu.net/art/art_eng_SL_hollander.htm.

Hollander, Charles, Hollander, Charles. "Pynchon, JFK and the CIA: Magic Eye Views of *The Crying of Lot 49*." *Pynchon Notes* 40–41 (1997): 61–106.

Horne, Gerald. *Fire This Time: The Watts Uprising and the 1960s*. Charlottesville and London: University Press of Virginia, 1995.

Horowitz, Daniel. *Betty Friedan and the Making of "The Feminine Mystique": The American Left, The Cold War, and Modern Feminism*. Amherst: University of Massachusetts Press, 2000.

Huey P. Newton Foundation, The. *The Black Panther Party: Service to the People Programs*. Edited by David Hilliard. Albuquerque: University of New Mexico Press, 2008.

Hume, Kathryn. *Pynchon's Mythography: An Approach to Gravity's Rainbow*. Carbondale: Southern Illinois University Press, 1987.
"Views from Above, Views from Below: The Perspectival Subtext in *Gravity's Rainbow*." *American Literature* 60, no. 4 (December 1988): 625–42.
"Books of the Dead: Postmortem Politics in Novels by Mailer, Burroughs, Acker, and Pynchon." *Modern Philology* 97, no. 3 (2000): 417–44.
"Thomas Pynchon: Reading from the Margins." *Studies in the Novel* 37, no. 1 (Spring 2005): n. p. http://gateway.proquest.com/openurl?ctx_ver=Z39.88-2003& xri:pqil:res_ver=0.2&res_id=xri:lion&rft_id=xri:lion:ft:abell:R03544941:0.
"The Religious and Political Vision of *Against the Day*." In Severs and Leise, eds., *Pynchon's "Against the Day,"* 167–89.
Hutcheon, Linda. *A Poetics of Postmodernism: History, Theory, Fiction*. London: Routledge, 1988.
The Politics of Postmodernism. 2nd ed. Oxon: Routledge, 2002.
Huxley, Aldous. *The Doors of Perception: Heaven and Hell*. London: Thinking Ink, 2011. First published 1956.
Jardine, Alice A. *Gynesis: Configurations of Woman and Modernity*. Ithaca, NY and London: Cornell University Press, 1985.
Jeffries, Judson L. *Huey P. Newton: The Radical Theorist*. Jackson: University Press of Mississippi, 2002.
Jenson, Arthur R. "How Much Can We Boost IQ and Scholastic Achievement?" *Harvard Educational Review* 39, no. 1 (Winter 1969): 1–123.
Jones, Charles E., and Judson L. Jeffries. "'Don't Believe the Hype': Debunking the Panther Mythology." In *The Black Panther Party [Reconsidered]*, edited by Charles E. Jones, 25–55. Baltimore, MD: Black Classic Press, 1998.
Kaufman, Marjorie. "Brünnehilde and the Chemists: Women in *Gravity's Rainbow*." In Levine and Leverenz, eds., *Mindful Pleasures: Essays on Thomas Pynchon*, 197–227.
Kermode, Frank. "Decoding the Trystero." In Mendelson, ed., *Pynchon: A Collection of Critical Essays*, 162–6.
Kerouac, Jack. *On the Road*. London: Penguin, 2003. First published 1957.
"Essentials of Spontaneous Prose." *Evergreen Review* 2, no. 5 (1958): 72–3.
"On the Road Back: How the Beat Generation Got That Way, According to Its Seer." Anonymous interview. *San Francisco Examiner*, 5 October 1958, *Highlight* sec., 18.
"St. Jack (Annotated by Jack Kerouac)." 1959. Interview by Al Aronowitz. In *Conversations with Jack Kerouac*, edited by Kevin J. Hayes, 10–36. Jackson: University Press of Mississippi, 2005.
Jack Kerouac to Lawrence Ferlinghetti, 25 May 1961. In Charters, ed., *Selected Letters 1957–1969*, 290–2.
Jack Kerouac to Fernanda Pivano, early 1964. In Charters, ed., *Selected Letters 1957–1969*, 377–8.
Kharpertian, Theodore D. "*The Crying of Lot 49*: History as Mail Conspiracy." In *A Hand to Turn the Time: The Menippean Satires of Thomas Pynchon*, 85–107. Cranbury, NJ: Associated University Presses, 1990.

Kinna, Ruth. *Anarchism: A Beginner's Guide*. Oxford: Oneworld, 2005.
Klinkowitz, Jerome. *The American 1960s: Imaginative Acts in a Decade of Change*. Ames: Iowa State University Press, 1980.
Kohn, Robert E. "Seven Buddhist Themes in Pynchon's *The Crying of Lot 49*." *Religion and Literature* 35, no. 1 (Spring 2003): 73–96.
Kouwenhoven, John A. *The Beer Can by the Highway: Essays on What's American about America*. Garden City, NY: Doubleday, 1961.
Kropotkin, Peter. *Anarchism: A Collection of Revolutionary Writings*. New York: Dover, 2002.
Lam, Melissa. *Disenfranchised from America: Reinventing Language and Love in Nabokov and Pynchon*. Lanham, MD: University Press of America, 2009.
Leary, Timothy, Ralph Metzner, and Richard Alpert. *The Psychedelic Experience: A Manual Based on The Tibetan Book of the Dead*. London: Penguin, 2008. First published 1964.
Leary, Timothy, *The Politics of Ecstasy*. 1968. Reprint, Berkeley, CA: Ronin, 1990.
Flashbacks: An Autobiography. Los Angeles: J. P. Tarcher, 1983.
"Meeting Thomas Pynchon." Interview by unidentified interviewer. YouTube video clip. http://www.youtube.com/watch?v=tSJ1Pzzhwmw.
Leary, Timothy, "Timothy Leary Revisited." Interview by Paul Krassner. In *Paul Krassner's Impolite Interviews*, edited by Paul Krassner, 301–9. New York: Seven Stories Press, 1999.
Lerner, Michael. "Anarchism and the American Counter-Culture." *Government and Opposition* 5, no. 4 (October 1970): 430–55.
Levine, George. "Risking the Moment: Anarchy and Possibility in Pynchon's Fiction." In Levine and Leverenz, eds., *Mindful Pleasures: Essays on Thomas Pynchon*, 113–34.
Levine, George, and David Leverenz, eds. *Mindful Pleasures: Essays on Thomas Pynchon*. Boston: Little, Brown and Co., 1976.
Lindbeck, Assar. *The Political Economy of the New Left: An Outsider's View*. 2nd ed. New York: Harper & Row, 1977.
Lott, Bernice E. "Who Wants the Children?: Some Relationships among Attitudes toward Children, Parents, and the Liberation of Women." *American Psychologist* 28 (July 1973): 573–82.
Luxemburg, Rosa. "The Militia and Militarism." 1899. In *Rosa Luxemburg: Selected Political Writings*, edited by Robert Looker, 76–92. London: Jonathon Cape, 1972.
Rosa Luxemburg to Karl Kautsky, 1 September 1904. Quoted in Frölich, *Rosa Luxemburg*, 70.
Luxemburg, Rosa, and Nikolaï I. Bukharin. *The Accumulation of Capital – An Anti-Critique: Imperialism and the Accumulation of Capital*. Edited by Kenneth J. Tarbuck. Translated by Rudolf Wichmann. New York: Monthly Review Press, 1972.
MacAdam, Alfred. "Pynchon as Satirist: To Write, To Mean." *Yale Review* 67, no. 4 (1978): 555–66.

Mailer, Norman. "The White Negro: Superficial Reflections on the Hipster." *Dissent* 4, no.3 (1957): 276–93. http://www.dissentmagazine.org/online.php?id=26.
Malcolm, Douglas. "'Jazz America': Jazz and African American Culture in Jack Kerouac's *On the Road*." *Contemporary Literature* 40, no. 1 (1999): 85–110.
Male Homosexual Workshop, The. "Statement of the Male Homosexual Workshop." In *We Are Everywhere: A Historical Sourcebook in Gay and Lesbian Politics*, edited by Mark Blasias and Shane Phelan, 402–3. New York: Routledge, 1997.
Marcuse, Herbert. *Counterrevolution and Revolt*. Boston: Beacon Press, 1972.
Marx, Karl. *Critique of Hegel's "Philosophy of Right."* Edited by Joseph O'Malley. Translated by Annette Jolin and Joseph O'Malley. Cambridge: University of Cambridge Press, 1977. First published 1843.
——— "The British Rule in India." *New-York Daily Tribune*, 25 June 1853, 5.
Mattessich, Stefan. "Imperium, Misogyny, and Postmodern Parody in Thomas Pynchon's *V*." *ELH* 65, no. 2 (Summer 1998): 503–21.
——— *Lines of Flight: Discursive Time and Countercultural Desire in the Work of Thomas Pynchon*. Durham, NC and London: Duke University Press, 2002.
Mayer, Martin. "Getting Alienated with the Right Crowd at Harvard." *Esquire*, September 1963.
McCann, Sean, and Michael Szalay. "Do You Believe in Magic? Literary Thinking after the New Left." *The Yale Journal of Criticism* 18, no. 2 (2005): 435–68.
McClure, John. A. "Do They Believe in Magic? Politics and Postmodern Literature." *boundary 2* 36, no. 2 (2009): 125–43.
McMillian, John, and Paul Buhle, eds. *The New Left Revisited*. Philadelphia: Temple University Press, 2003.
Mead, Clifford. *Thomas Pynchon: A Bibliography of Primary and Secondary Materials*. Elmwood Park, IL: Dalkey Archive, 1989.
Medoro, Dana. *The Bleeding of America: Menstruation as Symbolic Economy in Pynchon, Faulkner, and Morrison*. Westport, CT: Greenwood Press, 2002.
Mendelson, Edward, ed. *Thomas Pynchon: A Collection of Critical Essays*. Englewood Cliffs, NJ: Prentice-Hall, 1978.
Mendelson, Edward, "The Sacred, the Profane, and *The Crying of Lot 49*." In Mendelson, ed., *Thomas Pynchon: A Collection of Critical Essays*, 112–46.
Michals, Debra. "From 'Consciousness Expansion' to 'Consciousness Raising': Feminism and the Countercultural Politics of the Self." In *Imagine Nation: The American Counterculture of the 1960s and '70s*, edited by Peter Braunstein and Michael William Doyle, 41–68. New York: Routledge, 2002.
Millett, Kate. *Sexual Politics*. 1970. Reprint, Urbana: University of Illinois Press, 2000.
Molloy, Seán. "Escaping the Politics of the Irredeemable Earth – Anarchy and Transcendence in the Novel's of Thomas Pynchon." *Theory & Event* 13, no.3 (2010): n. p. http://muse.jhu.edu. ezproxy.sussex.ac.uk/journals/theory_and_ event/v013/13.3.molloy.html.

Moore, Thomas. *The Style of Connectedness: "Gravity's Rainbow" and Thomas Pynchon*. Columbia: University of Missouri Press, 1987.

Morgan, Robin. "Goodbye to All That." 1970. In Albert and Albert eds., *The Sixties Papers*, 509–16.

Going Too Far: The Personal Chronicle of a Feminist, 163–9. New York: Random House, 1977.

Mortenson, Erik R. "Beating Time: Configurations of Temporality in Jack Kerouac's *On the Road*." In Myrsiades, ed., *The Beat Generation*, 57–75.

Myrsiades, Kostas, ed. *The Beat Generation: Critical Essays*. New York: Peter Lang, 2002.

National Organization for Women, The. "Statement of Purpose." 1966. In *"It Changed My Life": Writings on the Women's Movement*, by Betty Friedan, 109–15. Cambridge, MA: Harvard University Press, 1998.

Newton, Huey P. "Speech Delivered at Boston College." 18 November 1970. In Hilliard and Weise, eds., *The Huey P. Newton Reader*, 160–75.

Revolutionary Suicide. New York: Harcourt Brace Jovanovich, 1973.

"A Spokesman for the People: In Conversation with William F. Buckley." 1973. In Hilliard and Weise, eds., *The Huey P. Newton Reader*, 267–84.

Nicholson, C. E., and R. W. Stevenson. "'Words You Never Wanted to Hear': Fiction, History and Narratology in *The Crying of Lot 49*." *Pynchon Notes* 16 (1985): 83–7.

Onions, C. T., ed. *The Oxford Dictionary of English Etymology*. London: Oxford University Press, 1966.

Panish, Jon. "Kerouac's *The Subterraneans*: A Study of 'Romantic Primitivism.'" *MELUS* 19, no. 3 (Autumn 1994): 107–23.

Patell, Cyrus R. K. *Negative Liberties: Morrison, Pynchon, and the Problem of Liberal Ideology*. Durham, NC and London: Duke University Press, 2001.

Pearce, Richard. *The Novel in Motion: An Approach to Modern Fiction*. Columbus: Ohio State University Press, 1983.

Petillon, Pierre-Yves. "A Re-cognition of Her Errand Into the Wilderness." In *New Essays on the Crying of Lot 49*, edited by Patrick O'Donnell, 127–70. Cambridge: Cambridge University Press, 1991.

Pitzulo, Carrie. "The Battle in Every Man's Bed: *Playboy* and the Fiery Feminists." *Journal of the History of Sexuality* 17, no. 2 (May 2008): 259–89.

Plamondon, Genie. "Hello to All That." 1970. In Albert and Albert, eds., *The Sixties Papers*, 520–3.

Plaskow, Judith. "The Coming of Lilith: Toward a Feminist Theology." In *The Coming of Lilith: Essays On Feminism, Judaism, and Sexual Ethics, 1972–2003*, edited by Judith Plaskow and Donna Berman, 23–34. Boston: Beacon Press, 2005.

Plater, William M. *The Grim Phoenix: Reconstructing Thomas Pynchon*. Bloomington: Indiana University Press, 1978.

Primeau, Ronald. *Romance of the Road: The Literature of the American Highway.* Ohio: Bowling Green State University Popular Press, 1966.
Prothero, Stephen. "On the Holy Road: The Beat Movement as Spiritual Protest." *The Harvard Theological Review* 84, no. 2 (1991): 205–22.
Proudhon, Pierre-Joseph. *What is Property? An Inquiry into the Principle and Right of Government.* Edited by Donald R. Kelley and Bonnie G. Smith. Cambridge: Cambridge University Press, 1994. First published 1840.
Pynchon, Thomas. *V.* 1963. Reprint, London: Vintage, 2000.
   The Crying of Lot 49. 1966. Reprint, London: Vintage, 2000.
   "A Journey into the Mind of Watts." *The New York Times Magazine,* 12 June 1966, 34–5, 78, 80–2, 84.
   Thomas Pynchon to Thomas F. Hirsch, 8 January 1969. In David Seed, *The Fictional Labyrinths of Thomas Pynchon,* 240–3. Basingstoke: MacMillan, 1988.
   Gravity's Rainbow. 1973. Reprint, London: Vintage, 1995.
   Introduction to *Been Down So Long It Looks Like Up To Me* (1983), by Richard Fariña, v–xiv. 1966. Reprint, London: Penguin, 1996.
   Slow Learner. 1984. Reprint, London: Vintage, 1995.
   "The Heart's Eternal Vow." *The New York Times,* 10 April 1988. http://www.nytimes.com/1988/04/10/books/the-heart-s-eternal-vow.html?scp=1&sq=heart%27s+eternal+vow+pynchon+marquez&st=nyt#.
   Vineland. London: Secker & Warburg, 1990.
   Introduction to *The Teachings of Don B.: Satires, Parodies, Fables, Illustrated Stories, and Plays of Donald Barthelme* (1992), edited by Kim Herzinger, xv–xxii. Berkeley: Counterpoint, 2008.
   Mason & Dixon. London: Vintage, 1998.
   Against the Day. 2006. Reprint, London: Vintage, 2007.
   Inherent Vice. London: Jonathan Cape, 2009.
Reich, Charles A. *The Greening of America.* London: Penguin, 1971.
Roszak, Theodore. *The Making of a Counterculture: Reflections on the Technocratic Society and Its Youthful Opposition.* Doubleday: New York, 1969.
Rothstein, Richard. "A Short History of ERAP." University of California Calisphere. http://content.cdlib.org/view?docId=kt4k4003k7.
Rubin, Jerry. "Yippie Manifesto." 1968. In *Takin' it to the Streets: A Sixties Reader,* edited by Alexander Bloom and Wini Breines, 323–4. Oxford: Oxford University Press, 1995.
   "Yippie Manifesto." 1969. Pamphlet published by The Not Guilty Bookshop.
Rudd, Mark. "The Death of SDS." http://www.markrudd.com/?sds-and-weather/the-death-of-sds.html.
Ryder, A. J. *The German Revolution of 1918: A Study of German Socialism in War and Revolt.* Cambridge: Cambridge University Press, 1967.
Schaub, Thomas H. *Pynchon: The Voice of Ambiguity.* Urbana: University of Illinois Press, 1981.

"Influence and Incest: Relations between *The Crying of Lot 49* and *The Great Gatsby*." In Abbas, ed., *Reading from the Margins*, 139–53.
Sears, Julie Christine. "Black and White Rainbows and Blurry Lines: Sexual Deviance/Diversity in *Gravity's Rainbow* and *Mason & Dixon*." In Abbas, ed., *Reading from the Margins*, 108–21.
Severs, Jeffrey. "'The abstractions she was instructed to embody': Women, Capitalism, and Artistic Representation in *Against the Day*." In Severs and Leise, eds., *Pynchon's "Against the Day,"* 215–38.
Severs, Jeffrey, and Christopher Leise, eds. *Pynchon's "Against the Day:" A Corrupted Pilgrim's Guide*. Newark: University of Delaware Press, 2011.
Sherard, Tracey. "The Birth of the Female Subject in *The Crying of Lot 49*." *Pynchon Notes* 32–33 (1993): 60–74.
Slade, Joseph W. *Thomas Pynchon*. New York: P. Lang, 1990.
SNCC. "SNCC: Founding Statement." In Albert and Albert, eds., *The Sixties Papers*, 113.
"SNCC Position Paper: Vietnam." In Albert and Albert, eds., *The Sixties Papers*, 117–18. Reprinted from *The Movement*, January 1966.
Solanas, Valerie. *SCUM Manifesto*. Edinburgh: AK Press, 1996. First published 1967.
St. Clair, Justin. "Binocular Disparity and Pynchon's Panoramic Paradigm." In Severs and Leise, eds., *Pynchon's "Against the Day,"* 67–88.
Strandberg, Victor. "Dimming the Enlightenment: Thomas Pynchon's *Mason & Dixon*." In *Pynchon and "Mason & Dixon,"* edited by Brooke Hovarth and Irving Malin, 100–11. Newark: University of Delaware Press, 2000.
Students for a Democratic Society. *The Port Huron Statement*. Chicago: Charles H. Kerr, 1990. First published 1962.
Thomas, Paul. *Marxism and Scientific Socialism: From Engels to Althusser*. New York: Routledge, 2008.
Thomas, Sam. *Pynchon and the Political*. New York: Routledge, 2007.
Thompson, Hunter S. *Fear and Loathing in Las Vegas*. London: Paladin, 1972.
Turner, Victor. *The Ritual Process: Structure and Anti-Structure*. New York: Aldine, 1969.
"The Center Out There: Pilgrim's Goal." *History of Religions* 12, no. 3 (1973): 191–230.
Van Gennep, Arnold. *The Rites of Passage*. Translated by Monika B. Vizedom and Gabrielle L. Caffee. London: Routledge & Kegan Paul, 1960.
Vonnegut, Kurt. *Slaughterhouse-5, or The Children's Crusade*. 1969. Reprint, London: Vintage, 2000.
Warren, Jenifer. "Former Black Panther Eldridge Cleaver Dies at 62." *The Los Angeles Times*, 2 May 1998. http://articles.latimes.com/1998/may/02/news/mn-45607.
Weisenburger, Stephen. *A "Gravity's Rainbow" Companion: Sources and Contexts for Pynchon's Novel*. 2nd ed. Athens: University of Georgia Press, 2006.
Wells, Simon. *Charles Manson: Coming Down Fast*. London: Hodder and Stoughton, 2009.

Wilde, Alan. "Love and Death in and around Vineland, U. S. A." *boundary 2* 18, no. 2 (1991): 166–80.
Wilson, Steve. "The Author as Spiritual Pilgrim: The Search for Authenticity in Jack Kerouac's *On the Road* and *The Subterraneans*." In Myrsiades, ed., *The Beat Generation*, 77–91.
Witzling, David. "The Sensibility of Postmodern Whiteness in *V.*, or Thomas Pynchon's Identity Problem." *Contemporary Literature* 47, no. 3 (2006): 381–415.
— *Everybody's America: Thomas Pynchon, Race, and the Cultures of Postmodernism*. New York: Routledge, 2008.
Wolfe, Tom. *The Electric Kool-Aid Acid Test*. New York: Bantam, 1969.
— "Radical Chic: That Party at Lenny's." *New York Magazine*, 8 June 1970. http://nymag.com/news/features/46170/.
Wolfey, Lawrence C. "Repression's Rainbow: The Presence of Norman O. Brown in Pynchon's Big Novel." *PMLA* 92, no. 5 (October 1977): 873–89.
Zinn, Howard. *SNCC: The New Abolitionists*. Cambridge, MA: South End Press, 2002.

Index

Acker, Kathy, 2, 167n3
Alpert, Richard, 65, 67, 73, 75, 178n15
Alternative realities, 25, 76, 79, 81, 83–85, 86, 87, 90, 91, 92
Anarchism, 2, 7, 10, 11, 64, 83, 92, 94–101, 156, 158, 159, 160, 164, 173n64, 183n26, 189n2
  and anti-structure, 34, 95
  and capitalism, 89, 90
  and family, 145, 146
  and jazz, 34
  and literary modernism, 20
  and political theory, 94, 95
  and spontaneous synchronicity, 55–56, 145, 181n66
  and the Black Panther Party, 106, 125
  and the Chums of Chance, 89
  and the counterculture, 8
  and the psychedelic movement, 99
  and the road, 162
  and the sixties counterculture, 95, 99
  and the Youth International Party, 10, 64, 123
  and the Yz-les-Bains group, 97–98, 160, 181n71
  and unity, 139
  and violence, 95–97, 145, 181n65
  and visionary experience, 91, 93, 163
Anti-authoritarianism, 1, 6, 94, 141, 158
Anti-pornography movement, 152
Anti-structure, 9, 11, 29–30, 31, 32, 33–36, 38, 39, 66, 95, 98, 101, 127, 159, 172n54, 173n64
Ashe, Frederick, 4, 55, 115, 116, 173n5, 175n33, 186n41
Atheism, 27
Atkinson, Ti-Grace, 142, 143
Attewell, Nadine, 47, 49, 144

Bad Priest, 25, 26, 27
Baker, Jeffrey S., 4, 79
Bakunin, Mikhail, 94, 98, 181n58
Baldwin, James, 103
Barthelme, Donald, 161

Basnight, Lew, 83, 90–91, 93, 180n54
Beat Generation, 14–18, 20–21, 37, 131, 171n45, 172n56, 172n58, 179n26
  and anarchism, 98
  and anti-structure, 30
  and communitas, 30
  and its legacy, 40, 102
  and liminality, 32
  and literary modernism, 14, 20, 170n19
  and motion, 15–17, 18, 24, 25, 27, 29, 88
  and pilgrimage narratives, 28
  and politics, 37, 38, 68, 159
  and racial stereotyping, 33, 34
  and religion, 25–26, 27, 30, 41
  and the hippie counterculture, 26
  and the New Left, 41
  and the psychedelic movement, 65, 66
  and use of drugs, 21
  as politically naive, 37
  as proto-countercultural, 13
  obscenity trials, 20
  origins, 14
  Pynchon's comments on, 9, 37
Benton, Graham, 80, 95, 101
Bergh, Patricia A., 80
Bersani, Leo, 47, 48, 61
Black Panther Party, 8, 11, 13, 105, 106, 114, 182n12
  and communism, 58
  and Eldridge Cleaver, 118–20
  and media misrepresentation, 123–24
  and political theory, 106–10, 114
  and revolutionary leadership, 117
  and revolutionary suicide, 112
  and social climbing, 63
  and the Democratic Convention (1968), 45
  and the Federal Bureau of Investigation, 122
  and the Schwarzkommando, 114, 116
  and violence, 45, 119–20, 122, 123, 160
  causes of its failure, 116, 122, 123, 124
  history, 106
  relations with white student Left, 105, 119

Black Power, 40, 45, 103, 105, 116, 186n23
Blicero. *See* Weissmann Lt.
Bodine, Pig, 27, 61, 63, 154
Book of the Dead, 69, 75, 170n26, 179n27, 179n28
Briggs, Estrella, 92, 93, 97, 113
Brown, Norman O., 46, 47, 67, 174n28
Buddhism, 1, 25–26, 27, 30, 81, 82, 83, 84, 86, 92, 134, 171n37
Burroughs, William, 14, 17, 18, 19, 20, 30

Calvino, Italo, 7, 164
Capitalism, 49, 86, 92, 93, 100, 136, 163, 180n56, 181n58, 182n12, 182n5
  and alienation, 33, 135, 159
  and anarchism, 90, 96, 97, 100, 136, 163
  and colonialism, 59, 87, 103, 110
  and communism, 51, 58
  and escapism, 51, 86
  and false consciousness, 87
  and feminism, 135, 136, 137
  and invisibility, 85
  and light, 10, 87
  and objective consciousness, 78
  and pornography, 50, 54, 62, 86, 153, 160
  and racism, 105
  and social mobility, 17
  and structure, 9, 32, 96, 150
  and the Beat Generation, 37
  and the Black Panther Party, 105
  and the Chums of Chance, 89
  and the Counterforce, 62, 63
  and the road, 23, 33, 162
  and the university campus, 42
  and time, 21
  and violence, 163
  Pynchon's criticism of, 2, 6, 12, 59, 95, 100, 136
Cassady, Neal, 15, 169n11
Castro, Fidel, 57, 105
Catholicism, 25, 26, 27, 117
Chapman, Wes, 50
Chastain, Darryl Louise, 148, 149–50, 151
Cherrycoke, Reverend Wicks, 82, 104
Christianity, 75, 85, 87, 96, 107, 111, 117, 121, 122, 147, 183n32
Chums of Chance, 83, 86, 88–90, 93, 97, 155
Civil Rights, 38, 102, 105, 116, 159, 169n1
  and student protest, 40, 44
Cleaver, Eldridge, 8, 118–20, 122, 123, 139
Clellon Holmes, John, 16, 26
Cold War, 37, 38, 57
Colonialism, 11, 58, 87, 103, 104, 110, 111, 115, 183n24
Communes, 41, 46, 48, 65, 68, 69, 98, 147, 149

Communism, 49, 51, 158, 181n58, 182n13, 186n41, 189n2
  and activism, 10, 53, 58–59, 111
  and anti-communism hysteria, 52
  and colonialism, 110
  and dialectical materialism, 11
  and feminism, 140–41, 147
  and the Black Panther Party, 105
  and the New Left, 10, 45, 57–58, 111
Communitas, 9, 29–32, 98, 113, 140, 161, 172n54, 172n57, 172n58, 173n64
  and anarchism, 139, 159
  and family, 12, 144
  and political action, 10
  and the psychedelic movement, 66, 81
  existential, 34, 56
Corso, Gregory, 16, 37
Counterculture
  core values, 9, 13
  definition of, 12–13
Counterforce, 62, 63, 109, 121, 183n24
Cowart, David, 3, 4, 160, 168n22

Davidson, Cathy N., 130, 135
Debord, Guy, 11, 87, 88, 121
Democracy, 17, 38, 40, 79, 94, 136, 159, *see also* Participatory democracy
Democratic Convention (1968), 45, 52
Derrida, Jacques, 150
Dialectical materialism, 58, 106, 107–11, 114, 162, 182n13, 183n26
Dixon, Jeremiah, 55, 104, 165
Driblette, Randolph, 133, 134

Economic Research and Action Project, 44
Educational functionalism, 128, 132, 184n6
Ego-loss, 36, 76, 81, 82, 91, 99
Eisenhower, Dwight D., 14, 17, 131
El Espinero, 91–93
Eliade, Mircea, 26
Empty Ones, 115, 117
Enlightenment, the, 3, 78
Enzian, Oberst, 115, 116–18, 119, 120–23, 159
Escapism, 8, 55, 80, 85, 88, 89, 109, 127, 134, 158, 163
  and activism, 163
  and capitalism, 86
  and fantasy, 49, 54, 57, 80, 159
  and feminism, 132, 150
  and love, 48, 49
  and use of drugs, 80, 162
  in *On the Road*, 33
Ewball, Oust, 97
Expressive politics, 60, 164

Index

False consciousness, 87
Family, 12, 68, 91, 93, 97, 104, 131, 140, 143–46, 148, 161, *see also* Motherhood; Fatherhood
Fantasy. *See* Escapism, Politics
Fariña, Richard, 42, 57, 174n7, 199
Fatherhood, 12, 33, 143, 145–46
Federal Bureau of Investigation, 11, 45, 59, 106, 118, 122–24
Fellahin, 32–33
Female Liberation Cell-16, 148
Female sexuality, 127, 128, 133, 144, 151, 152, 153
Feminism, 11, 130, 134, 135, 138, 146, 148–49, 151, 154, 156
  and capitalism, 137
  and female sexuality, 151
  and gender, 129, 139–40
  and pornography, 152
  and the counterculture, 127
  and the Fall narrative, 147
  and the New Left, 126, 137, 139
  moderate feminism, 128, 129, 137
  radical feminism, 8, 12, 139–41, 147, 148, 149
Ferlinghetti, Lawrence, 16, 23, 32, 37
Firestone, Shulamith, 140, 142, 143
First World War, 144
Free Speech Movement, 42, 62
Freud, Sigmund, 75, 115, 129
Friedan, Betty, 11, 12, 126, 128–30, 131–37, 184n6

Gates, Frenesi, 55, 141–42, 143–44, 147, 149–50, 151, 157, 187n46
Gay Liberation Movement, 51, 150, 175n32
Gender, 53, 127, 129, 131, 133, 134, 148, 149–51, 152, 154, 159, 187n58
  and feminism, 130, 134, 135, 137, 139–40, 149
  essentialist notions of, 12, 139, 146, 149, 150, 154
German revolution (1918–19), 59
Ginsberg, Allen, 14, 16–17, 20, 21, 25, 30, 35, 37, 65, 68, 172n57, 179n26
Gitlin, Todd, 4, 57, 60, 68, 77, 105, 119, 127, 137, 138, 162, 186n34
Greb, Rollo, 28, 29, 34, 35
Greer, Germaine, 140, 143, 149

Halfcourt, Yashmeen, 83, 93, 97, 144–45, 153
Harvitz, Ester, 27, 81
Hayden, Tom, 38, 186n34
Hedonism, 8, 9, 19, 26, 31, 40, 45, 66, 79, 96, 143, 162
Herero, 103, 104, 110, 114–15, 117, 118, 121
Hesse, Hermann, 4, 26
Higgs, John, 74
Hilarius, Dr., 69, 71, 73–75, 81, 133

Hinduism, 81, 82, 84, 92
Historiographic metafiction, 6, 167n1, *see also* Hutcheon, Linda; Postmodernism
Hite, Molly, 60, 61, 62, 130, 148, 185n14, 187n55
Hoffman, Abbie, 60
Hollander, Charles, 7
Horowitz, Daniel, 128, 136
Hume, Kathryn, 3, 112, 165, 176n45, 188n63
Hutcheon, Linda, 1, 5–6, 80, 163, 179n40
Huxley, Aldous, 67, 91

Imperialism. *See* Colonialism
Indians. *See* Native Americans
Inverarity, Pierce, 22, 23, 32, 75, 76, 88, 129, 131, 132, 133, 134, 135–36, 137
Invisibility, 29, 38, 84–85, 86, 89, 91
IT, 9, 28–29, 30, 33, 34–35, 65

Jardine, Alice, 130
Jazz, 14, 28–29, 32, 33–34, 55–56, 97, 98, 102, 164, 172n62
Jeffries, Judson L., 116
Johnson, Lyndon B., 43

Kant, Immanuel, 108
Karenga, Ron, 106
Kennedy, John F., 17
Kerouac, Jack, 14–17, 18, 20–21, 28, 29, 30, 31, 32–34, 37, 38–39, 66, 169n11, 172n57, 172n62, *see also* Spontaneous prose
  and myth-making, 21, 23
  and politics, 37–39
  and religion, 125–26, 27, 28
  and the road, 19, 21, 23, 162
  On the Road
    Pynchon's comments on, 9, 14, 102
  views on LSD, 65
Kesey, Ken, 66, 69, 77, 177n13
King, Martin Luther, 46, 111
Krassner, Paul, 60, 75
Kropotkin, Peter, 95

Lang, Fritz, 54
Latewood, Cyprian, 93, 96, 97, 145
Leary, Timothy, 8, 66, 69, 72, 76, 77, 79, 82, 83, 84, 90, 91, 92, 93, 100, 162, 168n12, 177n10, 177n13, 178n13, 178n19, 178n26, 179n26, *see also* Psychedelic Experience, The
  and controversy, 69, 73–74, 123
  and LSD's revolutionary potential, 67–68, 162
  and politics, 10, 65–66, 79, 162
  and rationality, 78, 79, 104
  and spirituality, 75, 92, 99

Leary, Timothy, (cont.)
  and the psychedelic movement, 65, 68
  comments on Pynchon, 4
  comparison to Dr. Hilarius, 73–75
L'Heuremaudit, Mélanie, 31, 155
Light, 10, 84, 86–87, 93, 106, 157, 180n56
Liminality, 9, 29–30, 31–33, 35, 36, 39, 81, 172n54, 172n58
Literature
  and its political role, 2, 22, 164, 167n3
Luxemburg, Rosa, 56, 58–60, 64, 111, 159, 176n45

Maas, Oedipa, 24, 39, 81, 87, 88, 91, 153, 164, 180n54, 185n12
  and activism, 42
  and alienation, 19, 24
  and community, 31–32
  and ego-loss, 24, 36, 81
  and fantasy, 81
  and feminism, 128–30, 131–37, 185n14, 185n19
  and LSD, 69–72, 73, 74–77
  and spirituality, 25
  and the road, 22–23
  and visionary experience, 34, 35
  as reader, 77–78, 100
Maas, Wendell "Mucho", 69–72, 76–77, 131, 133, 134, 137
Maijstral, Fausto, 22, 26
Mailer, Norman, 14, 17, 102
Malatesta, Errico, 96
Manson, Charles, 48
Marcuse, Herbert, 46, 60, 61, 113, 174n28, 183n29
Marvy, Major Duane, 61, 124, 164, 177n60
Marx, Karl, 11, 58–59, 107, 108, 110–11
Marxism, 11, 58–59, 87, 89, 99, 101, 105, 106, 108, 111, 114, 162, 179n37, 182n12, 182n13, 183n26, *see also* Communism; Marx, Karl
Mason, Charles, 48, 55, 104, 145
Mass media, 10, 11, 45, 48, 60, 66, 71, 73–74, 87, 105, 116, 118, 123–24, 150, 160
Mattessich, Stefan, 3, 4, 51, 154, 185n13
Mayer, Martin, 73–74
Mendelson, Edward, 25
Merry Pranksters, 15, 66, 69, 177n13, 178n13
Mexico, Roger, 47–48, 57, 61, 63
Modernism, 6, 14, 20, 170n19
Molloy, Seán, 6, 100, 163, 167n5, 181n65, 181n71
Morgan, Robin, 138, 139, 141, 147, 152
Moriarty, Dean, 9, 15, 19, 23, 26, 28–29, 30, 32, 33, 34–35, 39
Motherhood, 12, 127, 128, 130, 139, 140–44, 156

National Organization for Women, 126, 136
Native Americans, 17, 87, 91–93, 98, 104
New Left, 4, 9–10, 43, 44, 45, 98, 162, 163, 169n32, 173n5, 183n29, 186n34
  and Civil Rights, 44, 102
  and communism, 57, 58, 59, 60, 111
  and feminism, 12, 126, 137–39
  and the Black Panther Party, 105
  and the counterculture, 12, 13, 40, 65
  and the psychedelic movement, 66, 68
  and the Vietnam War, 45, 57
  and violence, 39, 52, 53, 60, 77, 113, 160
  core values and methods, 41
Newton, Huey P., 105, 111, 123, 124, 125, 126, 139, 182n16, 183n29
  and BPP theory, 107, 108–10, 113, 116–17
  views on Eldridge Cleaver, 118–20
Nixon, Richard M., 41, 57, 73, 175n38, 176n38
Non-violence, 39, 45, 46, 60, 160

O'Rooney, Wolfe Tone, 97, 98
Objective consciousness, 78, 84, 104, 120, 122, 147, 160
Oust, Ewball, 96, 97

Paradise, Sal, 15, 19, 21, 22, 24, 26, 28–29, 30, 31, 32, 33, 35–36
Participatory democracy, 40
Petillon, Pierre-Yves, 15, 33, 73, 75, 170n26, 172n58, 178n19
Picaresque form, 16, 17
Pilgrimage, 17, 27–30, 171n45, 173n64
Plamondon, Genie, 139, 141
Plaskow, Judith, 147
Pointsman, Ned, 54
Pökler, Franz, 54
Pökler, Leni, 49, 52–55, 59, 111, 140–41, 142, 143, 144, 147
Police brutality, 10, 52, 53, 64, 82, 103, 105, 168n22
Politics
  and art, 10, 44, 60, 164
  and fantasy, 79–81
  and reading, 78
Pornography, 12, 50–51, 54, 86, 121, 151–53, 159, 160, 174n28
Port Huron Statement, 10, 38, 39, 88
Postmodernism, 1, 2–3, 4, 5–6, 39, 72, 78, 81, 150, 154, 163, 170n19, 179n40, *see also* Modernism
  and politics, 1, 5, 6, 80, 163
Post-structuralism, 1, *see also* Postmodernism
Profane, Benny, 21–22, 31
Prothero, Steven, 28, 32, 33, 171n45, 172n57, 172n59

Proudhon, Pierre-Joseph, 94, 181n58
Psychedelic Experience, The, 10, 69, 73, 75, 84, 91, 99, 180n55
Pynchon, Thomas
and campus politics, 42
as apolitical, 39
as post-Beat, 20, 34, 73, 90
clarity of his political values, 6–7, 168n22
formal qualities of his writing, 1, 23, 81, 101, 163
his non-fiction, 7, 8, 9, 10, 14, 43, 44, 58, 70, 80, 103, 112, 158
literary criticism pertaining to his work, 2–5
popularity within the counterculture, 4

Quaternionism, 99–100

Race, 11, 13, 32, 34, 43, 92, 102–4, 107, 110, 116, 121, 157, 158, 181n3, 182n5, 184n42
Racism, 13, 38, 102–3, 107, 115, 117, 124, 154, 168n22, 188n65, 188n66
and capitalism, 105
and Karl Marx, 11, 58, 110
and Watts, Los Angeles, 43
Rationality, 8, 9, 13, 35, 54, 77, 86, 87, 96, 104, 120, 121, 146, 147, *see also* Objective consciousness
and dialectical materialism, 108, 109, 110, 114
and fantasy, 80, 85
and the psychedelic movement, 41, 66, 78–79
Reactionary suicide, 107, 117
Reich, Charles A., 102
Revolutionary suicide, 106–8, 109–10, 111–14, 116–17, 119, 123, 161, 182n16
Rite of passage, 29, 35, 36, 172n58
Rodia, Simon, 44, 164
Roszak, Theodore, 12, 13, 78, 104, 179n37, *see also* Objective consciousness
Rubin, Jerry, 60, 61–62, 64, 149, 177n59

Sachsa, Peter, 52–53, 54, 140
San Narciso, 19, 23, 24, 36, 135, 137
Schaub, Thomas, 5, 7
Schwarzkommando, 11, 106, 112, 114–18, 119–20, 122, 123, 124, 182n12, 183n32
Seale, Bobby, 105, 118
Second World War, 1, 11, 16, 26, 47, 54, 59, 63, 74, 90, 106, 115, 116, 124, 126, 128, 131, 186n41
Second-wave feminism. *See* Feminism
Severs, Jeffrey, 3, 155–56
Sexism, 12, 130, 138, 144, 148, 152, 153–56, 185n14, 188n66
Shambhala, 83, 86

Sherard, Tracey, 130
Sisterhood of Kunoichi Attentives, 147, 148, 149
Situationist International, 11, 25, 62, 87, 88, 107, 176n55
Slade, Joseph, 21
Slothrop, Tyrone, 49, 51, 57, 61, 62, 153, 164, 177n60
Snyder, Gary, 25, 68
Solanas, Valerie, 126
Spartacist revolt, 59
Sphere, McClintic, 34, 70
Spirituality, 25, 27, 28, 31, 104, 115, 118, 119
and alternative realities, 25, 76, 83–84, 85, 92, 161
and motion, 25, 26, 27, 29, 34
and the Beat Generation, 25–26, 28, 32, 37, 41
and the psychedelic movement, 65, 68, 99
aspirituality, 13, 26, 30, 31, 107
in *On the Road*, 9, 26, 35
Spontaneous prose, 16, 21, 170n11
Spontaneous synchronicity, 11, 55, 98, 145, 160, 181n66
Sportello, Doc, 48, 106, 146, 153, 165, 177n60
Stalin, Josef, 110
Stencil, Herbert, 21, 31, 164
Strandberg, Victor, 3
Student Non-Violent Coordinating Committee, 40, 44, 45, 46, 65, 102, 119
Students for a Democratic Society, 10, 38, 39, 40, 41, 44, 45, 46, 57, 58, 65, 88, 102, 119, 126, 137, 138, *see also* Port Huron Statement
Swanlake, Jessica, 47–48, 57, 63

Tchitcherine, Vaslav, 106, 107–8, 109, 111, 117
Technology, 23, 24, 108, 112, 120, 121, 123
Terrorism, 95–97, 120, 145, *see also* Violence
Thomas, Sam, 2, 3, 4, 5, 80, 85, 160, 163
Traverse, Frank, 91–93, 113, 114
Traverse, Kit, 85–86, 99
Traverse, Lake, 151, 155
Traverse, Reef, 93, 96, 97
Traverse, Webb, 85, 92, 97, 145, 187n48
Trystero, 22, 25, 31, 33, 39, 42, 70, 76, 77, 78, 81, 83, 103, 134, 164, 181n3, 186n23
Turner, Victor, 9, 28–30, 36, 171n45, 172n54, 173n64

V., 21, 26, 31, 56, 130, 164, 185n14, *see also* Bad Priest
Van Gennep, Arnold, 29, 172n58, *see also* Rite of passage; Liminality
Vanderjuice, Professor Heino, 84, 85
Vectorism, 85, 99–100
Vibe, Scarsdale, 85, 96, 97, 165

Vietnam War, 13, 38, 40, 45, 49, 51, 57, 74, 103, 139, 157, 158
Violence, 2, 18, 39, 43, 45, 48, 103, 110, 126, 143, 146, 150, 158, 160, 161, 163, 168n22, 176n45
　and activism, 8, 11, 47, 52–54, 56, 59, 63, 111, 125, 160
　and anarchism, 94, 95–97, 181n65
　and Black Power, 104, 106, 119–20, 123, 124
　and colonialism, 103
　and LSD, 77
　and the New Left, 10, 39, 45, 52, 60, 105, 122, 160
　as last resort, 59, 120
　justifications for, 112–13, 161
Visionary experience, 82, 85, 90–94
Vond, Brock, 142, 143, 144, 148, 150, 186n42
Vonnegut, Kurt, 2, 4, 167n3

W.A.S.T.E., 31, 32, 33, 39, 42, 76
Waddell, Helen, 14
Watson, Charles, 48
Watts, Los Angeles, 43–45, 55, 80, 81, 103, 112, 113, 160, 164, 181n4

Weather Underground, 45, 58, 59, 120, 160, 175n33
Weavers' rebellion, 55
Weimar Republic, 2, 10, 49, 56, 57, 58, 59, 82
Weisenburger, Stephen, 61, 175n32
Weissmann, Lt., 111, 117, 121
Wheeler, Prairie, 141, 143, 145, 148, 164
Wheeler, Zoyd, 141, 143, 145, 148, 150, 157
White City, 86–87
Whitman, Walt, 17, 23
Wimpe, 106, 107, 109, 111, 112, 114
Wittgenstein, Ludwig, 22
Witzling, David, 104, 106, 116, 120, 183n24
Wolfe, Tom, 15, 18, 63, 99, 177n13
Wolfmann, Mickey, 153

X, Malcolm, 105, 181n3

Youth International Party, 6, 8, 10, 13, 45, 123
Yo-yoing, 21–22, 31

Zen. *See* Buddhism
Zombini, Luca, 87

Lightning Source UK Ltd.
Milton Keynes UK
UKHW012312270521
384518UK00001B/23